WHY CAN'T
WE BE
GOOD?

ALSO BY JACOB NEEDLEMAN

The American Soul

Time and the Soul

The Wisdom of Love

Money and the Meaning of Life

The Heart of Philosophy

Lost Christianity

The Way of the Physician

A Sense of the Cosmos

The Indestructible Question

The Sword of Gnosis (editor)

Sorcerers (a novel)

The New Religions

WHY CAN'T
WE BE
GOOD?

JACOB NEEDLEMAN

JEREMY P. TARCHER/PENGUIN

a member of Penguin Group (USA) Inc.

New York

JEREMY P. TARCHER/PENGUIN
Published by the Penguin Group
Penguin Group (USA) Inc., 375 Hudson Street, New York, New York 10014, USA •
Penguin Group (Canada), 90 Eglinton Avenue East, Suite 700, Toronto, Ontario M4P 2Y3,
Canada (a division of Pearson Penguin Canada Inc.) • Penguin Books Ltd, 80 Strand,
London WC2R 0RL, England • Penguin Ireland, 25 St Stephen's Green, Dublin 2, Ireland
(a division of Penguin Books Ltd) • Penguin Group (Australia), 250 Camberwell Road,
Camberwell, Victoria 3124, Australia (a division of Pearson Australia Group Pty Ltd) •
Penguin Books India Pvt Ltd, 11 Community Centre, Panchsheel Park, New Delhi–110 017,
India • Penguin Group (NZ), 67 Apollo Drive, Mairangi Bay, Auckland 1311,
New Zealand (a division of Pearson New Zealand Ltd) • Penguin Books (South Africa)
(Pty) Ltd, 24 Sturdee Avenue, Rosebank, Johannesburg 2196, South Africa

Penguin Books Ltd, Registered Offices:
80 Strand, London WC2R 0RL, England

Most Tarcher/Penguin books are available at special quantity discounts for bulk purchase for
sales promotions, premiums, fund-raising, and educational needs. Special books or book
excerpts also can be created to fit specific needs. For details, write Penguin Group (USA) Inc.
Special Markets, 375 Hudson Street, New York, NY 10014.

Library of Congress Cataloging-in-Publication Data

Needleman, Jacob.
Why can't we be good? / Jacob Needleman.
p.   cm.
ISBN 978-1-58542-541-9
1. Good and evil.   2. Ethics.   I. Title.
BJ1401.N44   2007   2006037104
170—dc22

Printed in the United States of America
1   3   5   7   9   10   8   6   4   2

This book is printed on acid-free paper. ∞

Book design by Meighan Cavanaugh

While the author has made every effort to provide accurate telephone numbers and Internet
addresses at the time of publication, neither the publisher nor the author assumes any responsibility for errors, or for changes that occur after publication. Further, the publisher does not
have any control over and does not assume any responsibility for author or third-party websites
or their content.

To my students

ACKNOWLEDGMENTS

I have many people to thank, starting with those whose generosity with their time, attention and goodwill has allowed me over the years to write this book in an indispensable atmosphere of human warmth: Tonyja Duffield Blakeslee, Maril Blanchard, Christina Florkowski, Richard Hodges, Marc Liotta, Dean Ottati, John Piazza, Gregory Porter, Tanya Silva, Shivanii Singh and Frank Cordes, Sara Swan and Ben Blankinship, Jordan Sudy, David Tan and Alexis Vincent. In the same spirit, I wish to thank those who read this book in varying stages of completion. Their encouragement, suggestions, and criticisms have meant a great deal to me: Rabbi Jack Bemporad, Edward Grieve, Barbara Hart, Nancy Larson, John Miller and Dennis Pence.

I am grateful to Frank Gati who, working with David Tan, has been extraordinarily generous in helping to create a remarkable filmed record of class lectures and discussions.

I am also deeply grateful to Steve Bileca, Paul Druzinsky, Peter Esty and Steve Henrikson for the privilege of working with them to deepen the study of ethics and human life with the students of the Branson School in Ross, California. It has been a revelation to witness the moral passion of these high school students and how it is being met at this exceptional school.

Although the students and librarians named in this book are in varying degrees fictitious, I have tried to portray the essence of what transpired between us as faithfully as possible. I can only hope that what I was able to bring to my students has been to some extent adequate to what they brought to me by their unfailing intellectual honesty and thirst for understanding.

My editor and friend Mitch Horowitz was with me at every stage and phase of the writing of this book. What is a great editor? An impartial critic, an intimate coconspirator, a shelter in a storm, a sounding board, a reality check. Above all, a midwife for whom the process of bringing to birth begins at the moment of conception, and even before. Thank you, Mitch.

As for my wife, Gail, I think of the wise words of Ludwig Wittgenstein— "Whereof one cannot speak, one must remain silent"—and the even wiser words of the musicologist Victor Zuckerkandl: "What we cannot speak of, we can sing." It is impossible to speak well and truly about the nobility of her mind, her heart and her conscience. If I am the author, she has been, day in and day out, the author of the author. If I could sing on this page, that would be my song.

CONTENTS

THE ONE QUESTION

I t was the question of Socrates.

It was the question of St. Paul.

It is the question that calls to us in the sacred writings of the world, and which defines the pathos of all serious art and literature. It is the well from which the great reformers of mankind draw all their passion.

And now, in this place and time, it cries out to us as clearly and solemnly as Wisdom long ago cried out to man:

> She crieth at the gates, at the entrance of the city, at the coming
> in at the doors. . . .
> O ye simple, understand wisdom; and, ye fools, be ye of an
> understanding heart.
>
> PROVERBS 8:3, 5

The question has taken many forms throughout the ages, but the words that cut through all the worlds and across all the epochs of human history are simply these:

Why do we not do what we know is good?

Why do we do what we hate?

It is the question we never really ask; and it is the only one that can make a difference.

For all the vast religious and ethical literature available to us today, for all the evidence of the futility of violence and hatred in our lives and in the world; for all our efforts to find the help we need; for all our yearning to be men and women capable of love, the question remains:

Why can't we be good?

~~ *One* ~~

THE FIRST STEP

Woven into the immense tapestry of Judaic story and lore, peopled as it is by vast branching histories of families, kings and nations and by the fierce dramas of war and passion and the thundering justice of God, there exists, as it were, one quaint and tender image whose great importance may easily be overlooked.

Two men, one young and the other old, are facing each other. The younger man is balancing himself on one leg. The other, whom we may picture wearing a modest skullcap, holds his right hand over his heart and halfway extends his left hand, palm down, toward the first man.

The older man is Hillel the Elder, greatest of the rabbinic patriarchs. The place is Jerusalem, sometime in the forty-year period between 30 BC and 10 AD—during the reign of the hated Herod the Great and his son Herod Antipas.

The story in question is from the Talmud and is given there in very few words:

A man approaches Hillel in a nervously defiant attitude. "I will embrace Judaism," he says, "on the condition that you can teach me the whole of the Torah while I am standing on one foot."

Straightaway, Hillel replies:

"What is hateful to you, do not do to your neighbor. That is the whole Torah. All the rest is commentary. Now, go and study."[1]

This is the entire story. We are told nothing further about this man.

Perhaps, pensively lowering his foot, he wonders to himself why he has been told to "study." Has he not just been given the essence of the teaching in one simple directive: "What is hateful to you, do not do to your neighbor"? Could anything be clearer?

And also for us: could anything be clearer? We, too, hear those words, or words like them, and are ready, even eager, to embrace them as a moral ideal. Consciously or semi-consciously, we believe we know what is good. Our only question is whether we will act upon it, whether we will put it into practice. It does not seem to be a matter of "study," it seems to be solely a matter of action. What is there to *study*? And why?

Of course, in some ethical situations we may need access to certain kinds of knowledge—scientific or medical information, for example, or the details of someone's personal life circumstances. But, once we have done our homework, so we feel, our duty is just to act, just to do the right thing. The moral principle seems simple and clear, whether in the form given by the gentle teacher in the story, or as it was given a few years later by his younger contemporary, Jesus: "Love thy neighbor as thyself."[2] So much is obvious, is it not?

Or is the truth of the matter quite different? Is a specific preparation of the mind needed—a specific kind of education—before one can carry out any serious intention at all, much less an intention involving moral action? And if so—what kind of education, what kind of *study*?

We are asking a fundamental question about the world of ideas. We are asking about the whole meaning of knowledge as it relates to our ability to be good.

One often hears it said that knowledge in and of itself is morally neutral, depending solely on who uses it and for what purpose. But here, too, the truth of the matter may be quite different. Is it possible that all knowledge, whether in the form of universal ideas or simple, down-to-earth "facts," is inhabited by ethical forces, ethical assumptions, ethical implications? Could it be that our very concept of "neutral" knowledge and "simple" facts is itself a deception?

We dream, perhaps, that once we *"know,"* then we can act. But what if what we now call "knowledge" actually prevents us from acting in any humanly significant sense of that word? What if the kind of ideas in our mind and the quality of the information we value as "facts"—what if it all imprisons us in a dream, in the illusion of free, moral action? It could be that the way we use our mind, and the ideas that we allow to take root in our mind guarantee that we will never, ever, act from the human center of ourselves. And if action does not emanate from one's own authentic self, can it ever be free? And if not free, can it ever be moral? If we wish to be good, if we wish to be what we are meant to be, we have no choice but to question, deeply, our relationship to our own mind and its contents.

Do we imagine that the young man in the story, who certainly represents ourselves, puts down his foot and is then able to do what is good? Or does he perhaps take to heart what he has been told and begin to study the Torah?

THE WORLD OF IDEAS

What is this "Torah"?

In its technical meaning, it is the name given to the first five sections of the Old Testament, known as the Five Books of Moses: Genesis, Exodus, Leviticus, Numbers, and Deuteronomy. And in its broader meaning it refers to the whole Bible, the whole tradition. As such, it represents the core of the Judaic religion, embracing everything from its most profound and universal conceptions of God, the moral law and the nature of reality, to details and rules of behavior, many of which are often regarded as pertaining only to another kind of culture existing under radically different social conditions.

But the broader meaning of Torah takes us beyond sectarian considerations, pointing all of humanity to a fundamental vision of man in the universe, along with a highly developed teaching about the structure of the human psyche and the nature of the inner struggle that is offered to everyone who seeks to become a "servant of God." In this sense the "Torah" means a great body of ideas, a comprehensive vision of reality. Such a comprehensive and genuine worldview is the indispensable foundation and support for the development of individual moral power.

IDEAS ALONE ARE NOT ENOUGH

But to know these ideas only with the mind is not enough. They must be allowed to penetrate a man or woman's heart and soul down to the very tissues of the body. Struggle with and within oneself is necessary to allow the inner opening to what is called God, a force which alone makes possible a sense of responsibility to one's neighbor, and hence genuine moral action. The Ten Commandments, for example—the moral teaching that lies at the heart of the Torah—places the need to remember the One God as the first obligation and possibility offered to man; it is only after conforming one's heart and mind to the true perception of God that the individual and the community come under those commandments which deal with right action toward one's neighbor. But, again, and in its turn, simply to hear it said that one must "have no other gods before me" is not in itself enough. A preparation of the mind is needed—a degree of understanding of what is meant by this word "God." All of the knowledge contained in the Torah has as one of its fundamental purposes to point human beings toward the study of what is necessary for us to know about the meaning of the word "God."

Finally, concerning this struggle to become *able* to be good, a modern commentator offers this reading of Hillel's response:

"The first part of [Hillel's] answer," he writes, ". . . sounds like a short-cut to the core of religion, to a happy morality and to the good life." But it is not so simple:

> The addition, "Go, study" points to the long way that has to be taken, patiently and persistently. In order to recognize the other fellow as my neighbor, as my equal, as one who is like unto me, my naked, undirected Ego has to undergo radical change. Training of will-power, self-renunciation, loving understanding, is needed before a person will be ready to make room for the other. *Such training is part of the study which cannot be done while one stands on one foot.*[3]

BUT IDEAS ARE THE FIRST STEP

Our main point here, however, is that even to begin this "training," this indispensable inner struggle, a preparation of the mind is necessary. Moral action is never automatic; it presupposes intention, free choice. And intention inevitably either begins or must pass through the mind. Sooner or later, the mind has to assent in order for any action to be free.

Of course, it may sometimes happen that our actions are right and good without our seeming to have made any decision whatever. But for most of us, apart from rare moments of great crisis and demand, when the whole of our inner being may rise up in a surge of intuitive will and moral force that simply overrides our everyday personality, such apparently spontaneous behavior may simply be automatic, conditioned behavior. It cannot be called moral. It is not what we wish for when we wish to be good.

For most of us, most of the time, the free assent of the mind is necessary in order for any action to be moral. And the free assent of the mind is enabled principally by ideas and logic. For most of us, and certainly for most of us born and raised in the modern world, shaped as it is by the ideal of scientific, i.e., mental, knowing, it is absolutely essential to examine the ethical and moral coloration of all that we call knowledge, both as a society and in our personal lives.

Do the contents of our minds support moral action? Do our ideas about nature, about the human self, about the universe, about history, language, the origins of religion, the human body—about time and space, war and peace—empower us to do—or even to know—what is good? Is our mind, with all its beliefs, opinions and "certainties," moral, immoral or ethically irrelevant?

We are in front of a fundamental, but embarrassingly difficult nest of questions: What ideas and opinions actually inhabit our minds? How did they get there? What are they worth?

Consider the following picture of the contents of our mind. Imagine a large bric-a-brac shop that sells anything and everything brought into it. The place is crammed with old household objects and pieces of furniture, mostly scarred or broken and covered with dust, which the eager manager pompously refers to as "antiques." There are numerous small appliances—old radios, toasters, record players—which do not work and maybe even never have worked. There are old lamps with no shades and age-darkened lampshades with no lamps. There are glass cases full of "jewelry"—mostly cheap, decades-old costume jewelry. Covering the walls are hundreds of paintings, ranging from gigantic, smeary landscapes that would require a truck to transport, to tiny miniatures consisting of wormy strokes of color that represent scenes of life or human faces only when one squints or maybe even shuts one's eyes entirely. And as for the thousands of dog-eared old books and magazines, phonograph records, old postcards, and framed photographs of movie stars or other people's family members, one has the impression of an abandoned madhouse or a dungeon once peopled by bored lunatics.

Such are the ideas, concepts, views and opinions that reside in our minds—ideas, views and opinions about anything and everything in the universe. No matter what the world presents to us, no matter who or what we meet in the course of our day, or what is said to us or even what or who glancingly passes by, the moment we attend to it, we instantly have an opinion about it, an idea about it, a "point of view," as we sometimes pretentiously describe it. Our bric-a-brac mind is constantly serving us up its furnishings, pictures and appliances in all their disconnected, dusty glory. Yet very few, if any at all, of these ideas, views and opinions that color and shape our experience and our very lives have ever been examined and weighed as to their truth and worth. Very rarely, if ever, are we even aware of them. We are, perhaps, never aware that this or that passion or decision or anxiety or fear or hope or resolute action is not "mine" at all, but actually belongs to some disconnected idea, view, or opinion that has taken up lodging in my mind and is actually doing my "thinking" for me. It is not *I* who take this passionately held moral stance, let us say, and am ready to sacrifice my all for it—it is an appliance in my mind that *feels* like *me*, like *I*, only because my real *I*, my real self, has never stepped forward to look at it, examine it, and decide whether to keep it and use it.

In this bric-a-brac shop, however, one does occasionally come across some precious article—a beautiful old cameo hiding in a clutter of rhinestones and plastic pearls; the first edition of a great book; an exquisite Meissen statuette surrounded by a dozen bourgeois imitations; an antique Sarouk carpet, its regal splendor obscured amid a pile of cheap, machine-made "Persian" rugs. Such are the profound ideas introduced into human life by far greater minds than our own—by men and women who had attained the ability to see the truth about man and the world, and who devoted themselves to passing on to future generations signs and indications of this truth and the path that leads to its realization in the life of mankind. But in our bric-a-brac minds even these great ideas lose their value—their moral power—because of their association with the cheap objects that are offered for sale throughout the shop.

Great ideas are never meant to enter the mind alone. They are always part of a tissue of ideas, an organic whole. *No idea can exist alone.* If an idea is not related to other ideas that altogether form the whole of a living teaching, it will inevitably become associated in a misleading and even dangerous way with imitation, "bric-a-brac" ideas—the concepts, "views" and opinions that now infest our minds.

We need to look at these two kinds of inhabitants of our mind: ideas that come from a higher source than our ordinary thought, and the concepts and opinions which are conditioned into us by the influence of education, society, media, and which are unconsciously and uncritically accepted as our own thoughts and views. We need to understand the power that our thoughts and opinions have to determine our ability to be good. That power is at least as important as being aware of the food we eat. Ideas and opinions and the perceptions, experiences, and impressions they allow us constitute the food of the mind. Our actions, that is, our moral health, are affected by the quality of this food we put into our mind no less than our physical health is affected by the quality of the food we put into our bodies.

THE GOOD UNIVERSE

Strange-sounding words, "the good universe," but this phrase sums up one of the first and most central ideas that the skeptical young man of our tale will encounter when he begins his study of the Torah.

But before we follow his study further, we need to remember that we are taking the Torah—the fundamental expression of the ideas of the Hebraic tradition—as an exemplar of what is offered to humanity in every great spiritual teaching the world has known. To make our point, we could just as well have chosen the essential ideas of Christianity or Buddhism or Islam or any of the world's articulations of wisdom. Every spiritual teaching brings with it a great body of ideas, although they are not always expressed in abstract language. Most often, the ideas of a spiritual teaching are originally communicated to the world through symbolic forms which are designed to reach the more hidden levels in us of instinct, feeling, and intuition: this it accomplishes through myth and story, visual images, architecture, music, dance, ritual. But in one way or another, at one or another stage in the process of moral and spiritual development, man's independent intellect with its function of abstract, logical thought needs to be fully engaged, needs to consent to the demands and invitations of the teaching. In a culture such as ours, in which mental knowledge, disconnected from the sensitivity of the body and the feeling, occupies such a dominant place in our lives and our sense of identity, the confrontation with great ideas is central to the process of moral development. This is true even for the fortunate among us who as children received genuine moral nourishment in our young hearts through the influence of an ethically healthy family atmosphere. However, as adults compelled to act amid the influences of the modern world, almost all of us need the moral support of our thought and mind.

Here, then, is our "one-legged" pupil as he encounters the Hebraic vision of Creation.

From the very beginning he is met by the force of a great contradiction—as are most of us when we first study the Bible. This great contradiction is nothing other than the existence of evil and the disobedience of man—an event seemingly written into the very structure of the universe, the very structure and essence of reality itself. Here is the universe, here is creation in all its awesome immensity and infinity of purpose and beauty; here are the lights of the heavens, the sun, moon, and stars; here is life and the great flowing forces symbolized as "waters" above and below the heavens; here is all that the Creator has made—the whole living universe, the whole realm of Being itself. And here are the "days" of creation, indication of a process in which the Eternal enters into the realm of time, one "day" or step, at a time. And as the creation proceeds, starting with the third day, God repeatedly steps back and looks at what He has made, "and God saw that it was good." But when the whole of nature and the world are created, it is as though God pauses and ponders, and says to Himself, "Let us make man. . . ." "So God created man in

His own image, in the image of God created He him; male and female created He them" (Genesis 1:27). And now God shows the man and woman the whole of the world He has created and offers it to them, for insofar as man is made in God's image, the creation that is God's work is in some sense also the work of man.

But with this, the drama of the world of nature, time and free will begins. And it is at the beginning of this drama that God gives His creation a deeper, fuller blessing: "And God saw every thing that He had made, and, behold, it was very good" (Genesis 1:31). By bringing man into the universe, God is able to say that now it is *very* good, exceedingly good—which means complete, finished. And yet, at the same time, it is a drama, a movement; it is a struggle that is about to begin. Uncertainty enters the world, freedom enters the world. One might have imagined— as our young student might have imagined—that the world is *exceedingly* good because human consciousness has been brought to it. But he soon finds—as we who read this Bible soon find—that God has also brought *evil* into the world. With the movement of life, and especially the movement of conscious life—with man—the profound drama, the unfathomable mystery of good and evil enters the world.

An entire universe now unfolds: a history of God, as it were, in the form of and through the instrumentality of man, the self that we are, though we know it not. The Torah is speaking of man not simply as a particular being inhabiting a particular tiny planet in the great universe. It is also speaking of man as the center of the universe. Both of these contradictory ideas together!—as in the rabbinic saying, "Every man must carry two pieces of paper with him and look at each of them every day. On one it is written, 'You are as dust and ashes.' And on the other: 'For you the universe was created.'"

The universe cares about man, needs man, needs the essence of man— that which a human being really is and is meant to become. The man or woman who looks up at the night sky and experiences the sense of wonder is perceiving reality accurately. In such a moment an individual is equally humbled by two realities: the great world above and the fact of his own awareness and presence in that great world. In this primal experience of wonder—holy awe—we are infinite and finite at once; both eternal and temporal, as is God when He creates the universe and enters into time. I am here, just myself, this small being now penetrated by greatness, this man or woman who usually lives under the sway of fear and confusion. But now, in this moment of genuine wonder, I know that I belong to the sacred wholeness of reality and, if I am very attentive, I see that I yearn for my duty toward what I am and what has created me.

But the moment of wonder is often only a moment. In the very next moment, I will turn my head, I will move, and then—suddenly—I no longer sense my sacred essence. I am no longer Man: I am a desire, a fear, an impulse, a reaction. I like and dislike; I might even steal or kill, if not in fact then in thought. I am no longer Man; I am simply this man or this woman. What will I choose? To be Man? Or to be this distracted man or woman?

The principle of choice has been injected into the heart of creation. With the principle of choice, there enters the real question of good and evil. Nothing exists neutrally; nothing exists without being embraced by the question of the power of choice, of perceiving good and evil and acting upon it. Reality is charged with ethical forces. Everything *matters.* A man who sees or acts without primary reference to the inner power of will and intention is not a man.

Picture now our young pupil sitting at the knee of the great Hillel. Why, he asks, is the Torah so full of contradictions? Why are the first ideas he meets there so confusing? God creates Man—very well. He places Man in the Garden of Eden, paradise, and shows him the tree of life. Also—very well. And God also shows Man the tree of the knowledge of good and evil. But this is not so very well; here begins confusion.

Here begins evil. But why? Why the serpent? Wasn't it God Himself who placed the serpent in the garden? Did God not know what the serpent would do? And why the disobedience of Eve and then, after her,

Adam? And why does God forbid them to eat of the tree of the knowledge of good and evil?

Our young questioner is not asking merely out of curiosity. He is a serious seeker. His seemingly whimsical gesture of standing on one leg was in fact an act of desperate need: let us see him that way, see him as we ourselves are in our most stormy moments of inner questioning about ourselves.

THE TEACHER WAITS

The teacher quietly studies the student in front of him. He waits. He does not give the kind of instant response that was an appropriate initial "shock" when the young man first came to him in an act of bold, holy impatience. The teacher lets the question sound *within himself.* The teacher and the pupil are now within one of the primal sacred forms in which the transmission of truth has always taken place throughout the ages: the face-to-face encounter of the seeker and the guide.

The teacher waits and lets go of his own first associations to the question—all of the ideas he has studied and mastered, the ideas that await the questioning pupil before him. The teacher does not want to cover the question with words; he does not want to kill the sacred state of the questioner with an "answer." He wants, among other things, to help prepare the pupil for the ideas that he will encounter in the years ahead of him, to prepare him to value the state of questioning that will allow the ideas to enter him in the right way, as his own discovery. He wants to help the student receive deeply the help of the teaching, the energy the teaching can carry into his mind and heart.

The teacher waits—until he himself becomes empty of his "wisdom." Until he himself is even more deeply in question than the pupil. And then, perhaps, the teacher is given the response, because it is now *his* question.

The question is: why did Adam and Eve obey the serpent instead of God?

Hillel—the Hillel of our imagination—replies:

"And what do *you* obey?"

The response hangs in the air. As the teacher knew it would. Such a response stops the serious seeker. He will not answer back easily or quickly. Even now, perhaps, he senses the weight of this seemingly unsatisfying, almost irrelevant response to his question. In any case, the pupil is being prepared in his heart and mind to face part of the great answer that the teaching gives to the existence of evil in the world—that man is born with two lives within him, two forces that are opposed to each other, and that the task and meaning of our life is to bring them together through a freely chosen struggle, so as to allow the reconciling force of God to enter into the human community.

In this demand placed upon man lies the story of the world; that genuine evil (not sent by God) arises from an inner "choice," a refusal to accept the struggle that will show us the nature of the forces within ourselves, and the sacrifices required of us in order to place our powers in the service of the Eternal.

"What do *you* obey?"

Does the pupil glimpse, suddenly, that his need, his human situation, the confusion and the profound *unsatisfactoriness* of his day-to-day life, are not due only to something missing in him, but to something missing in Man? The great original disobedience of Adam and Eve is the story of Man. Our individual situation is the whole situation of humanity; it is not just my problem, my difficulty; it is the problem and the sorrow of man on earth. Does the student hear that? Perhaps not yet. He needs to hear more, other ideas that speak about the laws of God, the demands of God, the possibilities that God "had in mind" when he created Man. Our young pupil cannot know about these things. No one knows about them, apart from those who have long struggled to awaken to the truth.

IDEAS LIVE IN PEOPLE

The whole of the Torah, the whole body of ideas now stretches out before the pupil, waiting for him, calling to him. It will be, it must be, that everything he learns about the world and man will be received in the light of the question of service to the Eternal. The world now becomes charged with ethical meaning.

But first the fundamental ideas of the teaching must begin to be received. They must be admitted into the storehouse of his mind, where through logic and reflection and through the indispensable help of the guide, they gradually expose the opinions, imitation ideas, and unconsciously accepted concepts that clutter his mind and pre-condition his fundamental perceptions of the world and his fellow man. He will begin to realize that almost everything in his life and in his world has until now been brought to his awareness already stained by opinion. No sooner does he try to think about something, no sooner does he try to decide what he ought to do, than the opinions in his bric-a-brac mind are writing the menu of his options and, unknown to him, dictating the direction and quality of his actions.

But now the ideas of the teaching begin their work. The very nature and existence of the world becomes a new question and a new idea for him—that is to say, for *us.*

The world? The universe? Does it exist for no reason? Did it just spring into being from nowhere? Do things just happen to be arranged with such incomprehensible order—with life upon life, life within life, purpose within purpose surrounding us and penetrating through all the reaches of space and time? Is not the fact of existence itself, being itself, a mystery—an inescapable mystery: that is to say, a question that must be wholeheartedly confronted?

We cannot escape this question. In fact, we *must* not escape this question. Before any commandment from above is formulated, the great teaching demands of us that we confront the mystery of existence itself.

The psyche of every man or woman entering the "temple of the mind" is constructed to ponder this question. The more we explain the world, whether through science or any other modality, the greater appears the mystery of the world's very existence.

We are born to look, examine, explain; but hovering over all our explanations that show us the intricate interconnectedness *within* the world, hovering over it all in the structure of our mind is the ever-deepening mystery of the *fact of the world,* the origin and meaning of existence itself, order itself, the cosmos itself—and, finally, the corresponding mystery of the existence of the mind that sees all this and feels all this: the question and the mystery of *oneself.*

God created the world! Suddenly, the words are new. The world is charged with mystery—mystery defined as intelligence beyond my intelligence; as higher order, an order that I cannot understand, but which I am *obliged* to understand.

GOD IS ONE

Here is what the pupil is told about the chief characteristic of this God who created the world:

Hear O Israel! The Lord our God, the Lord is One.

God is One. What is this *monotheism* that is presented as the fundamental commandment to man, the commandment—or, as we may say, the *possibility*—of seeing and respecting the wholeness of God and the wholeness of the world? All too easily, it slips away into a mere concept. Or an article of blind faith. Or even a war cry. That is: an imitation idea, or a sentimental dream, or an inflammable slogan.

There is one God and one God only. Why is this so important?—or, rather, why, when it is so easy to say the words, is this idea presented in the form of a *commandment,* or a sacred invitation, something that we must struggle or inwardly prepare ourselves to accept?

Consider this story, recorded nearly two thousand years after Hillel.

Another teacher and another pupil and again the aching question—this time concerning what the Torah commands about the oneness of God:

> Hear O Israel! The Lord our God, the Lord is One.
>
> And thou shalt love the Lord thy God with all thine heart, and with all thy soul, and with all thy might.
>
> And these words which I command thee this day: place these words upon your heart:
>
> And thou shalt teach them diligently unto thy children, and shalt talk of them when thou sittest in thine house, and when thou walkest by the way, and when thou liest down, and when thou risest up . . .[4]

The pupil asks the rabbi, "Why are we told to place these words *upon* our heart? Why does it not tell us to place these words *in* our heart?"

In fact, the question already lives within the differing translations of the text. The Hebrew, *al-levavekha,* means "upon your heart," but in the vast majority of the English translations it is rendered as "*in* your heart." It is as though the translators, like the pupil in the story, cannot understand why it is said "*upon* your heart."

Why, then are we not told to place these words, these root words of the entire teaching, *in* our heart?

The rabbi answers: "Because," he replies, "we are unable to put these words into our heart. All that we can do is to place these words *upon* our heart."

THE PUPIL WAITS

The pupil waits. He has come to understand that the teaching is about himself, *myself,* one's own life, one's own being. The ideas are about me, here, in front of the question of myself. Hearing the rabbi's reply, more of the question begins to form on the pupil's lips: *Then what am I to do? What are we to do?* But before he can speak it, the rabbi answers.

"Our hearts are closed. All we can do is to place these words *upon* our heart. And there they stay . . ."

". . . until one day the heart breaks . . . and the words fall in."

ONE GOD; TWO HEARTS

The idea of the One God leads the pupil to the idea of the human heart—that at one and the same time the human heart wishes both to receive and to reject what is offered to it. Here, in front of this contradiction, the pupil—we, ourselves—confront the great idea of man's "two hearts," his two natures, or, as it is called in the Hebraic formulation, the *yetzer tov* and the *yetzer ha-ra,* the good impulse and the inclination toward evil. The Torah calls us to inform both of our "two hearts" about the oneness and the greatness of God. It calls us to serve God with both the good impulse and the inclination toward evil, just as, at the root of His creation of the world, the good and the evil, the angel and the devil, were created to further the action in the world of the One-Without-a-Name, the God beyond God—what the hidden tradition-without-a-name refers to as the great *In-Itself,* the *En-Sof.*

The two hearts of man must be penetrated and reconciled by the truth of God. As we are now, one impulse affirms and the other impulse denies. The practice of the teaching will involve bringing these two movements into harmony—through submission to the One-Without-a-Name within ourselves.

God is One—yes, but also, and of highest importance: God is *Oneness.* God is Unity. The pupil is obliged to understand what this means. The pupil—man—does not understand this idea—because, in order to understand it, he must himself be on the way to unity within his own being. Without a taste of the experience of unity within himself, the idea remains only a noble ideal, a noble concept which the good impulse with him accepts—like an "obedient" follower, a "good Jew." But it is not enough to be a "good Jew." Or rather—it is impossible to be a "good

Jew," a good man, without including in one's consciousness all that resists the impulse toward Good.

THE PROBLEM OF EVIL

Here the pupil once again meets the great idea of evil: Evil exists not only within himself, but in the whole of mankind—and in the whole of the Creation. And yet: *God is One. God is Unity.* How to understand this? How to *begin* to understand this? The Torah stretches out before the pupil. The history of mankind begins. Everywhere and in everything there is the struggle between good and evil. Everywhere, and in everything, God commands and man resists. Man, *Man:* who is this? Who or what is he? Sometimes he is Pharaoh, the tyrant, enslaving the people of Israel, drawing his power from idols. Sometimes he is Moses, extracting the truth hidden in the secret temples obscured by Pharaoh; Moses visited by God, leading the people of Israel—Man in all his multiplicity and passivity—out of the state of slavish obedience to the false king, Pharaoh. Yes, Man *is* the people of Israel wandering through the desert, the austere path that leads from slavery, degrading submission, to the land of "milk and honey"—the realm where the essence-food of Man is prepared by the Creation itself. Man-in-the-desert: Man on the *way:* Man severed from the foods of the land of slavery, severed from the life of slavery, but not yet in the state of freedom and conscious service that is his right and destiny. This, too, is Man: Man in between sleep and awakening, Man in whom the two natures contend with gathering force, Man in between the *yetzer tov* and the *yetzer ha-ra.* On this path, Man is provided with a food that comes from above—the food, *manna.* God will provide—God is providence in many senses, but here emphasizing the sense that from above, Man will be provided with the essential sustenance needed by his developing soul.

. . .

Here we take leave of our one-legged pupil. He will return to us later in his work of studying the Torah, his task of admitting all the great ideas into his mind, and laying them "upon his heart." The vastness of what he will study is beyond summary and description, being one of the fundamental expressions of the vision of man and the universe that has guided human life since mankind first appeared on the earth. Every word, every image, every story will call him to stop inside himself and look out at the world with new eyes. He will learn again and again that he, Man, is a being created for right action, a being who is meant to step into the stream of human life and create causes, create effects: *to be, to know, to love* and *to do* in the human world, just as God, the *Creator of Causes*, is *Being, Wisdom, Mercy* and *Demand* in the life of the universe.

He will learn, in short, that his essence is the power of conscious action, and that all genuinely conscious action is moral action. He is not a stone, he is not a tree, he is not an animal, he is Man. A stone exists, a plant lives and senses, an animal moves and feels and may even "think." But only a man can act.

He is Man. Yet, at the same time, he is not yet Man. He is not yet united with his own essence.

Moses leads the people of Israel to a promised land that he himself cannot enter. The pupil will learn that no one knows where Moses, the greatest of men, is buried. Does this mean that not even Moses attained to Man? Or does it mean that no one of us can ever discover the hidden Moses, the hidden truth?

He will learn that so great was the attention to God of Abraham, Isaac, and Jacob that God defines himself to the people by their names. After naming Himself to Moses as the awesomely mysterious and concrete: "EHYEH ASHER EHYEH," "I WILL BE THAT I WILL BE," a phrase that has been subject to many interpretations, one of which we may propose as *"I Am my actions when there is holy need for Me,"* after defining Himself for Man as the Creator of Causes acting within Time (human life)—after defining Himself as the God whose Being is Doing— He speaks further to Moses, saying, "Thus shalt thou say to the children of Israel, The Lord God of your fathers, the God of Abraham, the God of Isaac, and the God of Jacob, hath sent me unto you: this is my name for ever, and this is my memorial unto all generations."[5]

He will learn that he is both terrifyingly estranged from his essence and incomprehensibly close to it. He betrays his nature and at the same time he tastes within himself and in the demands placed upon him that he is the son of the Creator. There is a passage between what he in fact is and what he is created to be, a passage that is very far and long, and at the same time immediate and nearly instantaneous. It is like an electric arc between now and the future, between what I am now and what I AM in eternity. Eternity and temporality, infinity and finitude, past and future, the very meaning itself of time and history stretches before the pupil, stretches before Man, before oneself, myself, yourself.

And the bridge is action, manifestation, doing—action rooted in the contemplation of Being, in inner stillness, inner submission, inner attention to Truth, an inner attention to truth and wisdom that begins in the mind, in thought.

His primary question takes form. Our primary question takes form. It is the question of Man in our era, now, here, in this burning world and this burning life we live.

What activity of the mind leads us toward the power to be good? Man is the being meant to act and at the same time the being unable to act. Modern man lives in his mind, asleep to the power to act that resides in the whole of his being. But within the prison of the mind there is an action that leads toward conscious action. Within the mind there is a power of relationship to my neighbor that leads toward love of my neighbor. The mind alone cannot make us able to do what we know is good. But the mind alone can take us toward that power.

Great ideas show us the possibility; they touch the heart of the mind. They are instruments that show us where we are and where we are meant to go, but by themselves they cannot give us the power we need and yearn for, the power of conscious action, the power of love.

Great ideas call us—not to act, because they tell us we cannot yet act.

But they call us to another kind of action that is within our power, just as we are. And that action is the work of the mind, the work of thinking, pondering.

What kind of thought, what kind of relationship to great ideas will actually take us toward what we are searching for in relation to our neighbor and the life of man? The answer is right before us. The answer is in you, my neighbor. The first step toward the power of moral action lies in the power we have to *think morally*. But this does not mean necessarily to think specifically about moral or ethical issues—it means the work of *thinking together* with my neighbor, with you, about any essential question of the heart and mind. A new meaning of human relationship now appears—in fact, an old, an ancient meaning of love. The ancient meaning of friendship appears—to work together at thinking.

Which means: to work together at speaking from the heart of the mind and listening with love and rigor. It is the work of allowing language to be born between us, real language that carries the vibration of thought.

We are speaking of an entirely new realm of ethics—a pre-ethical realm, as it were, that is a step toward the life of conscious moral action. But it is an ethics we can practice just as we are—with work and guidance. It is not impossible for us. It is our step toward the possibility that we yearn for, but which we cannot as yet attain.

We are speaking of the ethics of thinking together, of philosophical love.

Enter Socrates.

Two

THE SECRET OF SOCRATES
or THINKING TOGETHER
AS A WORK OF LOVE

Visible objects are to be seen only when the sun shines upon them;
truth is only known when illuminated by the idea of good.

REPUBLIC, BOOK VI[6]

et us, finally, imagine this man differently. Our attitude toward
him has become shamefully comfortable—even where we see
him in his legendary last hours surrounded by his pupils, calmly
holding the executioner's cup to his lips. Not to mention the static picture we have of him mingling in the marketplace, fishing for seekers of
truth. Or discoursing with divine objectivity on the mysticism of love
while his table companions are sinking into wine-drenched sleep.

So comfortable have we become with our picture of this man that we
give the name "Socratic" to almost any kind of intellectual conversation
at all—as though we understood what *he* meant by "dialogue" and as
though we could even do it ourselves!

We need to imagine him now for what he really was, and what we
need him to be for us: *the destroyer of "thought" and the inseminator of mind,*
for whom love was the conjugal act of human beings thinking together,

for whom truth was born not in the answering, but in the deepening of questions—in the exchange of heart and mind between the teacher and the pupil and *within the pupil himself.*

His great pupil, Plato, carefully scripted him within the vastness of what was to become the Western world's most powerful system of philosophical ideas—ideas that have moved the entire life of the earth, radiating their formulations into the Hebraic revelation, lending it a logic and a language that enabled it to speak to all minds in all nations. Through this marriage of Judaism and Greek philosophy, both Christianity and Islam, each in its turn and in its idiom, transmitted their revelation to the intellect of the world. Yet embedded in the middle of it all stands Socrates, a mystery in broad daylight—the man who "understands nothing" and who shows all who wish to hear that they, too, do not understand. And who whispers to us that real thought demands freedom from thought-in-quotation-marks.

The formulations of his pupil, Plato, flow through the blood and tissues of our culture. The idea of the real world behind the world we see, a real world accessible only to the soul; the idea of levels of mind, corresponding to levels of reality: these ideas come from Plato. The idea of wisdom as virtue, and virtue as wisdom, comes from Plato. The very distinction between opinion and understanding comes from Plato, as does the idea of authentic learning as deep inner "remembering." The idea of the yearning for truth as an organic element in the structure of the human psyche comes from Plato. And above all, from Plato we are given the astonishing idea that the source of all that exists in the whole of the great universe is the radiating light of Goodness, a Goodness hidden deep within the world of appearances—that unstable world where humanity sleeps in the darkness of "forgetfulness"—a world from which, however, we can awaken through the effort to know ourselves. All such formulations, and much, much more, came to the world through Plato.

But Plato came from Socrates.

ENTER SOCRATES

Socrates is the symbol and the reality of the work of thinking *together.* It was a work that was unknown to those around him in Athens. And it is a work that is unknown to us today.

Thinking is an ethical act. Such is the fundamental message that Socrates offers to our world. Thinking is an ethical act—real thinking, the thinking of a man, of a being who is born for moral action, but who is not yet capable of it, who is not yet able to be good.

What Socrates brought was a work of the mind that is a preparation for morality, a rehearsal for moral action. What takes place between Socrates and those who occupied the place of his pupils is an *intermediate* movement between moral impotence and moral power. What he offers us is a way of finding the stepping-stone between a life driven by egoism and a life based on conscience.

You do not understand what it means to be moral—so he is telling us from across the millennia. You do not understand what virtue is; what justice is; what love or beauty are; you do not understand friendship; you do not understand responsibility either toward your neighbor or God or toward yourself. You do not understand what real freedom is, or courage, or compassion; you do not understand what happiness is. And, above all, you do not understand what you yourself are. You do not understand your own soul.

Because you have no understanding of these things, and because you are not aware of your ignorance, your life is wretched and chaotic. You believe you ought to be good, but you do not see that you are not yet *able* to be good. Your being does not allow it. Your mind and heart are in the thrall of your appetites and your actions are in the thrall of your tyrannized and tyrannizing mind. Within you, deeply buried, is an immeasurably higher force of thought and mind, a soul, your Self, which has the power to put your being in order and which can give you the power to know what is true and to will what is good. But, as you are, these possibilities beat their wings in vain.

THE SECRET OF SOCRATES

Come, says Socrates: what is your question? What is it you wish to understand? Consider it carefully: about what do you wish to think?

This is already a very great and deeply *ethical* issue: what *ought* we to think about? To what end should we put the energies of our mind, our defining human quality? This is the first question of Socrates and the first question of man, the being for whom being itself is in question. How we respond to it is of immeasurable importance. How we respond to it will determine the course of our entire life.

What is your question? What do you need to think about? What do *we* need to think about together? For it is only by working together that we can approach the answer to the mystery of our existence. It is only in the life of the exchange of mind and heart between people and within ourselves that we will taste the demand of the Good, that we can hear the call of the Good, that we can struggle to obey the Good and confront all in ourselves that resists the Good. Thinking together is a preparation for living together. Thinking together is a school for conscience, an "academy" in which individual human beings can in fact struggle to act as though they were moral, as though they were able to hear and obey the call of conscience.

To think together is not yet to be good, far from it; but neither is it to be entirely lost in the egoism and imaginary morality of our everyday life. To think together is to step into the realm of intermediate morality, a moral life that we can in fact practice—as opposed to the actual moral life in the world that we only imagine we can practice. The work of thinking together is only a step toward the power to be good, but it is a real step and therefore of immense value. It is a step we can take; a step we must take. This is the secret of Socrates.

THE TASTE OF THINKING

I have called it a secret in broad daylight. Let me explain what I mean by those words.

I remember very clearly the day I first encountered this "secret." It was the beginning of my freshman year at college. Only a week before, I had been at the window of my dormitory room in Harvard Yard, waving good-bye to my mother and father as they drove off toward Philadelphia in our 1950 Chevrolet. But now I was walking toward the first of my classes, a large General Education course in the Humanities. I had stayed up half the night reading our first assignment: Plato's *Apology,* consisting of Socrates' defense of himself before the Athenian court. The court has charged him with corrupting the young and subverting traditional religious belief—serious indictments, tantamount to the charge of treason.

I did not feel that Socrates and Plato were strangers to me. As I joyfully walked to class under flaming leaves, I mused absently about the love affair I had had with philosophy during my high school years.

Starting around the age of fifteen, I read every philosophy book I could get my hands on, often understanding almost nothing—sometimes hardly more than a sentence or two. But when I did understand something, even if only a very little—as I did, for example, reading the lucid essays of Bertrand Russell or the *Meditations* of Marcus Aurelius—I felt a sense of homecoming: So! I was not the only one who had such questions!

It was a feeling which I did not and could not put into words, a sense that I had found companions in another life, another world in the midst of my everyday world. I might even say that I had fallen in love with the very word "philosophy," which evoked in me a sort of movement within myself, an inner "taste" of the mind.

I remember again and again encountering that word "mind" in the books I was reading. And as I read the arguments and questions of the philosophers—and kept stopping when I didn't understand, or stopping even more radically when I *did* understand—then I saw that in the stops between the deep thoughts, in the stops between the deep questions and the proposed answers—I saw that in those stops, which took place in me automatically—in those stops, I saw, I *knew* that I was experiencing my *mind*. I was *thinking*. And this *thinking* had a completely different sense, a different taste, a different quality than when I was puzzling over my homework, or trying to figure out an algebraic equation, or trying to decide what movie to go to, or how to understand why someone didn't like me or how to ask my father for something.

And at the same time, I noticed very strongly—yet without really knowing it in words or being able to see it explicitly—that the same "taste," the same movement was what occurred in my love of nature and science: looking up at the night sky, watching the ant crawl through the "forest" of hair on my arm, studying the laws of chemical equilibrium or the axioms and proofs of Euclidean geometry or the pattern of spore propagation in mushrooms or, above all, the wonder of the human body.

It was same taste as in listening to certain kinds of music—something in me would come to a stop, even as the momentum of emotional ex-ultation poured through me—while listening, say, to Beethoven's Seventh Symphony or the Franck Symphony in D minor: I would come to a stop, in the midst of which I would wonder how it was that a mere sequence of sounds brought me in touch with another reality in myself, a reality whose name philosophy was now showing me: *mind*.

In this way, my adolescent love of philosophy allowed me to recognize the connectedness of special attractions in my life, special "moments" of looking, listening, observing, wondering, including certain special qualities of quiet sorrow and quiet joy—all of them were the movement and the life of my *mind*. And all of them appeared as a *stop*, an interior stop. It was not that a new thought appeared or a new insight or a great answer. It was that the momentum of thought had been brought to a stop. That was as far as I could see—and even putting it that way occurred to me only much later in my life, when I was helped to understand that the *stop* is the doorway to a new *kind* of thought, leading to a new possibility of action and care.

Philosophy had brought me to the brink of recognizing that I was searching for something in my life. Searching for what? I certainly *wanted* many things, but this was completely different. Not "success"—which I certainly wanted; not recognition, which I certainly craved; not success with girls, which I certainly yearned for; not physical prowess, not "fun," not rest, not excitement . . . None of these, but only "something" having to do with *mind*.

THE MOUNTAIN OF PLATO

But what was I to do about Plato? There it was: two massive volumes with a name as intriguing to me as the contents were indigestible: *The Dialogues of Plato.* I must have renewed those books twenty times at our school library until, finally, our librarian, a tiny, white-haired elf-woman named Miss Yoder (I never learned her first name, or thought of her as having one) stunned me by actually telling me to keep them. I later learned that she had the library order a new set, because the way I was struggling with them and lugging them back and forth appealed to her. May God give us more such librarians!

It was not simply that I could not understand Plato. I could not understand *why* I could not understand him. And I found that unbearable. Everywhere I turned I was being told about his importance, his greatness. I understood of course that he lived about 2500 years ago in ancient Athens, that he was born into an aristocratic family and as a young man became a devoted pupil of the great Socrates. I understood that his philosophy was written in the form of intellectual dramas called "dialogues," most of which featured Socrates examining deep philosophical questions and challenging the assumptions and beliefs of all who came his way. Fine and good, but what did it all mean—any of it?

The easiest thing to grasp—and even then only up to a certain point—was Socrates' last days. I could more or less understand that he had been unjustly accused and sentenced to be executed because his influence on young Athenian aristocrats and his way of questioning everything was threatening to the faction that had seized political power in Athens. I could read Socrates' famous defense of himself with a certain amount of interest, but without really feeling what was at stake. Was I supposed to be deeply moved by the injustice of it? How could I be? His argument before the court was so smooth, and he himself seemed so untroubled by what could happen to him—namely, death!

Again and again I would pick up a heavy volume and try to read one or another of the "dialogues," with their strangely beautiful names—many of them sounding to me a little like the mysterious names of the distant stars and constellations in the night sky: *Charmides, Meno, Phaedrus, Timaeus, Hippias Major, Philebus* . . .

In the margins of the text the translator had provided brief running summaries of the themes treated in each of the dialogues, and these summaries, coupled with the mysterious Greek titles, made them all the more fascinating to me and raised my hopes of finding whatever it was I was searching for. Even to list a few of the themes mentioned in these marginal notes evokes in me the memory of what I felt approaching these writings and what over fifty years ago I hoped for from them: "The Immortality of the Soul," "The Meaning of Friendship," "Wisdom and Pleasure," "What Is Knowledge?" "The Creation of the Universe," "Justice and Happiness," "True Courage."

Disappointment! Individual sentences and sometimes even whole pages I could easily follow and they often intrigued me. But what did they really mean? It was deeply frustrating to me. Not because the words were obscure or technical or the line of argument logically complicated; I could easily accept that in the works of the other philosophers I had tried to read—Spinoza, Kant, Hume and others—there was specialized terminology and complexity that I could not grasp, just as I could not grasp the specialized language and references in scientific books. But this was not how it was with Plato—quite the contrary! I recognized all the words and would quite easily be following, and even enjoying, the back-and-forth between Socrates and his companions. But after two or three pages I would invariably begin to realize that I had no idea what was going on. At this point, I would simply put the book down in frustration—maybe picking it up a little later and peeking at the place where I had left off in the hope of catching the real meaning, as it were, on the sly. To no avail. It was like being spoken to in a foreign language in which you perfectly well understand every word that the person is saying, but have no idea what he means to say!

THE MISSING PAGE

One day my frustration boiled over. I was sitting at a table in the big, sunny reading room of the school library. Classes were over and, it being a beautiful spring day, the library was almost deserted—save for one or two other students and, of course, the two librarians: the tiny, white-haired Miss Yoder and her second-in-command from a wholly other tribe of elves: the lanky, towering, gray-haired Miss Clarissa (she had a long Polish last name that no one ever remembered). Miss Clarissa was almost twice as tall as Miss Yoder, and much more of a demon about rules and regulations.

I had been sitting stock still for well over an hour on one of the library's slippery chairs. In front of me Volume One of the Plato was open to the dialogue called *Meno,* the theme of which was "Can virtue be taught?" This theme did not attract me at all. The word "virtue" meant nothing to me—I doubt that I had ever once in my life used it in a sentence or even spoken it aloud. But in another book I had read that this was Plato's and Socrates' most essential question. If so, it was frighteningly meaningless to me. Much later in my life, of course, I realized that in these wooden words lay the whole question of how to become able to be moral and how one who has this capacity can help another to develop it in him- or herself.

But here the translator had signaled another major theme of the dialogue—and this interested me immensely: the idea that real knowledge does not come to us from outside, but lies hidden within us and needs to be "remembered." How this was connected with virtue I neither knew nor cared to know—even though that was the fundamental issue at hand. What excited me was the idea that within myself there lay the depths of great knowledge and wisdom; that inside myself there was something called the soul, and this soul was something that knew, that understood, that had wisdom. I didn't care about virtue; I cared about knowledge and understanding. About the soul and virtue I had had enough in the suffocating books and sermons of religious leaders and writers with their talk of the soul going to heaven or hell because of so-called good or bad deeds or thoughts. Who could take that kind of thing seriously?—apart from some Catholic classmates of mine who *said* they took it seriously and who then said, in a kind of guilty whisper, well, maybe, maybe not.

But the equation of the soul and the *mind*—that was thrilling. That was my *self*! That was my real identity! That was what I was tasting when I *stopped* inside myself!

Or was it? Did I really understand what Socrates was saying in words so clear, but in a progression of argument that was becoming unreal to me? My fingers were gripping the edge of the table. Little by little my head was bending down to the open book until my nose was inches away from the page where Socrates offers actually to *demonstrate* to his patrician host, Meno, that every human being already has within himself, within his immortal mind and soul, the true understanding of everything.

In what has become one of the most oft-cited passages in Plato's writings,[7] Socrates asks Meno to select any one of his servants for the experiment. A young, uneducated boy is asked to step forward. "Attend now to the questions which I ask him," says Socrates to Meno, "and observe whether he learns of me or only remembers."

"I will," says Meno.

Socrates now proceeds to draw a simple geometric figure, a square divided into four smaller squares, and, in very simple language, asks the boy what he thinks would be the measurements of a square twice as big—that is, a square with an area twice as large as the original figure. It seems obvious to the boy—as, at first glance, it would seem to many of us—that a square twice as big as the original would simply have sides twice as long as the original. But, of course, that is not true. A square with sides twice as long as the original square would actually be four times as large.

Through guided, step-by-step questioning, Socrates now elicits from the uneducated servant boy the insight that a square twice as big will not, as it first may seem, have sides twice as long as the original square, but will in fact be a square figure with sides whose length is the length of the original square's diagonal.

The conversation between Socrates and the boy occupied several pages in the text and was accompanied by clear, simple diagrams. But even so, it took me many readings and the exertion of all my attention and patience to follow Socrates speaking to the boy in such a way that his questions did not give the boy any answers, but only allowed him to discover the true answer for himself, from his own mind, his own thinking. After many readings, I still could not escape the impression that Socrates was "cheating," leading the boy on so precisely that he was practically putting the answers into the boy's mouth. But, at the same time, perhaps I was wrong; perhaps the example really was showing what Socrates said it was showing. It was so often this way reading Plato! Was the "dialogue" doing what it was supposed to be doing? Or was it a ruse, a kind of intellectual comic strip with the superhero Socrates always winning and only pretending he was just "questioning"?

At the same time, I very well recognized something in what was happening with the servant boy. It was just that year, my sophomore year in high school, that I was taking geometry. Every day we would be working the Euclidean theorems and proofs and diagrams about angles and lines and areas. And almost every day, in class and at home working out my lessons, I would end up intoxicated with joy at the beauty of the proofs. At the beauty and purity of geometry. At the wonder of certainty, the happiness of seeing a pure, ultimately real world and sensing, knowing that my mind, the mind, could be allowed to move and dance and follow laws, patterns, lines that defined, that undergirded everything in the universe, everything real, everybody in the world, every living thing, every volume, every object, every star, every galaxy. Everything was geometry! Geometry was the bones of God's creation! And my mind didn't have to sweat and puff to understand it, to memorize anything, to stuff itself with words and boring facts. The work of geometry was not "work" at all; the work of the mind here was to work at allowing the mind to dance! And the dancing mind, the joyous, liberated mind, was pure geometry. The dance was Euclidean. The dance was precise, exact, irrefutable, completely certain and it was all about the real world out there and in here! Was this a taste of wisdom? Was this something of what all knowledge should be? Was this the mind? Yes and no. Was this something to guide my life? No and yes.

I read on and on, not budging from my chair, my breathing becoming audible. Socrates turns back to Meno, and the question of knowledge and wisdom and the soul is picked up again. Who cares about the servant boy now! Now we were turning back to wisdom and the soul and we were going to find out if the beauty and the dance and the love that the mind finds in proofs and angles—we were going to find out whether that was what all knowledge and wisdom was like and we were going to find out whether inside myself there was wisdom and knowledge as clear and certain as geometry—but now about the world and life and the universe and—all right, "virtue," if you wish, if you must—but wisdom and knowledge about *everything*. I was going to find out who I was, I was going to understand my own soul!

I had to be careful not to turn the pages too rapidly. The arguments were compactly stated, but not hard to follow if one took time and was attentive. So I raced on, but very carefully, holding the table tighter and tighter.

And again, but now like a blow in the chest: *disappointment*! I couldn't believe it! Suddenly, the text came to an end! Suddenly, it was the last page!

For a moment, I just sat there, staring at the page. Then I desperately flipped the pages back to see if by chance I had skipped whole pages at the end. But I had not.

I was now too agitated even to read the last two paragraphs of the text, where Socrates says we will only know how to become virtuous when we understand what virtue itself is, and where he says that someone who understands how to help another become virtuous would be like a real man in the world of shadows—Hades, the realm of men who have no being; where he says that a real man is one who remembers his *mind* in the world of diminishing being . . . these magical last paragraphs that show the attentive reader the clue to the deeper purpose of all Plato's writing, that show the secret of Socrates and the work of thinking together . . .

But I was not in a state to even want to appreciate such niceties. I was blinded with disappointment and only saw that the dialogue was ended. Or was it? Idiotically, I actually had the thought that the last page must be missing! And even more idiotically, I stood up, book in hand, and stormed over to the librarians' desk in the center of the big reading room. With only her head and shoulders visible from behind the high circular desk, the gentle eyes of tiny Miss Yoder beamed warmly at me as I charged at her like an angry bull.

She did not seem the least bit perturbed when I all but slammed the Plato volume down in front of her. As I did so, I realized how stupid I was being. I realized that of course there was no missing page.

So there I was—a total idiot, and an angry idiot at that. Miss Yoder just continued to beam at me. That was hard to swallow. She could have at least acted concerned. What made it worse was that right next to her, a little to the back, Miss Clarissa was seated at a filing table looking up at me with fierce disapproval. Miss Clarissa seated was exactly as tall as Miss Yoder standing. So there was the gray head and the white head. There was the stern scowl of Miss Clarissa and the all-knowing, inexplicable motherly warmth of Miss Yoder. I might have been able to deal with either alone, but not both together.

I stood there for a moment without being able to say a word, staring openmouthed into two sets of eyes: the smoldering dark eyes of Miss Clarissa boring into me and the sparkling, pale blue eyes of Miss Yoder welcoming me in.

And then something happened. Suddenly, I don't know why, I became very, very quiet inside myself. And the more quiet I became, the more Miss Yoder's eyes seemed to glisten with warmth and kindness.

After a moment or two, Miss Clarissa swiveled herself back to her filing desk and I was left alone in front of Miss Yoder. I stood there like that—maybe for ten or fifteen seconds, but it seemed like an hour—completely calm from the top of my head down to the tips of my toes. My whole body was vibrating with the same happiness, but deeper, that I experienced in geometry class or looking at the night sky.

I have no idea whether Miss Yoder knew was happening in me or not, whether she made it happen or not. It would be interesting to think that she knew at least something of what she was doing, but whether she did or not, she certainly knew something of what was happening in me. Because at a certain point she simply picked up the Plato book from the circulation desk and handed it back to me in a gesture of such intentional power that I will never forget it, and then she turned away to attend to her librarian business.

After all these years, I now have the words to describe what had happened to me. My mind had entered my body and my body had gratefully received it.

Do any of us really understand how the mind needs the body in order really to think, really to understand what it means to act, to be, to serve the good? Do any of us understand why we human beings need each other in order to find our own real mind, the mind of the lover of wisdom, the mind that is the source of virtue?

It is now necessary to go deeper into the secret of Socrates: thinking together as a preparation for being good. The secret is that in his *way* of questioning whether virtue can be taught, Socrates was in fact teaching men how to be virtuous.

But let us proceed carefully. We are at the edge of something quite new, something that could actually make a difference in our lives.

FREEDOM FROM ANSWERS

It was a different person who walked away from Miss Yoder. He was not the young egoist who moments before had angrily charged up to the desk. His mind was now quiet. His body was alive with a vibrant sensation of weight and attention. And as for his emotional state, the best way to describe it is to say that he was now, suddenly, open to the world outside of himself. It was an entirely new quality of feeling. A quality of feeling not noticed in our psychology books. Or, rather, noticed only in a roundabout way, mixing it up with theories and assumptions about human nature that cloud over its enormous significance. The point is that for a few moments *I was seeing the world without reference to myself.* Without reference to my opinions or to my problems or to my thoughts about this or that, and—and this is of great importance—*without reference to my emotions.* The capacity to feel had been liberated from the web of emotional reaction.

It was a glimpse of something of such enormous significance that Plato came at it over and over again, each time from a new direction, in his great philosophical dramas. It was a glimpse—a fleeting glimpse—of the real world. A glimpse of the secret of Socrates: *When the mind and the body receive each other, a new capacity of feeling is liberated in man, a feeling that sees all things under the idea of the Good.* It is a glimpse of objectivity— true objectivity that sees what is good and real. There is no objectivity without the perception of the Good. This is the essence of the Socratic revolution.

Granted, these are opaque statements. But let them stay where they are, there on the table before us. They will clarify themselves soon enough. And when they do, we will begin to understand why we human beings must work hard to be able to allow in ourselves the power to feel, to see, with the whole of our minds, the objective world outside ourselves—including especially the man or woman in front of us. We will understand why our culture and the life of our minds are infected with an ethical relativism that is a prison for our hearts and souls, or, in reaction to it, a fanatical absolutism that is little more than a fever in the brain.

Is this new feeling, this access to the root of love and therefore virtue, what the noble Meno felt as Socrates walked away—leaving him with only the question he started with—"can virtue be taught?"—but with that question so deepened, so emptied out and thereby so open to new life that it leaves one, for the moment at least, transformed in heart and soul? Or what the young Charmides felt? Or Gorgias? Or Lysis, Ion, Phaedo, Theaetetus? Do we know what any of these individuals experienced after Socrates applied to them his power of awakening dialogue? Always and again the dialogue ends with the return of the original question emptied of all associations, of all "answers."

We are asking about the inner state of being of those who stayed with the dialogue until the end, and who allowed its action to cleanse their minds. We have many descriptions of those who could not see it through. We have Thrasymachus in Book I of the *Republic,* hysterically storming out the door when his cynical opinions about justice are exposed as self-contradictory. We have Callicles in the *Gorgias* angrily holding on to his view that happiness comes not from self-mastery and the striving for wisdom, but solely from the satisfaction of the appetites, leading Socrates to end the dialogue by saying to him:

> Then let us follow the guidance of the argument . . . which reveals to us that this is the best way of life—to live and die in the pursuit of righteousness and all other virtues. Let us follow this, I say, inviting others to join us, not that which you believe in and commend to me, for it is worthless, dear Callicles.[8]

Yes, Plato often allows us to see the resistance to the work of thinking together, the work that Socrates brought of cutting away all presuppositions and assumptions in order to allow the new mind to present itself (as a baby "presents" itself in coming to birth). But has Plato shown us the inner world of those who stayed with the dialogue—who voluntarily suffered themselves to be emptied by the great "midwife" and destroyer of "opinion"?

There is an obvious answer to this question—the question of what was it like to stay with Socrates until the end of the dialogue. The answer lies first and foremost in the testimony of the love that his pupils felt for him. For over two thousand years that testimony has broken the heart of every reader of the dialogue called *Phaedo* in its masterful depiction of Socrates' serenely active mind during his last hours in the company of friends. And it lies in that most "alive" of all the dialogues, the *Symposium*—just at the end of Socrates' overwhelming discourse on conscious love, with the raucous, glorious testimony of the blazing adventurer Alcibiades, who confesses the unique fusion of joy and anguish that was the action of Socrates on his mind and heart. It is, he shows us, the joy and anguish of seeing oneself between two contradictory inner currents within the soul: the movement toward truth and Being on the one hand and the allure of falsehood and self-indulgence on the other— the joy and suffering, that is, of genuine conscience, the one and only source of moral power in man.[9]

BREAD AND STONE

But enough of textual commentary. We need to find the work of thinking together in our own lives *now and here.*

Please, now, come with me into my classroom, where I am about to make my own new discovery about this work.

It is the middle of December, the last day of classes. Outside, the sky is darkening and the wind is rattling the windows.

The course is called "The Nature of Religious Experience." We have been reading from the *Upanishads,* the *Life of the Buddha,* the Zen Buddhist *Sutra of the Sixth Patriarch,* the *Tao Te Ching, The Book of Job,* Isaiah, *Matthew,* the sermons of Meister Eckhart, and the poetry of two great masters of Islamic spirituality, Rumi and Hafez. We have been speaking *about* religious experience—we have not been trying to *have* religious experience. But, of course, throughout the semester students have been asking the great questions of the heart; and I have been trying to maintain a necessary balance between my academic responsibility on the one hand and, on the other hand, my personal feeling not only for the intimate metaphysical needs of the students, but for the fundamental questions themselves about life and the search for truth, questions that are bound to arise in oneself—in myself—in the presence of such texts.

I had promised the students that on the last day of class, after they handed in their final essays, they should feel free to speak about anything, anything at all—free of all concerns about grades or tests or performance. Attendance in this final class meeting was understood to be purely voluntary—and usually about half the students would remain after dropping off their exams. Today, perhaps because of the threatening weather, only about a dozen students stayed. I invited them all to come forward and form a half circle of chairs in the front of the class.

We could hear occasional rumblings of thunder in the distance.

Teaching such material, I have over the years felt a duty to my students to provide some kind of forum, even if just as a token, relatively outside of academic considerations, that could, so to say, more directly acknowledge the personal metaphysical sensitivities that draw so many of these young men and women to such a course in the first place, sensitivities which are inevitably activated by the class discussions and the powerful readings.

In these "unofficial" sessions, however, there would always arise one specific question that I found impossible to respond to in any adequate way. On this occasion it was the first question asked.

I groaned inwardly when I heard it:

"How do you recognize a real spiritual teacher? How do you tell the difference between someone who really knows something and someone who's just a charlatan?"

As is well known, the San Francisco Bay Area has for decades been the breeding ground of many new religious movements. Everything good and bad about the now widespread culture of "New Age" spirituality had its origin here—everything from the entry into our society of authentic teachers from the ancient traditions of Asia and the Middle East to spiritual fantasists from every nook and cranny of the world. The joke used to be that if you threw a brick out of any window in San Francisco, you would probably hit a guru. Amid teachers and practitioners of Christian and Jewish mystical spirituality; teachers of Zen, Tibetan and Vipassana Buddhism; Sufis, yogis and saints; healers and therapists of every stripe, color and price; amid men and women offering methods reflecting deep, esoteric truth alongside peddlers of psychospiritual superstitions and deceptively marketed forms of self-manipulation and self-inflation, what man or woman in search of the *way* would not be confused and bewildered? Of course these students need to ask this question!

And of course I need to respond to it. Having exposed them to teachings that have the power to awaken the hope that in this heartbreaking world there may actually exist Truth and guidance that leads to Truth, I am morally obliged to offer whatever help I can when this question is put.

Over the years I had put together a number of formulations about this question which, taken as a whole, was usually enough to pass for a satisfactory reply. But each time it left me with the hollow sense that they had asked for bread and I had given them a stone. And each time, I tried to justify myself by reasoning that it was not my place to imagine I actually had any "bread," in the form of personal guidance, to give them. Nor was it my place to express my personal opinion about this or that teacher or group or religion. I am a professor of philosophy, not a preacher or a guru. But these rationalizations, although perfectly valid as far as they went, only increased my sense of failure in front of an honest, real question for the arising of which I was to some extent responsible. Yes, I am a professor, not a preacher or a guru—but I am also a man, a human being. And simply as a man, I am morally obliged to try to do justice to this question of the heart. But how?

THE ETHICS OF COMMUNAL THOUGHT

I began in my usual way by acknowledging the seriousness of the question, citing references in world literature describing the "marks" of a genuine spiritual master. A spiritual teacher, we are told, seeks only the good of the pupil; he or she uses no seductive methods or tricks that play on human weaknesses such as suggestibility, spiritual pride, or emotional vulnerability. A true teacher in this realm has been "authorized" by his or her own master, or in any case is connected to a lineage in which the mysterious current of divine efficacy—called variously *baraka* in Islam, *chi* in Chinese tradition, or "the grace of the Holy Spirit" in Christian traditions—operates to ensure the authenticity of the teacher and his methods. And as for the personal qualities of the true spiritual guide, we are told that he or she is tranquil, humble, unconcerned with material things such as money, and is, above all, compassionate and all-loving, never given to egoistic anger or self-serving personal emotions of any kind.

But this time—perhaps it was because of the loud sounds of the approaching storm—I could not really put myself into this response. In fact, I never really was able to believe in such an answer. It was, in fact, pretty worthless, but I had never known exactly why.

A flash of lightning brightened the room for an instant—but long enough for me to see my students' faces as if for the first time, long enough for me to feel shame. I was answering this heartfelt question in a way that gave them nothing—while making them think they were receiving something useful. And the reason I was doing this—leading them round and around through a revolving door of mere words and academic abstractions—was that I very simply did not know *how* to answer it. What I was giving them were somebody else's answers, however much they were hallowed by time and tradition. But what I owed them, with their expectant, upturned eyes, was *myself,* my own conviction.

But what *were* my convictions? The answer appeared immediately—like another kind of lightning flash which, from that moment on, illuminated the whole world of my future work as a teacher of ideas. An answer, as I now understand it, that offers a genuine ground of preparation for a life ruled by conscience.

I was standing by the blackboard facing the students. I put down my chalk and leaned a little against the blackboard. It seemed to me as though the question about an authentic teacher had been hanging in the air for a long period, although in fact it had only just been voiced by Timothy Grattin, a bulldog-like senior who throughout the semester had both irritated and pleased me by the way he never let go of his questions.

For what seemed a very long period, I said nothing. And nothing occurred to me. But what was entirely new in the situation was that I felt no panic whatever. I did not inwardly scramble to find any words or ideas or references. I don't know how I must have looked to them, but inside myself I was receiving with all of my presence the experience of my emptiness in front of this question. And this sense of emptiness was like a gift. It was a gift that I was accepting and—here is the main point—*it was what I owed to them.* Finally, I understood that I was in the realm of ethics, the ethics of communal thought. I put all my trust and faith in the honesty of accepting my ignorance. Mentally, intellectually, and also in my heart. I now had no doubt that I was trying to do the right thing by them.

THE TRANSFORMATION OF THE QUESTION

"I don't know the answer to that question," I said. "Let's think about it."

That is what I said, but what began to happen in me was that I tried to allow the question to "come down" inside me.

I continued: "All those qualities of a true teacher—they can all be imitated, obviously. Anyone can say they are authorized; anyone can say they are sent by God; anyone can pretend to be serene and compassionate, at least for a little while and to a certain extent."

All eyes were on me.

"So what are we to do?" I said. "What are we to do? We need help and genuine guidance, but we don't want to be fooled. We want to be open, but not gullible. We want to be critical, but not cynical."

And suddenly I saw that I was *feeling* the question as my own; I was feeling it and thinking it at the same time; *I* was the one who needed to know the answer, both for their sake and my own. I too was in need and in search of wisdom and guidance.

But now the next question arose in me with great intensity: how much do I really wish for wisdom and guidance? How serious is that need in me—or in any of us? The question of how to recognize a real teacher was transforming itself into a question of what it means to be a real seeker, what it means to search for wisdom and guidance.

All eyes were on me.

It was so clear now. I stopped in front of Timothy. "We all have this question," I said, acutely aware that everyone was waiting. "But how intently do we search for a teacher or for wisdom? Is our need really as deep as we say or imagine?"

Why had I never before thought like this? I had only to look in myself in order calmly to see the action of the question—in the world of my own inner impressions and inner memories; in the world of my doubts and certainties—as well, of course, as in the world of my own intellectual associations and previous insights. I had only to allow the functioning of my whole psyche, mind and feeling, to deliver to me associations that corresponded to the question, which was now my own, and to the need of the questioners in front of me. Their need—my sense of duty toward them—made it nearly impossible for me to lie or pretend, and at the same time made it possible for me not to be afraid to expose to myself my own uncertainty in front of such a question of the

heart. I had only to feel my community with my students in order to allow the functioning of my sense of obligation to impact the contents of
my mind—and thereby to allow my own psyche, as it were automatically,
to scroll appropriate thoughts in front of my consciousness. In short, I
had to allow not only their question, but their being—their personhood,
their eyes and look—into myself while setting aside all merely mental
"answers" and while opening my own attention to the responses to them
and their questions that were inevitably transacting deeply within my
mind and heart. I had to be *in* question while responding *to* the question. I was *choosing* this approach—instead of automatically answering in
my usual way. Is this not a matter of ethics? The ethics of communal
thought? And doesn't it lead not only to truer insights, but, perhaps even
more important, to serving the good of the other? Isn't thinking together
a platform where morality and truth begin to meet? A platform—that is
to say, a preparatory theatre of life according to conscience?

But I am getting ahead of myself.

I am standing there in front of the circle of students and in this state
of responding to them from within my own inner questioning, I suddenly remember an old insight, about one of the great questions of philosophy, that came to me years before. An old insight suddenly breathing
entirely new life.

This needs some explanation.

THE WORLD OF APPEARANCES

For many, many years—ever since as a teenager I precociously began to
study philosophy—I had been fascinated and troubled by the idea, found
in almost all great philosophical and spiritual teachings, that man lives
in a world of mere illusions and appearances. While respecting all the
great teachers of the past, I could never understand what they meant
when they said that the world I was living in could be considered illusory. Wasn't this cup I was holding real? Perhaps I did not understand

much about the cup, perhaps I lacked all kinds of scientific and other knowledge about it, but nevertheless, it was not an illusion in any normal sense of the word. This cup, poorly understood though it may be, is real—as is this pencil, that house, that person, this pain in my tooth, this mother and father, the sun and moon in the sky, this fact of death. . . .

Yet so many of the wise teachers of old spoke of the world as a mere tissue of appearances, behind which existed, hidden from our sight, the world as it really is. And, so they said, no amount of information or inspired scientific theory could bring us any closer to seeing this real world behind the appearances. And as to how this real world was to be perceived they were frustratingly vague and often dogmatically "metaphysical."

And though I never could really understand this idea, I could never shake it off either. I could never accept the clever proposals of so many fashionable modern philosophers and writers who simply defined the problem away, usually claiming that since there was no experience (at least none that they had) of the supposed real world behind the appearances, the only sensible view, the only honorable and courageous view, was to concentrate our attention and our life on the world we actually saw and touched, and boldly declare that the world of appearances *is* the real world, and that the idea of another reality hiding behind it arises in us due to a mental aberration, or an unwillingness to live the life we actually have or, perhaps, simply from a disease of language.

It was only after many years of living with my inability to grasp this idea that the approach to a solution finally presented itself. And, as a matter of fact, it, too, presented itself in a classroom when another aggressive student, this time a dark-eyed, husky-voiced young woman with a misleading name—something like Angelica or Celestina—persisted in asking the question in exactly the same way I was experiencing it within myself. It just so happened that in the previous class just an hour before, I had been discussing another of the central ideas of the ancient traditions—the idea, namely, that our ordinary sense of self-identity, what we call our personality, is not our true identity. As taught in the philosophical traditions of India, for example, the idea is that hidden within ourselves—or what we call our "selves"—is a deeper, divine Self, which is our true identity, our true "home," in the language of the ancient mythology. It is only through contacting, by experience and not just in theory, this deeper Self that we human beings can find the true meaning of our lives and the real experience of peace, the attainment of freedom from the fear of death and loss.

The same idea in different language is found in every great spiritual teaching and philosophy—Buddhism, Hebraic, Christian, and Islamic mysticism, the teachings of Plato and the great Stoic thinkers of Rome. Everywhere and in every culture the idea is there. So much is this the case that it is no exaggeration to say that this idea in its many diverse expressions, along with the maturely developed idea of God, comprises the one central doctrine of all the wisdom of mankind, the idea around which all the great spiritual teachings revolve, as planets revolve around the sun.

I remember very clearly what then took place as I tried again and again to come up with an explanation of the concept of the world of appearances that would satisfy the dark-eyed, persistent student, whose mind I greatly appreciated, however uncomfortable her persistence was now making me feel. Then, as in the present instance facing the question of recognizing an authentic teacher, my own mind finally came to a stop, having temporarily run out of "answers." The only difference between now and then was that at that moment in the past I did not willingly accept my inner situation. On the contrary: in a state of embarrassment at my inability to answer her question, I heard myself babbling whatever words or phrases were popping into my head from the countless books I had studied in the field of comparative religion and philosophy—words and phrases that were no more than so many various forms of restating the idea in question, rather than offering any real elucidation of it. Once again, I was leading a sincere student through and around a revolving door of mere academicism.

TWO HALVES OF ONE GREAT IDEA

But suddenly I saw and deeply felt what I was doing. And, seeing myself with unusual impartiality, my embarrassment sharply diminished, overshadowed by the arising of a strangely quiet mixture of intense interest and a tincture of honest remorse, a uniquely profound and bittersweet mixture of joy and sorrow—all permeated by a powerful awareness of myself present watching over everything in myself and outside myself. In a word: for a moment, a long moment, the experience of *I am* appeared. And next to this sense of *I am* all of my impulses of embarrassment and panicky grasping for an "answer" seemed as though they belonged to someone else. They did not trouble me or seduce me at all.

And all at once I realized how to respond to her question, which, as I say, was also my own question and had been such for many years. It was so obvious! Why had I not thought of this before? I suddenly understood that the ancient idea that we live in a world of appearances veiling the real world was only half of an idea. *And as such, it was impossible to make sense of it.* Without the other half of the idea it was inevitable that all "answers" could appear only in the form of bloated pseudo-metaphysical speculation which, in turn, would inevitably be justly demolished by a positivistic "realism" of one sort or another that simply refused to honor the relevance of the idea at all.

And what was the other half of this idea—which fit into the first half with the precision of the pieces of a Swiss jigsaw puzzle? Simply this: Like the great surrounding world, one's own self was also a tissue of appearances, beneath which there existed a real Self. *And it was only through contact with this real Self behind the appearances of one's own socially conditioned surface personality that the real world outside oneself could be experienced and known!* Only the real internal Self hidden within could know the real external universal world hidden behind the appearances.

THE REAL WORLD CAN BE KNOWN
ONLY BY THE REAL SELF

That is to say: hidden behind our own, my own, ordinary thoughts, feelings and perceptions; hidden behind our own sense of identity, which has been thrust upon us by the accidents of upbringing, social caste, education, reading, media, advertising and peer pressure—that is, through our identification with and attachment to the thousand and one influences of external conditioning—there exists another consciousness which is our real consciousness, whereas the consciousness we live in day by day and which we tragically sense as our real self is, in fact, only a transitory, fabricated surface phenomenon by no means to be considered as our genuine self. Call this surface phenomenon the "ego," perhaps, or the "me." And call the real Self just that: the real self, the real I which alone has the right to say *"I am."* It is this real Self which has the intellectual intuitive power actually to verify the idea of the world behind the appearances. It is the real Self which has the power to see this real external world and to understand it and, eventually, to merge with it. The surface self can know only the surface of the world.

THE QUESTION OF THE HEART
IS A MORAL DEMAND

Such, or something very much like it, is the other half of the great idea of the world behind the appearances. But—and here in the present context is the most important point of all—*I was able to come to this deeply realized insight only under the pressure of a moral demand,* the demand, the duty, to respond honestly to a heartfelt question put to me by a sincere and serious student.

This was fundamentally a moral, ethical transaction, make no mistake about it. This was the action of the mind working (and making its own kind of intellectual sacrifices) in intense relation to the needs of another person's mind. This tiny moment of *thinking together* was a beginning moment of moral action involving two *minds*. In that sense, it was the realm of what might be called *intermediate morality,* something in between an ethical action in relation to another individual and a purely private act in relation to one's ordinary self alone.

Before proceeding to clarify this, at least to me, profound discovery, we need to take note of one other factor, one other result of the work of thinking together. It is a result of unsurpassed significance in the possible moral development of man, a result which our one-legged man was sent off to discover by the great Hillel and which glows in the heart of the method, if it can be called a method, of Socratic conversation, and which gives the only real justification for suggesting that for many of us the road to becoming capable of moral action must begin in the mind with the study of great ideas. The point is that through this act of accepting and suffering one's own total inability to respond to a genuine question put by the other; by accepting and suffering the hollowness of all one's "answers"; by taking the risk of standing blankly in front of one's own know-nothing mind, what can then be given is a response, an insight, an idea that is profoundly felt in the heart as well as known by the head! That is to say, to a small extent, but resonant with immense hope and significance: the ideas of the mind merge with the intuition and energy of the heart. To a small extent, *one then feels what one knows.* And the significance of this event, slight as it may be and transitory as it may also be, is, as we shall see, incalculable. It is incalculable because it is only when we feel what we know that it becomes even remotely possible intentionally to act upon what we know. We cannot do what we know we should, because we do not know the good with the whole of ourselves.

THE AUTHENTIC TEACHER AND
THE AUTHENTIC SEEKER

We are back again in front of Timothy Grattin and his question of how to recognize an authentic spiritual teacher. The lightning is flashing more frequently, accompanied by thunder. The rain is loud and steady. Thick sheets of water are streaming down the windows.

I am standing silently at my chair confronting Timothy's question. Having let go of all my inadequate answers, I willingly allow the silence to continue. I am not at all afraid that the class will see that their "wise" professor is at a loss. A unique feeling of freedom begins to flow through me. Many seconds pass; a minute, two minutes. The roaring sounds of the storm seem only to increase, and even sweeten the silence. It is very clear that the whole class, all twelve of the young men and women seated in the circle, are to some extent sharing the tranquility of the silence with me.

Had I gently ended the class just then without saying anything further, no one would have been disappointed. Had I myself been a spiritual guide, perhaps that is what I would have done, so as to allow the question to sink down into them. But I was being drawn to something else; I was being drawn to the sense of an unknown act of faith. I was, somewhere in my mind and heart, quietly choosing to have faith in the act of simultaneously accepting both my own incapacity and the inescapable duty to respond with honesty to the genuine need of another human being's mind. It was now not at all difficult to stay with this faith; there were no temptations that I had to fight off, no new "answers" slithering out of my professorial memory. I was as though saying to myself— or, to be precise, I was as though saying to the silence inside me: "Here I am. I do not understand. But I *must* understand." Never had I felt simultaneously so alert, as though there were danger everywhere; and so relaxed, as though I were also protected from any harm or failure.

If I now relate how I finally did respond, it may sound disappointingly evasive. But, in fact, even now, long after the event, it seems the only honest and practical beginning of an answer to this question—of course, when the question itself is honestly asked.

I started by saying, "How are you searching?"

The class looked at me expectantly.

I continued, speaking exactly as my thoughts came to me, without weighing my words:

"We want to know how to recognize a real teacher, but do we ever ask ourselves in what way we are searching for a teacher, in what way we are searching for truth? Could it be that we can only recognize a teacher when we are in a state of need, when real need pours through us and sensitizes our powers of perception? A hungry man looks for food in a very different way than a full man. Need can attract intelligence.

"We say we are searching. That is a very great thing—to search for truth. But what are we actually doing? We read books—sometimes, when it pleases us—or we listen to lectures—sometimes. But otherwise we may go through our day-to-day lives with no thought at all of this question, with no sense of need for something deeper in our lives, something that we cannot name. In that sense, we are really flattering ourselves when we say we are seeking truth. It is not so. We are seeking it *sometimes, occasionally,* when 'it occurs to us,' or for a deep moment or two when something chances to remind us—like an encounter with death or shocking injustice or personal loss or when looking up at the night sky—but then the moment passes and it is gone, the 'search' is gone. It is unwise and dishonorable to call such a haphazard process a *search*.

"Just as it is only the real Self that can see the real world behind the appearances, so it may be that it is only the real seeker who can recognize a genuine man or woman of wisdom.

"Does that seem right to you?" I asked Timothy. And then I turned to the others. They were looking back at me with great attention, but I couldn't tell what they were thinking or feeling. The only thing that was immediately clear was that although they had become extremely attentive, they were not agitated; they were not "excited." Their eyes were not roving the ceiling for objections or clarifications.

I continued: "Imagine a condemned man in prison. Nothing matters more to him than the possibility of escape. This need is always with him, no matter what he is doing, poised inside his mind like a hungry animal. People come to this prisoner, or he hears of people, who have a plan of escape. He listens to them all. He is open to them all. He listens to these plans with great care. And he studies the people who offer them. Who are they? Are they solid? Or are they just crazy? Can they control themselves? Or will they break apart at the first difficulty? And does the plan make sense? Does it take everything into account—including the inevitably of shocks and dangerous surprises? Or is it only wishful thinking? Only a fantastic gamble insanely depending on luck?

"Some plans he can see through immediately, but as for the rest, he neither rejects nor accepts anything *a priori*—because it is his very life that is at stake. His need gives him the power to be open and critical at the same time. His need is so great that it makes him cool and patient, yet at the same time ready, if necessary, instantly to mobilize himself for action."

Suddenly, I felt that I was now starting to talk too much, that I was on the verge of becoming a little intoxicated, allowing a metaphor to lead, rather than serve, my thought. I paused, and, with a certain effort, stopped my mind for a second, in order to let in the impression of myself as I was. The perception of silence, which had already drifted into the background, then returned, along with the sounds of the storm. And the unknown faith also returned from out of the background. But faith in what? Not faith in my now completely depleted mind. I understood that I needed to say more, to think more, to give more, but did I have anything more to give?

Had it all been a fantasy—this sense of the ethics of thought? I realized that I now had nowhere to go inside myself. Had I been fooling myself all along? The new faith was being shaken. A kind of despair was beginning to creep in, saying to me: "Look, it's not such a big deal; you're making too much of this. What do you expect? This is only a classroom. What you've said is quite adequate. Lighten up!"

Nevertheless, the demand to go further was becoming increasingly urgent. What had been said was not enough, not nearly enough. But from where in myself could the next step come?

A KIND OF LOVE

The answer soon appeared—and, of course, *it did not come from anywhere in myself at all*. It came from *them,* the students, from the other half of the ethical transaction. How could I have forgotten that? How could I have begun to speak in a way that left so little room for questioning, so little room for the other, for my "neighbor"!

I nearly laughed with joy at this realization.

Not Timothy, but another student, a brilliant woman named Adriana Waters, with crystal-blue eyes and a forehead like a white sail, asked, very simply:

"But suppose we don't have such a sense of need? Suppose it is too buried? What should we do? The question is still there—how can we know who to trust?"

A moment passed. I started to pace, then stopped.

One thing and one thing only came to me—the faith that intelligence can appear not from anything I can make happen, but only from staying in front of the truth and the need of the moment. The faith had returned, faith in attention, not in words or concepts. I was about to enter a kind of experience that was to be repeated many times after this—the experience, namely, that when we are at an ethical crossroads, when we are at the end of our ethical resources, it is through the awakening of conscious attention to our lack that a right action—in this case, simply a right thought—may be given to us.

"Can we stay with that?" I said to her.

"What do you mean?" she said.

"I mean, can you—can we—stay with the truth of our situation? The truth, in this case, is this: Let's say that here is an individual who is offering, or who seems capable of offering, spiritual guidance, wisdom, a *way*—call it what you like. Let's say I am very interested in him or her; let's say there seems to be something special about this person. But I am not sure—either of him or of myself. I don't know if this person is what he seems. I don't want to turn away from something that might be what I wish for; nor do I want to follow something or someone only through self-suggestion or wishful thinking.

"What do I do?

"I stay with my uncertainty, which is now sensed as a need. It is not only he or she about whom I now have a question; it is myself who is in question. The need I now feel—maybe it is not the great hunger that creates intelligence and the power to choose. Nevertheless, it has its own degree of force and intelligence. . . .

"But now, perhaps, I see something else as well—an impatience, a kind of pressure inclining me to close the question, to get on with it all, to come to a judgment about this person before me.

"But if I stay with the truth of the situation, the truth that I don't know if I can really trust this man and that my hunger is not so deep as to bring me instinctive certainty—if I stay like that, what happens then?"

Adriana replied with an unusually relaxed voice: "I think I see where you are going."

"Here you are," I said. "You want to know the quality of this man or woman in front of you, who may or may not be a genuine spiritual guide. You want to know, but your wish is only of ordinary intensity; you do not have the desperate intuition of a great seeker. Yet you are not complacent either, although you sense in yourself the pressure of habit that at any moment may shut down the question. What is taking place in you?"

The class is allowing this strange conversation to take place. No one is interrupting, not even the bulldog Timothy Grattin.

And, for sure, it is a unique dialogue that is now taking place. It is not academic, but it is not "not academic" either.

Adriana and I are genuinely *thinking together.*

In fact, we are suddenly having exactly the same thoughts together. I have asked her a question, the answer to which I honestly did not know. It was a question to *us,* not to her. It was to us, the two of us, supported by the good attention of eleven other students.

Her reply, which now came to her exactly as the same thought came to me, was:

"I guess I . . . just wait. I really don't have to make up my mind right away. I just go on speaking to this person, watching him, wondering. *I don't have to decide!*"

I nodded—not to her, but to us. "And now what?"

"My God!" she said, and stopped.

What had she discovered? Now it was I who didn't know.

"What?" I said. "What is it?"

"My God!" she repeated—and then went on: "I am now more interested in how open my mind is than I am in knowing whether this person is or isn't a real teacher!"

A long pause. Sounds of rain. Silence.

Of course—I didn't say it, I felt it—*that's the answer.* Our dialogue has brought her and us to a faith in the mind, a faith in intelligence. A real question has been answered—not by words, but by an event in the mind, an event shared by two people. A kind of love; it was a kind of love. A creation.

So *that* is the secret of Socrates!

~ *Three* ~

THE WHITE DOVE

W here do we find ourselves? We have spoken of "rehearsing" the work of morality—which is the work of love—in thinking together. We are discovering that thought—serious thought about serious things—may be an intrinsically social act. We may need each other in order to think intentionally about the most important questions of our life, the otherwise unanswerable questions that can be confronted only through awakening *the heart of the mind,* an awakening that results from the shared need for truth. There, in the work of thinking together, we wish to and we actually can, in a certain sense, love our neighbor, the one who shares our question. We can even love our enemy, perhaps especially our enemy, the one who opposes our view, who argues with us, who disagrees. With this enemy we can "rehearse" the need for differences between people, and, through this, understand the need for genuine complementarity in our mutual relations, the need for the force of resistance as a necessary condition for the appearance of real unity.

I wish to illustrate what I am now speaking about by describing an experiment, an exercise, that any two people can try if they wish to verify the claim I am making about the immense and virtually unknown ethical significance of thinking together.

A REHEARSAL FOR MORALITY

I do not claim originality for this exercise—psychologists, counselors, and consultants have known about it for a long time, and I have been told that it or something very much like it was part of the ritual of dialogue in certain American Indian tribes. It is also possible that it lies near the heart of the ritualistic form of active debate that we now know exists in the Tibetan Buddhist tradition and in many other religions throughout the world and throughout history. And we may well imagine that the whole dynamic rite of Talmudic argument has its roots in what this exercise can teach us. Finally, and most poignantly, there exist in Christian art throughout the ages striking images of two monks speaking together being visited by a white dove, symbol of the Holy Spirit, descending from on high, or arising from out of their own mouths.

We are interested in that dove—for in it lies the secret intention of this exercise, an intention and result that were no doubt understood in the great spiritual traditions of the world, but only a faint echo of which has survived in its modern psychological usage. We may also surmise that its importance and even its very existence and form have been long forgotten or fatally altered in most of our religious institutions.

The exercise is simply described. Two people face each other who passionately hold diametrically opposed views about a given issue or idea, and they proceed to argue back and forth for their point of view. Let us call these people "Mary" and "John." The rules are that when Mary speaks, John may reply only after he has clearly repeated the essentials of what Mary has said. And it is entirely up to Mary to decide if John has given a fair and accurate statement of what she has just said. Only when this condition is fulfilled is John permitted to present his response and his point of view. And then, before Mary can answer John, she in turn is also obliged to summarize what he has said, to the point that he accepts her summary as fair and accurate. And this goes on, each answering the other under this rule that no one can express his or her own views until he or she has accurately summarized what the other person has just said.

My first full-fledged experiment with this exercise was full of surprises that showed me how little we really understood about the thought component of human conflict and about the possibility of resolving conflict through creating conditions within the mind. I am speaking about conditions that allow the unforced arising, however fragile, of the normal, intrinsic human feeling for one's neighbor—always remembering that this is still in the realm of "rehearsal." Yet what a stunning "rehearsal for morality"!

LIFE WITHOUT ETHICS?

I don't remember in which class I first tried it. It could have been any one of them—the introductory course in philosophy and religion or the Plato seminar or the advanced undergraduate course on Emerson and Thoreau or perhaps the course called Modern Religious Thought. I remember only that I was trying to introduce the general subject of ethics and that I was operating under the assumption that everyone in the class more or less understood the meaning of the word and that everyone had his or her own personal experience to draw on in order to think about it. And so, when I asked for examples of ethical dilemmas or conflicts from the students' own lives (without their going into too much personal detail), I was bewildered by the fact that not only did no one offer to speak, but that no one even seemed to understand what I was talking about. It even seemed that they had no concrete idea of what the word "ethics" meant!

How was this possible? Obviously, such situations had occurred in their lives, as they do in everyone's life—situations where one is painfully obliged to choose a course of action without being sure whether it is morally right or wrong; or where one knows what is right, but is strongly inclined to act otherwise; or where there is sharp disagreement between oneself and another person about the good and the bad in an urgent life situation. So why had these students become uncharacteristically tongue-tied? It was not as if I were asking them to divulge intimate secrets—I was asking only for generalities. What was their difficulty? Did they really not recognize the ethical dimension of their lives?

Suddenly, I began remembering certain things about my students. Over the years it had been like this: We would approach the subject of ethics, of good and evil, of right and wrong, and almost always they would speak of whether something made them "feel good" or made them "feel bad," or "feel guilty." Not whether or not they *were* guilty, but only whether or not they *felt* guilty. Not whether it *was* good or bad, but only whether it made them *feel* good or bad.

I had not paid much attention to this difference of language. Oh yes, I was always struck by the almost universal moral relativism of the young men and women that I tended to come in touch with. As in many other parts of our modern world, it is so much the fashion to deny the existence of absolutes in the ethical sphere that anyone who dares even to ask seriously about this possibility is immediately branded as naive or fanatical. Who's to say what's good or bad, right or wrong? What's good in one place or for one person may be bad in another place or for another person: these are the "ethical" certainties of our modernistic era, and so many of our children—and almost all students like mine—simply accept without any second thought that all morality is relative to time, place, ethnicity, religion, social class, nationality, and so on. This moral relativism is not ever in question, and many are the teachers and instructors who drill this point of view into them with a fervid dogmatism that easily rivals the dogmatism of any religious fundamentalist.

That much I understood about my students' opinions and beliefs concerning moral values. But what I hadn't seen until now was the possibility that, partly because of this fixed relativistic mind-set, they had never actually *experienced,* as such, the genuinely ethical element in human life! Or, rather, because they obviously did face choices and demands over and over again, as we all do, involving honesty and lying; the keeping and breaking of promises; stealing; injuring others; breaking and obeying rules, laws, and principles; self-sacrifice and self-gain; cheating; honoring or betraying trust—although they obviously faced situations involving these elements, such situations were in their consciousness immediately translated into matters simply of what "feels good" or what "feels bad."

These were my troubled thoughts the day that I first tried the exercise in question. My mind was reeling. I badly wanted to go somewhere and think more calmly about what I seemed to be seeing about my students. I wanted to think more carefully, more contemplatively about it. It was as though a powerful new vein of reflection about all our lives had suddenly opened up: it was now no longer a question only of correct or flawed philosophical beliefs and opinions about ethics, but of the existence or absence of actual ethical experience. Was the *experience* of the ethical momentously disappearing from our world, like some great endangered natural species?

I could not, however, go somewhere and reflect. I was obliged to continue with the class, and when I did—acting almost out of desperation because I was so unsettled by the apparent paucity of ethical experience in these young men and women—it led eventually to what was for me a revelation about the real causes of ethical conflict in human relationships. And about what, precisely, we must work at in our mutual human relations. It led me to understand, if only in the rehearsal theater of the mind, what is needed in order to call down into our threatened common life a genuine contact, however preliminary, with the reconciling force of non-egoistic love.

TURTLES

"Take an ethical problem that none of us is able to solve, a problem that our whole society, our whole world, is unable to solve," I said, as I started roaming around the classroom. "Take abortion—a completely intractable *ethical* problem. Logically speaking, each side has its uniquely compelling arguments and its uniquely good reasons—to the point that this very issue of abortion seems at the present moment to be the chief representative of the many-aspected *metaphysical* contradiction rooted in the fact of modern society, with its anomalous values, existing and seeking to perpetuate itself within the bosom of the great universal laws of nature and organic life that often oppose these anomalous values. In any case, no rational human being on either side of this question of abortion is entitled to just dismiss the other side. At the same time, nowhere, even among the most thoughtful individuals, is there more intense passion, more ferocity, more 'certainty' on each side."

Heads nodded in agreement.

"Our society simply has no generally acceptable solution to the ethical dilemma of abortion," I said as I returned to the front of the room.

I sat down at the metal table.

"So here is a test for us. This is *ethics*. We are in front of a painful and momentous question of right and wrong. How shall we try to think—to think, and not just wrangle—about it?"

The class remained quiet as I carefully explained the ground rules of the exercise and the standard of listening it demanded of everyone.

I then asked the class: "Who feels strongly that women should have the right to abortion?"

As I expected, almost all hands immediately went up. There were about fifty students in the class.

"Who volunteers to speak for this point of view?"

Slowly, one after the other, and to my surprise, all but three or four hands went down. I attributed this to "stage fright," but later I understood that something much deeper was involved.

"And who will speak for the opposite point of view—against abortion?"

Not a single hand went up. This was not too surprising, considering the makeup of the whole student body and the general political temper of San Francisco. But it was disappointing in terms of the experiment I wanted to try.

"Is there no one who thinks that abortion is wrong?"

I detected a slight twitching in three or four students.

"If you did feel this, would you be afraid to admit it?"

The twitching increased for a moment and then stopped.

"Well," I said, "that means we can't try the exercise."

At this, Janet Holcomb, seated to my right against the tall windows, said that, although she was pro-choice, she would be willing to argue for the other side for the sake of the experiment.

"No, it has to be a sincerely held opinion," I said. "Both sides have to believe in the rightness of their view with equal conviction. The forces on each side have to be equal and opposite—as they are in the world, and in our lives."

I waited, but no one came forth. I was sure there were one or two who held the view that abortion is morally wrong, but they had retreated into an intimidated silence. In fact, a gray pall had descended upon the class, a hollow silence. The men, in particular, seemed frozen.

"Why don't we take another topic?" sang out Elihu Andrews, a broad-shouldered, sweet-voiced black man.

"All right," I said. "What?"

After a few seconds, one proposal after another rose to the surface, looked around, and then immediately sank back out of sight into the gray silence.

"The war in Iraq," said Bernardo Di Giorgio.

"Gay marriage," said Agnes Huong.

"Globalization."

"Israel and Palestine."

But the hollow silence continued—an atmosphere of dull withdrawal. I was looking at fifty turtles peering out from deep inside their shells. Why? Why were these ordinarily vibrant and even volatile students now so passive?

Ah, but then one of the turtles stuck out her head and softly said: "Partial-birth abortion!"

PASSION AND ATTENTION

It was like watching a black-and-white movie suddenly turn Technicolor. Immediately the air became electric. Hands flew up like startled birds. It was astonishing. Everyone began talking—to me, to each other, to themselves. Arguments were already starting—men and women alike. Here, obviously, on this issue, was where the white heat of the problem of abortion had moved. Was it not now, at least temporarily, at that point in time, one of the chief points of concentration of the moral crisis of our whole world?

At this point there was no problem finding volunteers for the exercise. The only problem was which students to choose from among the many who were offering themselves on each side of the issue. I had to decide fairly quickly. Should I take a man and a woman? Or should it be two women? Should it be seen as a "woman's issue"? Or was it more deeply true that it was first and foremost a *human* issue?

But why even look at it like that? Or, rather, to look at it like that meant to choose the participants solely on the basis of both the urgency of their concern for human life and welfare, and the intensity of their desire for the truth, wherever it might lead. What was needed was passionate conviction existing side by side with the willingness to step back from one's passions without intending or even wishing either to deny or to justify them. My God! Here, right away, in the theater of the mind, the fundamental ethical imperative was already rising—namely, the willingness in the midst of emotion, in the midst of fear or anger or craving, to try to free oneself from total and complete "identification" or "absorption" by one's inevitable and automatically arising passions. Granted, it was only in the rehearsal theater of the mind—but wasn't that the whole point of this exercise: to *study,* within specially supportive conditions, the possibility and the laws of the struggle to be good, a struggle that otherwise seems such an impossibility in the concrete, complicated conditions of everyday life?

But was I being presumptuous in assuming I was able to make such a determination about the motivations of my students? Was I foolish to imagine that I could see into them in this way?

In fact, and surprisingly enough, it was not at all difficult. There was simply no mistaking the presence of this mysterious quality in them: the simultaneous existence of passionate conviction and equally intense self-questioning: a conviction that was not "certainty"—that is, it was not fanaticism; and a self-questioning that was not "self-doubt"—that is, it was not timidity.

It is not possible for me accurately to characterize this quality in words. Hovering above or within the powerful contradiction between their personal conviction and their inner self-questioning there existed another, a *third,* quality. It showed itself, if I may put it this way, in the *atmosphere* that embraced them, that gave a certain softening glow to their skin, and which worked a manifold subtle contouring of their features, a contouring that made them as beautiful, present and normal as an Egyptian Fayum portrait. And it expressed itself physically, this quality, in the fact that they were suddenly moving with the integrity of little children—the body and mind in one piece. I *knew* whom to choose.

It was two women—Janice Eberhart and Arlene Harris, both sitting in the front row.

Janice was in her early twenties, slight and quick as a small bird, with abundant henna-red hair that she wore in a braid behind her. She had the habit of sitting in her chair with her head bent forward, her chin touching her fingertips, which were pressed together as though in a posture of prayerful supplication—a posture she held tightly when she was trying to formulate a thought with special sincerity or logical precision.

Arlene Harris was a black woman whose age was difficult to determine—probably in her mid-thirties. Her skin was intensely, luminously dark, as were her large, steady eyes. A tall, raw-boned woman with close-cropped hair and high, wide cheekbones, she would occasionally come to class all smiles, wearing a blazingly beautiful Nigerian boubou that made her seem nothing less than an African tribal queen. She was a straight-A student.

Today she was dressed in her more customary crisp jeans and cardigan sweater.

I moved two chairs to either side of the metal table and motioned for the two women to come forward and take their places. "Remember," I said to them, "you must be rigorous about this. The other person must repeat, not necessarily in the same words, the exact gist and meaning of what you have said. Only then is she entitled to respond. It will sometimes be tempting to settle for less, but don't do it. It has to be a truly fair statement of what you have said, without anything essential left out."

Then, as the two women were taking their places and turning their chairs to face each other, I said to the whole class,

"You have an important role in this exercise. You have to be quiet and very attentive; you have to listen very carefully. The people in front need to be supported by the attention in the whole room. The exercise will not succeed without that."

THE SHOCK OF THE QUESTION

"The subject is partial-birth abortion," I said, still facing the class. "And just so everyone clearly understands what is at issue, will someone please define it?"

A man at the back of the class said something not very clearly, and immediately four or five people were calling out their definitions. Up front, Janice, who was taking the "pro-life" position in the exercise, sternly offered a precise definition. Speaking with some emotional difficulty, and with her palms pressed together and the tips of her fingers touching her chin, she said,

"Partial birth abortion is a procedure . . . where the doctor delivers the baby . . . up to the point where only the head remains inside the womb . . . and he then punctures the skull . . . and removes the brain."

No one moved. The clock on the wall suddenly seemed to be ticking very loudly.

After a long moment, I motioned to Janice to go on and begin the dialogue. Without a moment's hesitation, she started, speaking—as has now become a habit among many younger women—with many of her assertions curling up at the end as though they were questions:

"I am against partial-birth abortion. To begin with, I think it has to be understood why the woman has decided so late that she doesn't want to have the pregnancy? There are cases where continuing the pregnancy might be dangerous to her health—and that's where I might say there's a little bit of room. But if it's not a matter of her own safety, her own life, then I would say that there are a lot of families who need children and can't have them and who could adopt them—it's not as if the child would be unwanted. Of course, to do that causes terrible emotional turmoil, but it's going to be just as emotionally damaging . . . in a different way . . . to abort the child as to have the child and let it go. It's still . . . I mean, some child could have been around and is gone now."

She continued, pushing one thought out on top of the other:

"Sometimes the child is called a fetus, but we can't really say whether or not it is a living child? And I think calling it a fetus just smears the issue? And makes it easier to accept. And, look, suppose when a child is born early, a premature child, and they would try to save the baby's life . . . but suppose the mother decides she doesn't want the baby, so there is a period where you just call it a fetus? And you can kill it.

"And I've seen videos where it is done and they take the camera up close so you can look at it and it's . . . *alive*! It looks like . . . a *small child*!"

I interrupted her.

"Very good," I said, in a professorial manner that I hoped could keep everyone's attention mainly on the intellectual content of what was being said, and because I did not want to start the experiment with an overlarge demand on Arlene's memory. "Obviously, there's much more to be said; hold it for your next turn. Now listen to Arlene. And remember—she must give a fair summary of what you've said."

Arlene began speaking in a flat, matter-of-fact way. "It seems that your main concern is that the woman opts to abort this baby so late in her pregnancy. She should have made the decision earlier. But there are so many families who want to adopt children and they could have the child and raise it with the proper care." Arlene paused. "Is that right?" she asked with uncharacteristic hesitancy.

Janice quickly and warmly replied, "Yes, that's right."

"No," I said to Janice. "There was more. She's leaving out something. Say what Arlene left out."

Janice obeyed, repeating what she had said—but this time with much less emotion—about the baby being alive and about the hypocrisy sometimes involved in calling it a "fetus."

Arlene then repeated that part.

"Are you now satisfied?" I said to Janice. "Has Arlene given a fair and complete statement?" Janice nodded yes. "Then let's proceed."

I motioned to Arlene.

With her hands coolly crossed in front of her on the folded-down writing surface of the lecture-room chair, Arlene leaned forward. "It would never be something that I myself would do," she said, "but I feel that it is a choice that every woman should have, even if it is . . ." She searched for a word "not *correct*." She turned her steady dark eyes to me for a moment and then continued in a curious monotone: "I'm thinking of it from the point of view of the needs of the planet. There are so many people in the world, so little space and so little food—it is all out of control. If this were a poor Third World country, another nation, it wouldn't be a question at all. They don't have the option of having such a procedure. But here in America, where we consume way beyond our share of the world's resources, we have the ability to have such a procedure. So in America even though abortion of this kind might not be morally correct, it's a choice a woman should have."

Speaking now smoothly and effortlessly, Janice replied:

"So you're saying that it's a choice that all women should have, that it's not something you would personally choose, but that all women should be able to decide for themselves and that it would be especially important now, especially in America, because we have such an over-population issue in the world and such an issue of resources not being equally distributed to everybody that the choice is, maybe, not *good,* but maybe makes sense in relation to the whole society we have today."

Pause. "Is that a fair summary?" I asked Arlene. She nodded yes, but weakly.

"Are you sure?" She said nothing.

I began to detect something going on under the surface of this suspiciously calm exchange between the two women. In most other cases when I have tried this experiment, with issues involving politics, racism, religion—as well as with this general question of abortion—the students' struggle to step back from their passions was much more visible. Here this struggle had appeared only at the very beginning with Janice's definition of partial-birth abortion. After that, it had settled into an apparently lukewarm conversation and I began to wonder if I had paired the wrong people.

THE MORAL POWER OF LISTENING

But this was all about to change. It was about to change because of what always happens if this exercise is sincerely tried primarily as an exercise in the study of the moral power of listening. What may have seemed for a few moments to be a lukewarm conversation was actually the manifestation of a totally new effort of attention, each participant working in an unfamiliar way to listen carefully to the other without reaction, without judgment, without anxiety about winning or losing. And this mutual struggle for impartial attention brought about one of the most beautiful, visible results of this exercise—it gave both participants the sustained experience of intentionally separating themselves from their opinions, rather than simply holding them back like chained dogs. Moreover, this effort of genuinely stepping back—inwardly—from their own emotionally driven opinions in order to attend to the other person was deeply sensed by everyone in the class, even though they might not have been able to explain what was so unusually gripping about an apparently modest, quiet little discussion.

"Arlene," I asked, "are you sure you're willing to accept that Janice has given a fair summary of what you said? What about the matter of Third World countries?"

"Yes, that's right," said Arlene matter-of-factly, "she did leave that out."

Before Arlene could then repeat that part of what she had said, Janice jumped in.

"Okay," said Janice, "here it is: in Third World countries they really don't have the luxury or choice to have an abortion or not. But because in America we have so many things and so much money—which we take from the rest of the world—we are free to make these decisions."

"Is that fair enough now?" I asked Arlene. She said yes. "All right," I said to Janice, "now give your response. Take your time." She needed no time at all.

"Okay," she said, cheerfully, "in Third World countries, where abortion is not an option, mostly women do not have birth control and so have many children that they can't take care of—and it's true we don't want to recreate that situation in our society where we have so many resources available. So I do agree that we have the ability to make that choice where other countries don't have that option. But I'm wondering if just because we're so powerful it's okay for us to have that choice?

Like—the more powerful we get, the more choices we're allowed to have?—no matter whether they're ultimately for the good of people or not? And I wonder if there are other solutions to the problem of late abortions that people are not considering just because the choice of abortion seems so readily available here? Like in other countries maybe they would be obliged to figure out a way to do something positive with a negative situation—whereas here we sort of look for the quick fix out of it—like a magic pill to make it go away? And that attitude may be a block that is difficult to correct—and so maybe this issue won't be resolved for a long time, because that attitude is everywhere in American society."

And now Arlene: "She says that here in America we have so much power, and the more power we have the more choices are available to us and people have the ability to make these decisions. But because it's so easy to make these choices, people are being less than resourceful in finding other options that . . . that preserve . . . that are . . . better?" Arlene stopped. Something was happening.

"Are you all following this?" I asked the class, in order to allow some space in the process that was taking place between the two women.

Janice bowed her chin against her fingertips, nodded her head, and stated that this was a fair summary of what she had just said. At this, Arlene suddenly sat up very straight, tall and broad-shouldered in her chair. Her steady eyes glowed.

"Reply," I said to her, almost in a whisper.

"I agree with Janice," she said, "Americans as a whole are morally lazy and if abortion was not so readily available it would make people *think* more about it. And maybe that would be a good thing, a very good thing!" She waited a moment and then in a strong voice:

"But I still think the option should be available. It's just not *right*," she said, her voice rising, "to tell someone that they can't make a choice with their body. There's something going on inside of them and they should have *control* over that! Now, I'm not saying that you can never tell a person what not to do; there are complex issues involving the definition of fetus and about people being born or not being born and so forth—I'm not going into that right now. So, yes, certainly there are things you have to say no to. It's wrong to kill someone, obviously. But it is also wrong to tell a woman what to do with her body and this is what the dominant forces in our society have not yet understood. Me, the woman, the rights of my body, my rights . . ."

Here Arlene stopped. Again, the ticking of the clock became audible.

I turned to the class: "Please notice," I said, "that a new point, a new issue has just been introduced into the exchange."

A MOVEMENT TOWARD CONSCIENCE

But it was more than just a new point, it was a new and deeper part of the psyche that was emerging out of Arlene's mind and instincts, and it instantly affected everyone. Right or wrong in any usual sense was not the issue. The issue was the human heart, one's own self emerging, one's own feeling, one's own thought. Arlene's words had new authority, the authority that comes from the beginning of the movement toward conscience. *Toward* conscience, no more, but also no less. The *beginning,* no more but also no less. She was struggling for her conscience. Years of creating conditions in which I was able to demand of young men and women that they try to think honestly had sensitized me, perhaps excessively, to this element in them, this moment when they cast aside both the "acceptable" and the superficially innovative and began to speak simply from themselves, right or wrong. When this happened, it was never violent, never strident, and it was always full of quiet electricity.

Arlene continued: "This body remains mine until the day I die and during that time it must not be legislated with undue purpose. This is not just about fetuses, this is about me and every woman who wants her freedoms. We have been struggling for centuries for the rights that men enjoy. In *Roe* the Supreme Court decided that it was the parent who deserved the highest level of constitutional protection. This is what I'm focusing on. Women need to be respected enough to have the same rights as men, the right to decide what's best for our lives, best for our bodies, to be seen as equals, to be treated as equals. Of course, partial-birth abortion is a nightmare, but do the men making the laws understand the nightmare of unwanted pregnancy as it sometimes unfolds in the course of a woman's pregnancy? Have they themselves ever menstruated? Ever feared their own pregnancy? Have they ever had a uterus or had a Pap smear or a cervical exam? Have they ever borne children or felt one grow inside of them? Do they know what it's like for a woman who finds herself terrified and alone in her decision to abort a pregnancy? Who has no options that protect her health and who feels forced to take matters into her own hands? How can they propose to legislate something they will never understand? How can they make rules about my body, who have never lived in a woman's body? . . . and never really include the opinions and influences of most women in their decisions?"

Janice, still in the posture of a supplicant, kept her head bowed, her palms pressed together, her chin just touching the tips of her fingers. Only one thing had changed: her eyes were now tightly closed as she listened with great concentration to every word Arlene spoke.

What was now happening was something that sooner or later takes place every time I have tried this exercise, and every time it is like a miracle. It takes place when the deeper feelings begin to emerge—not the agitated emotional outbursts we all know only too well, but the deeper passions of the emerging conscience. The "miracle"—though in fact it is actually lawful—is that the stronger and more deeply felt the passions of conscience are, the more an individual also quietly witnesses him or herself—that is, the more dynamically calm the individual becomes. And this act of stepping back within oneself then spreads or echoes itself in the other partner of the dialogue, and also, to some extent, in the students in the class. Just as in our mutual relations with one another the agitation of emotionalism tends to evoke agitation in response, so too can the steadiness of attention that is the inner companion of essential moral feeling evoke the same state in one's neighbor.

In the class all heads were now turned toward Janice. How would she respond to this powerful statement by Arlene?

With her eyes remaining closed, Janice summarized as follows:

"Women should have the choice to do what they want with their bodies, just the same as men. And in women the fetus inside them falls under that jurisdiction. And there has to be a definition of what is wrong that we all understand and agree on. And therefore we have to accept abortion—late-term abortions have to be allowed under the principle that all people have the right to do what they wish to with their own bodies."

"Is that a fair summary?" I asked Arlene. Of course, it was and it wasn't. The content was "accurate," but Arlene's passion was absent in Janice's account, inevitably and justly so—justly all the more because the same quality of feeling was arising in Janice as well, although it was about to express itself in another form. And I can say without any hesitation that the feeling each woman was experiencing about the issue of abortion was, without their naming it to themselves, accompanied and balanced, or rather, in a strange way enhanced by another equally deep essential passion, another equally deep harbinger of conscience: namely, *the wish for truth, wherever it leads.* The love of truth. One has to see it to believe it, to know what it really is like. The love of truth is not what we believe it is when we start the process of thought and dialogue. The ordinary intellect alone cannot really love truth. It can be "interested" in truth, but what it really loves and serves is usually something else, something not so beautiful in us. As Socrates shows through the genius of Plato's art, the love of truth can appear only when it has to be paid for inwardly, only when one comes upon the resistance of one's "own" entrenched opinions. *When one comes upon this resistance and still presses on, abandoning the attachment to one's own thoughts, an inner action is taking place which Socrates presents as a foretaste of "dying."* The true philosopher, he taught, studies death and dying through the act of sacrificing attachment to an "important" thought as it is occurring within one's own mind.

SOMETHING EXCEEDINGLY FINE

And now Janice, her eyelids fluttering and then opening wide, turned her head toward Arlene and began her response. It was obvious to everyone that "something," something exceedingly fine, was now passing between these two women.

"Arlene has very clearly brought out one of the main points in this whole question," she said, looking directly at Arlene, but keeping her hands still pressed together in front of her. "Is the fetus part of a woman's body, or is it a separate entity inside the woman? And . . . we do have rights, but also responsibilities over our bodies. But I think there's a different kind of responsibility we have toward children, our own children. And I wonder if we really understand the difference between the two kinds of responsibility—and even what the word 'responsibility' means? So that if I have a child—I mean, if you get to the third term and a woman decides for whatever reason that she doesn't want to continue, then the question is: has she been irresponsible with her own body or irresponsible with another . . . *body,* somebody else's. Like when does the responsibility of motherhood take hold? I think that's the question and I think people sort of blur it off when they say, well that's a fetus and what does that have to do with motherhood?—there's no maternal instinct, there's none of that.

"Of course to say that motherhood or maternal instinct doesn't exist—is obviously wrong. But the question is when does it start? When does there actually come to be this relationship between a mother and her child? And I've known people who have had miscarriages and they feel this *bond* was severed; so when did the bond start? And that is, I think, a matter of taking responsibility for *something else* and not just your own body . . ."

Janice stopped in mid-sentence. Slowly and uncharacteristically, she placed her hands on her knees and quietly looked at Arlene. Arlene, for her part, also assumed an uncharacteristic posture, though the change was more subtle than Janice's. Her broad, proud shoulders gently relaxed and rounded themselves like folding wings. Her luminous black eyes held steady.

The students in the class, wondering who was going to speak next, were patiently turning their heads back and forth. For a moment, I was tempted to say something in order to break the silence. But just as I started, I realized how foolish that would have been. Whatever it was that was passing between the two women was becoming more and more palpable. It was something very fine and very strong—the word "sacred" would not be wholly inappropriate. And seeing that, sensing that, I suddenly remembered that it was this "something" that was the whole point of the exercise. I wondered to myself: how could I have forgotten that— even for a moment?

Finally, Arlene responded: "What I hear you saying . . . is that we're drawing a distinction between the woman's responsibility for her own body and the woman's responsibility for the body that she's growing inside of her. Saying that we have to look at where her responsibility for her own body ends and where it begins for her as a mother. Saying she has to decide when does it become *her child*."

Without waiting for me to say anything, Janice leaned forward and spoke directly to Arlene—in a strangely resonant soft whisper that was distinctly heard all the way in the back of the class. "That's right," she said.

LOVE AND LISTENING

There now took place what was in its way one of the most dramatic events I have ever witnessed in a classroom. Arlene just sat there, apparently thinking of how to respond. She just sat there without saying a word. No one was at all inclined to break the silence. A process was taking place within Arlene that was completely unknown to any of the students. Was she desperately struggling to find a counterargument? Maybe . . . and maybe not. Was she feeling "defeated"? "Bested"? There was no sign of that at all. Yet it was clear she was struggling.

What she finally said took us all by surprise.

She said only a few words:

"I can't really argue with that," she said, almost in a whisper.

Everyone caught their breath while the words seemed just to hang in the air. I could see Janice ready to rise out of her chair, perhaps to embrace Arlene. The class did not know what to do. It seemed that not even Arlene understood the change that had taken place in her and, through her, in the rest of us.

Perhaps because I had witnessed something like this before, in other kinds of conditions, I saw very clearly that for a moment Arlene had submitted herself to another quality of energy within herself. At the same time, I sensed the reflection of this inner action also taking place within myself. I sensed in myself a reflection of her inner freedom, a taste of the love of truth—truth not as words, but as a conscious energy that binds contraries together, that binds people together, truth as love. And it is because genuinely moral action in another person evokes in ourselves a taste of our own inner possibility,—it is because of that that we cannot help but feel genuine respect and love for a good man or woman. Her good action evokes a reflection of that action in ourselves. We ourselves become good when we sense another's goodness. And in that moment we see that we wish for that; we cannot help but wish for that. We are built for that.

Of course, special conditions are necessary in order for this force to pass between and within people. In the usual inner and outer conditions of our everyday life, our egoism either cannot allow such perceptions to enter, or else we are fooled by artificial goodness in another, or else— in the end—we simply schizophrenically bifurcate ourselves, and our down-deep love of the good goes into hiding while in our surface personality we are "good" only when it serves our interests; and in our mind we become either sentimentally naive about ourselves and others or nightmarishly cynical (or "realistic") about the way of the world. Or, even worse—and of course very common—the upsurge of evil and brutality in man evokes in us the same mysterious forces of subjective fear and hatred that are the sources of human evil always and everywhere.

We are speaking now of a specific moral triumph in and through this one woman, Arlene, and in and through these two women thinking together and working to listen to each other. The class had broken into confused chatter—Had Arlene "lost" the "debate"? But if so, why did everyone feel a victory had taken place? . . . with no "loser"? Why did everyone feel so elated? Why was there such a celebratory mood in the classroom? With absolutely no sense of anyone or any opinion being "right" or "wrong"?

Yes, it was "only" in the rehearsal theater of the mind, but what a moment it was! And yes, it wouldn't last for much longer than this moment and it might not influence the actions of anyone's life, but what a glimpse of human possibility, what a glimpse of the awesome demand of what we all too easily speak of as ethics! Such a moment—call it, if you like, a moment of moral mysticism, or a moment of communal moral power—not only brings the meaning of ethics closer to us, it also, and equally, shows us how far from the good we actually are in our everyday life and in our everyday state of being, in our everyday mutual relations.

"We can go on with this in another way," I said, finally.

"Tell us," I said, speaking to both women, "what are your observations about this process of listening? What struck you about it—either about the work of listening, or about how you're now *feeling* about your point of view on this issue? Is your position, your opinion, in any way changed? In what way?"

"It's a very powerful exercise," said Arlene, her voice still reflecting her vibrant state. "If you have to repeat precisely what the other person has said it means you have to listen very carefully."

"And what does that do to you, what does that mean, what does that act require of you?"

"It demands that I focus," said Arlene. "It means I have to really understand what the other person is saying . . ." Arlene's usually steady eyes were drifting toward Janice. It was clear that although she was addressing me, her heart was with Janice.

"And it really changes my perspective."

"How so?"

"I really can't hold on so tightly to what I believe if I'm constantly releasing it in order to listen to what she's saying."

At that I nearly lost my composure. "Fantastic!" I said. "We go through our whole lives getting into discussions and arguing about this or that—and never, not once, do we ever listen to each other like that!"

I then turned to Janice, whose hands were now completely relaxed on her lap and whose look was riveted on Arlene.

"Although Arlene was the one who gave way," I said to her, "I'm sure you must have been experiencing the same kind of thing that she was."

Janice looked at me and for a moment she started to bring her hands together, but then softly dropped them back onto her lap.

"Absolutely," she said. "Obviously, we both got to say a lot more than you usually get to say in a discussion, but I found myself listening to a person, not to an argument . . ."

Again I excitedly broke in:

"This is entirely the most important point in the whole exercise. Repeat what you just said!"

"I was listening to a person, not just to an argument."

I turned to the class. "Do you hear that?" I said. "Do you understand what they discovered? You can go on disagreeing forever with another person. You can have a point of view that is 180 degrees different. You can be as passionate about your opinion as you want. But as long as you recognize and feel that you are listening to a *person,* there will be no violence, there will be no war."

After a long silence, I said to the women: "Thank you. You were both wonderful."

Arlene stood up to go back to the rows, but Janice didn't move. "But wait," she said, bringing her palms together once again and lowering her chin to the tips of her fingers. "What happens when it comes down to actually making a decision? Actually having to choose what to do? What then? It's all well and good to have a discussion about this, but *what about when you actually have to act?*"

The class suddenly became quiet as stone. Arlene stood by her chair in the front row by the window and did not sit down.

The professor—myself—is also quiet as stone. The question, the *one question,* has descended into the classroom and hovers in the air like a great winged life. Due in large measure to what has just gone on in the class, the one question of how actually to live enters now into everyone equally and evokes in everyone an "essence-feeling" that is somewhere between wonder and despair. Wonder as when one looks up at the immensity of a sky laced with an infinity of starry worlds; despair as when one honestly confronts the course of mankind's criminal life on earth along with the seemingly intractable chaos and moral weakness of one's own individual manifestations in life.

Four

BETWEEN WONDER
AND DESPAIR

L ate afternoon, the beginning of December. The air is damp and
cold. Behind a veil of thin gray clouds, the sun is already near the
horizon. Soon it will be night.

As I left the classroom and walked toward my car, I continued to feel
the reverberations of the exercise with Janice and Arlene, especially the
way it ended—with Janice's tense outcry about what happens when we
have to decide, when we actually need to *do* what is right.

But what am *I* doing? I asked myself. What is this "one question" that
I am constantly evoking, or planting, in the minds and hearts of my students? And what do I really owe them?

The whole enterprise of philosophy suddenly seemed to me a colossal presumption, maybe even a sort of madness: one small man wishing
to grasp the universal world when even the smallest element of nature—
a single leaf, a raindrop, the sound of a bird—defies all understanding in

itself and in its connectedness to the whole of reality, the whole of Being.

And, in its way, even more awesome; in its way even more incomprehensible is man himself. At least, standing under the stars and turning one's attention to the natural world around us, we can instinctively sense and mentally accept that one and the same universal order embraces all things, the same great laws operating here on earth as in the boundless cosmic world. At such moments one can well believe the great philosophers and visionaries who tell us that all things emanate from and tend toward what is called the One, the Good, the Being of beings. But what of Man?

Taken in the abstract, as a being possessed of self-aware reason and the relatively independent power to act from love and duty, a being ordained to be steward of the earth, a free and conscious servant of the Source of all things—taken as such, our human existence, mankind, wherever in the universe such a being may exist, can be understood not only as part of the all-encompassing greatness of Creation, but as its crown jewel. But man in the concrete, on the other hand, man as he actually is and behaves on earth, ourselves as we actually are—no, this passes beyond all possible comprehension. Human evil simply cannot be contained in the same mind that contemplates the beauty and order of the universal world. The contradiction is too extreme.

How many times, standing in front of a class, have I lectured about the so-called "problem of evil" and the various religious doctrines about sin and ignorance, without actually feeling anything whatever about the horror of mankind's collective depravity and cruelty. And then, for a brief moment, an image appears, a memory, a fact, a glimpse, an item in the news, a fragment of history, a tale told by a grandparent or an old friend—an image of the objective obscenity of war, the intentional destruction of millions of human lives in the service of insane ideals or "noble" purposes concealing nothing more than greed for power, massive resentment, the neurotic "honor" of the false self, the false collective identity . . . Here an image from literature of a Cossack grabbing a baby from its mother and bayoneting it in the air; or there film footage of Nazi soldiers bulldozing a mountain of murdered flesh into a carefully prepared ditch, filmed footage of walking human skeletons being herded into the ovens to be gassed. . . . Or a statistic dropping out of a book into my mind and down into my heart and down further into my bones and guts: a report of numbers, numbers, thousands, hundreds of thousands, millions, tens of millions . . . Armenians, Rwandans—countless thousands of slaughtered human beings piled three or four deep over an acre of God-forsaken land. Listen to them shout and scream as they dive into the pit of death. Or the blinding image of Hiroshima and the robotic soldiers of Japan submitting their hollow, but still human, lives to the insensate "divine emperor," the massive, ingenious cruelty of the Japanese officers—or, in another place, of the Chinese soldiers, or, in another place, crushingly close to home, of the American murderers and betrayers of the American Indians, the fathers, the mothers, the children, the dreams, the symbols, the stories, the traditions, the life of the culture. Or then the images of the Middle Passage from the shores of Africa to the New World . . . hear them choke and cry, these noble bodies chained to their posts, sickening and in this rolling nightmare, the survivors to face a life of slavery—squeezing out of that destroyed living life a spirituality, a music, a sorrow and grief beyond all imagining; hear them sing, hear them dream of heaven, hear their ghosts in our minds.

And all this is only the visible tip of the buried mass of human depravity.

But what, then, of the greatness, the Good on the other side of the human ledger? What of the soaring, sunlit heights of human love, beauty, wisdom, intelligence? What of the millions upon millions of small, invisible sacrifices strewn through our lives and through the history of our race; actions of who knows what mothers and children and fathers and brothers and strangers; and who knows what acts of compassion, what carefully built schools of thought and practice, what consciously created symbols and cathedrals and harmonies communicating truth and hope to the world of man; what world-historical incarnations of God or the Good springing forth from the great dance and joyous work of spiritual transmission in the inner temples of India, Egypt, Jerusalem . . . ?

Where am I? It is already dark—how did that happen so quickly? Where is my car? I have walked around in a big circle without knowing it. Janice's cry comes and goes, Arlene's nobility warms my thoughts, her discovery, her humility, the raising up of the whole class into the light of a more human attention, a moral attention there on the protected stage of the mind—proof that there exists within man a source of moral power that has not been known or recognized or named by an entire civilization—evidence, a hint, a key to this riddle as big as the now dark-ening sky above me; the riddle of human evil—evidence that will not survive the first step outside the classroom, the taste of a hint of the source of moral power in man that will not survive the first attraction in the street, the first impression, certainly not the first irritation, the first worry, the first pang of hunger or impatience or anger or resentment . . . and then goodbye the attention of a man and hello the laughing, schem-ing, paranoid, giddy dreamer that we all are, as we are, we poor, morally impotent representatives of . . . *man*!

In the deepening twilight, I watch from across the street as dozens of students come streaming out of the Humanities Building animatedly laughing and talking to each other or talking into their cell phones as they are dispersing. The sight and sounds of them bring me—a man who has just unconsciously walked around in a circle—"back to earth." For a moment, I experience that special sensation of myself here and now in my body, not unlike what I have previously described in my en-counter with Miss Yoder at her desk in the Central High School library. And suddenly, the whole question of good and evil looks completely different, completely new. For a moment, the question moves to a new terrain. How could I have forgotten this? How could I have forgotten that which I have studied for so many years and verified in my personal life with such painstaking difficulty: namely, that the perception of evil in the world and in ourselves makes a specific demand upon us—a demand not only to *do* whatever we can, but *to be able* to do, to *be* what we are meant to be.

In this moment I see that I do not know or understand evil in the world or in myself. I do not understand what evil really is or why it exists. How to remember that, and how to draw the right conclusions from it? How to remember, how to see that being swallowed by moral despair (and its crippled spawn of guilt and passive helplessness) actually conceals from us the fact that we simply do not understand what Man is, what place he occupies in the cosmos. We do not know what we are, and we do not see or understand the forces on earth and beyond the earth that have brought what we call evil into being. And, of greatest importance, how to remember that such understanding cannot come from the mind alone, from ideas alone; nor can it come from emotion alone, not even from the searing realization of human evil when it presents itself right before our eyes.

Our morality? Is it anything more than the preaching of a flea riding the back of a rampaging elephant? I look at these young men and women and the things that they or I worry about from morning to night. Consider all our attempts to be good, decent people. Consider our moral vows, our golden rules, our laws and rules of civilization. And then consider the crimes we commit, the crimes of humanity, the depredations, the violation of children, the torture, the destruction, the genocide, the rape—and the deception, the uproar of revolution, the preaching of murderous ideology, murderous religion—can we really believe any of that is under human control? Of what universal forces are these crimes the result? Did not all these murderers and the millions of obedient murderers they lead—didn't they too have mothers and mentors who taught them what was good or bad? Didn't they too make moral vows; didn't they think they were doing the good? What awesome hypnotic force of self-deception enables us, compels us, to adopt our moral principles in the belief that we will be able to live them, or even to try to live them in our actual lives? What a monstrous deception of ourselves by ourselves—as individuals and as humanity! Is our morality anything more than organized self-concealment? And aren't the great cynics and skeptics of the world right when they say that man is nothing more than a ruined animal who needs to be held in check by the illusion of morality, backed by psychological threats of guilt and religious mythologies of heaven and hell, as well as the concrete threat of physical force and punishment?

And yet . . . and yet it cannot be that it is only in the theater of the mind that we can free our attention from its bondage to desire, opinion and fear; it can't be that it is only in the mind that we can consider our neighbor regardless of our own personal well-being or safety or satisfaction or goals. Is it really only in our mind—or, what is worse, only in our fantasy—that we voluntarily submit to the moral law, the law of conscience in our lives? Why is the stability of our lives such an illusion? Why does the slightest scratch from life or from my neighbor turn us upside down? What does it mean that our lives and the life of our whole society is, as has been observed, "a soap bubble that can only exist in a quiet medium"?[10]

And yet . . . what of the invisible acts of sacrifice and love throughout the world and throughout even one's own little life? Do they not serve, these invisible acts, these movements of human love and human attention freed from the ego—don't they and they alone sustain our lives and the life of our civilization, of humanity itself? Yes, we have heroes whose actions are like beacons to the world, but for every heroic action that makes the headlines of history there are thousands, millions, of heroic actions behind every other door and within every other human heart. Somewhere within mankind, within people we know, within ourselves, there are and have been these energy-transactions of love—perhaps even bordering on being unconscious, but they sustain the life of all of us. Like neural messages, they pass within the body of human history, unseen, unrecognized. We know they're there. Or do we? And are they?

Yet the crimes—now called maybe merely "failures," psychological distress, neurosis, mental disorder, depression: these are not only psychophysical "illnesses"—they are moral failures, moral failures of the society, of the world. Every wound caused by withheld or twisted love is a moral failure; every act of love, even at its most nearly neutral, even in the form of restrained violence or the restrained expression of malice and its brood—every such act or every such tiny mastery of anger and fear toward another—every such act has a moral dimension. *All actions between and among people are of the moral order,* although they have physical, neural, psychological effects. Don't we see that? Don't we see that we human beings, we men and women are living in a universe shaped, built, structured by the element of good, each element in the universe serving its purpose, doing its "good" in the whole cosmic scheme? Each element of nature, of creation, has its good—call it its function if you like—and each element lives and breathes from the interplay of ends and purposes that are uniquely good for itself and collectively good for the whole. The whole of nature is built on community, whether the community of species or even one-celled animals, or the community of man.

Such is nature, such is the cosmos, a vast cosmic organism—which means a vast cosmic community. And for man, this organic wholeness of the good is the human community. The human community has its own unique good and contributes, does it not, its own unique good to the universal whole.

I have not moved. Have I once again gone away from my own present existence, away from the sensation of presence? Have I once again flown out of my body into the little prison of my thoughts? Have I again become the poor being—Man-on-earth—whose moral impulses, whether confused or clear, cannot pass from his mind into the muscles of his body? Man-on-earth who reveres the commandments of his religion or the ethical teachings of his philosophers and saints or the inspired sacred sensations of his hymns and chorales and triumphant music or the heartbreaking mystical laments of his greatest poets; Man-on-earth who bows his head in humble sorrow in front of the Cross or the great legendary lives of Man-Gods, his great righteous teachers—who, yes, knows what is good, who feels what is good, but who, when he steps out into his actual life, acts in obedience only to his fears and angers and hurts and religious fantasies; Man-on-earth who can neither fight for the good nor even retreat into an honest contemplative escape from the world, who knows, but is powerless to *do,* powerless to act on what he knows or what he feels. *Why can't we be good?* That is why.

It is because there is no deep or real relation inside of us between our mind and that which moves us to action—the word for that power being in our language *emotion:* that which moves us to physical action or to the act of human speech or to the real wish to love and serve or to partake in the great struggle for what is objectively good and right and just. What is the courage we need to understand and then to hold on to our understanding as we move our body and our heart into the vortex of our lives and the life of our neighbor and community? Noble as it is to search for the truth, how can it be noble simply to cultivate the truth away from the battlefield of life that demands of Man-on-earth the courage to protect what God or Nature has put into our hands to serve and protect?

Little man, little woman, you and I, and the rest of us—isn't all our suffering moral suffering? Our wounded lives, our deep hurts, our disillusionments, our divorces and betrayals and abortions and blind sacrifices leading to no good; our good acts and small sacrifices serving only to throw clearer light on our metaphysical and psychological helplessness—isn't all of this a moral failure that must not induce guilt in us, but deeper than guilt, the taste of the true perception of our being or state of being?—which must and can be healed in stages corresponding to what is actually broken in ourselves and how it may be repaired.

How really to step from the theater of the mind into the streets and skies of actual life? Is there a moral power of our being, an attention that can gradually, in precise stages, free itself from the serpents of our opinions and hearts and bodies and our history and our cultural conditioning—a power that can move in toward God and out toward our neighbor in the service of what is Good and what brings to us and to our neighbor the real Good that, we are told, has been prepared for us in the very essence of our being as Man?

Can we ponder this together?

Five

ON THE WAY TO
GOOD AND EVIL

Our question is vast, vast beyond imagining. It concerns the entire history of mankind, of the world. Who can conceive the extent of man's inhumanity to man through all the ages of time? Even those among us who have been deeply and personally scarred and devastated by the unfathomable brutality of human evil— even they probably cannot imagine all the horror of this evil throughout the ages of human life on earth, from the "glories" of pharaonic Egypt and the "proud" conquering empires of ancient China and Persia and Alexander to the slaughtering hordes of Central Asia to all the countless genocides and near genocides of yesterday and today. The stain of human evil covers the earth and seeps into all man's achievements in art, science, and in the institutions of society. Religion as we know it cannot change it nor, it seems, even understand it. Our science of psychology, so full of hope only a few decades ago, cannot change it or understand it. Government cannot control it nor, most often, even refrain from manifesting it itself. And, as we know close to hand, our modern institutions of commerce and business, heedless of the cost to human life and welfare, continue to shock us as they violate the most fundamental canons of trust and honesty. Carried into the bloodstream of our modern culture by the great social technology of money and finance, the heartless calculus of exploitation and blind profit infects nearly every aspect of human life on earth.

The question is vast beyond imagining in its breadth and depth in human history. But it is equally vast, so to say, in its personal, individual intimacy. The force of human evil—call it by what name you will—reaches as deeply into the individual human heart as it reaches into the causal chain of human history. It is as much one's own, my own, central fact as it is a central fact of humanity, man-on-earth. The two aspects of evil, the inner and outer, the personal and the collective, reflect each other. And we cannot imagine, we cannot comprehend either aspect of the force of evil, just as we cannot imagine, cannot comprehend the greatness and goodness of what we are in our hidden essence and what we are meant to be: conscious instruments of the Absolute.

The great religious and philosophical spiritualities of the world teach that we men-on-earth exist between two infinities: the great cosmos around and above us and the cosmic world within us, each a reflection of the other. We are as deep inside as the universe in which we live is vast and deep outside ourselves. We might say, in this respect, that in order to know the universe, that is, in order to know reality, it is fundamentally necessary to know ourselves. In a sense, we could say that in this respect man exists between two Goods—the Goodness above and the Goodness within, or, as it is sometimes expressed, man is a microcosm. But now we must consider another aspect of this idea that is usually left out of its expression in the familiar presentations, an aspect that is there in the wholeness of the teachings, but has been, as it were, "re-located" in a place very distant from the idea of the microcosm. And that idea is what we must now consider as we begin to ponder the work of stepping out of the theater of the mind in order to try to live according to what we know to be good. That idea is this: man exists also between two evils: the evil without and the evil within: the sin and ignorance of mankind itself and the sin and ignorance of one's own self.

The Christian doctrine of "original sin" was no doubt intended as an expression of this idea. As such, it was perhaps intended to help men and women confront the degraded state of their being and by so doing support in them—in us—the healing action of remorse. Instead, it has had the effect of inducing a quite opposite response within ourselves, namely *guilt,* a response which masquerades as remorse, but which has become one of the main obstacles to the confrontation with oneself that is necessary in order for man to receive the reconciling force of what is called in Christianity the Holy Spirit (or "the Comforter"), and the idea of which exists in all the great traditions, under other names—that same Holy Spirit symbolized by the image of the white dove.

Metaphysically and psychologically, guilt is the opposite of remorse. Guilt is founded on the illusory premise that we should have and *could* have acted differently in this or that situation, with this or that person or in the light of this or that ideal. Remorse, on the other hand, is rooted in the objective perception that it is the state of our being that has been revealed, that this is what we are—contrary to what we have believed about our moral capacities. In guilt we may vow to do better—which is often a way the ego has of "quarantining" the momentary impression of deep-seated moral incapacity and preventing it from entering into us as truth. Remorse, on the other hand, brings with it no external or internal promises to do anything, but only the profoundly sorrowful acceptance of what we are, together with the physical and metaphysical relaxation of the ego's condition of tension, a relaxation that opens the heart and the body to receive a new quality of attention—an attention, or conscious energy, that in the Eastern Orthodox tradition has been called "the attention that comes from God." It is imperative that we study this difference in ourselves, for it is such emotions as guilt and fear, with their reflexes of self-pity and anger, that arise in us with such force outside the theater of the mind, in the "streets" of our everyday life; it is such emotions that we need to understand if there is to be any hope of manifesting in our actions the good that we discover in ourselves—even if it be only in "the theater of the mind"—when we try to touch or sustain in ourselves the power to love, which is the ultimate basis of all ethical action and principles.

Such ideas about human evil and its reconciliation in ourselves through the action of remorse may without difficulty be found in the discourses and writings of teachers and guides in all the great spiritual traditions, East and West, throughout the ages. But in this context there is one element in these teachings that is not often noticed, an element which in a strange way seems to have concealed itself even as it is expressed time and again in the literary and artistic transmissions that have come down to us. And it is safe to say that it is this that is perhaps the chief missing element in all our struggles to live according to what we know is good. It is an element that has been forgotten in most Western religions; and as for the religions of the East, even with all their psychological practicality, it is possible to say that they have this element, but they may not know that they have it. Or, if that is too presumptuous a statement, it is possible that they have not found the way to lift it out of the vast web of their teachings and show it clearly and plainly to the modern mind, with the result that, continuing to be confused with or obscured by other aspects of their practical and theoretical teachings, it persists in slipping away, unnoticed, like a shy maiden unwilling to risk being exploited or inappropriately handled.

And yet, without this element, ethics must ultimately remain what it has been in so much of human history and in our individual lives: little more than a grand self-deception, the dream of *doing*—an unrealizable ideal that at best enables society to function, but which in a deeper sense only masks our collective and individual moral impotence, to the point that now the world of nature and man is in real danger of complete destruction.

ON THE MEANING OF THE HUMAN BODY

We identify this missing element as the work of establishing a relationship between the mind and the body. But we are still no closer to understanding it. And that is because to come toward a new vision of the nature and meaning of the human body will require of us access to a realm of ideas, experiences and attitudes that we can neither invent nor discover by ourselves nor passively glean from what has accidentally been made available from the ancient traditions. At the same time, to speak of it clearly and directly entails the risk of entangling it in the machinations of our habitual mental explanations. This latter danger may explain what lies behind the hiddenness of this element in the ancient teachings, where one might surmise that the reason it was practiced without being explicitly conceptualized was to prevent its being trapped in the automatisms of the intellect. Nevertheless, one must ask: is the truth about the nature and purpose of the human body *too* hidden in the ideas, rituals, and ideals of spiritual teachings and practices available in our era?

Did our one-legged man find it offered in the spiritual community of Hillel? That is to ask: where in the Hebraic tradition can we find the teaching that the attainment of moral power—that is, the capacity for genuine and sustained moral action—requires a specific practice that leads to a transformed relationship to the physical body? And where do we find such a teaching in the Christian tradition? Or in the Islamic tradition? Or are followers of these traditions to be forever locked in the view that the body is simply and only the enemy of the good?—or, at most, is the positive view of the body, as we find in some surviving indications, limited to the view that it can provide the reward of sanctified pleasure associated with man's proper execution of his earthly duties and obligations, as, for example, in the sexual relationship between husband and wife?

The point is that nowhere in the known conventional views do we encounter clear indications that the body is meant to be a necessary element in a process leading to the development of man's *ableness* to do what is good. On the contrary, both our modern religious teachings and our secular, humanistic ethical teachings assume that the main element in morality is our intention, an intention which is absolutely under our control. Nowhere—or only very rarely and very obscurely—do we find a hint that although we are meant to act in accordance with the good, in fact we do not; not because of our intention, but because of our state of being, a critical aspect of which is our undeveloped or distorted relationship to the body, and another aspect of which—and these two aspects imply each other—is a lack of intellectual comprehension of what the human body really is and really means on all levels—physical, cosmic, and metaphysical.

And again, to repeat: where certain doctrines such as the notion of original sin seem to teach that man is not able to be good, no matter what his intention, the inculcation of the feeling of guilt takes away what surely is the essential meaning and purpose of such a doctrine— namely, to support and assist the arising of remorse of conscience in the mind and heart, and the concomitant relaxation of the soul which opens man to the reconciling grace of the Holy Spirit. Thus, when St. Paul cries out in Romans 7: "For the good that I would I do not: but the evil which I would not, that I do" and follows it soon after with the utterance: "O wretched man that I am! Who shall deliver me from the body of this death?" the ultimate answer that he gives is that the Spirit (*pneuma*) will "give life" to the body that is destined for death—if, and only if, man allows the Spirit to enter into the body. And when the Spirit does enter the body (through the action of *faith*), it takes the place of our vain striving to obey the religious laws and doctrines which have had the perhaps unexpected effect of showing us that by ourselves and as we are, our moral intentions and our actions are intractably opposed to each other.

THE SOCRATIC THRESHOLD

But what of Socrates? What of the influence of ancient Greece on our present civilization and our understanding of ourselves? Is our culture not the distant product of just these two historical currents: the Hebraic/Christian vision and the Greco/Roman vision? What, then, of the "secret of Socrates"? What of this "secret" concerning the fundamental role of uncompromising dialogue on the way to self-knowledge, and the fundamental role of the work of self-knowledge on the way to virtue? Do these practices, *can* these practices, bring us to the actual power to *do* what is good in our actual lives?

The answer, surely, is No, they cannot. They can only bring us to the threshold of moral power. But to cross that threshold, to actually live a life of virtue, something else is needed, and that "something else" is not made clear or explicit in the writings of Plato. The entire, vast corpus of the Platonic philosophy, with its immense vision of the cosmic order, and the nature of space and time which links these two mysteries to an all-embracing divine plan of creation, its doctrine of the Good as the Being of all beings, the ultimate conscious reality pervading the universal world; its teaching about levels of knowledge of understanding and the need to struggle in order to awaken from the cave-like dream of our everyday existence with all its violence and unreality and fear; its unequaled diagnosis of the communal and political life of unawakened man and the need for communities and states that seek justice to come under the guidance of inwardly developed rulers—all this only brings us to the threshold of virtue, the threshold of moral power. Beyond this is the secret of Socrates and the secret of his illustrious pupil, Plato. Neither the incomparable science of dialogue created by Socrates, nor the intellectual study of the all-embracing philosophical system of ideas articulated by Plato, can by themselves take us across the threshold of the power to act according to the good. And this is why surrounding all the

profound writings of Plato there exists an even more profound silence—
the silence dressed in the thin veil of the words "the oral tradition"—in
the thin veil of the teaching about the insurmountable limitations and
dangers of the merely written word. This is why the discourses and dialogues of Socrates almost always end with an unanswered question, *the*
unanswered question: what is virtue and how can we learn to live according to what is good?

We do not know—apart from the most slender and ambiguous
hints—what and how Socrates taught his pupils outside the process of
dialogue. Plato and, to a greater extent perhaps, Socrates' other illustrious pupil, Xenophon, allow us to see only a tiny glimpse of the way
Socrates behaved with those whom he sought to awaken beyond the
theater of the mind. Nor do we really know what, beyond words and
ideas, was being attempted in the thousand-year history of the Platonic
academy, which exerted such an enormous, and almost entirely un-
chronicled, influence in the ancient world and the world of late antiquity. It is enough to say that the whole principle of what is called the
"oral tradition" or the "hidden tradition" refers not merely to childish
ideas of secret doctrines and secret words, but to intensive emotional and
physical conditions intended to have effect on the being of man, not
only on the mind. But we do not and cannot have explicit records of
what those conditions were in the ancient world, or even if such conditions effectively existed or continued to exist past the lives of their creators and founders. And where the nature of such special conditions is
in fact described in the transmissions of the great spiritual traditions, it
is done in words and images (literature, story, art, architecture, music,
dance) that require a state of rightly guided inner struggle in order really
to be understood for what they are. That is to say, such transmissions
have inner levels of meaning that can be discerned only by the inner levels of human perception awakened in the process of the overall development of man's state of being.

Yes, our civilization is in large part rooted in the two traditions of
Hebraic/Christian religion and Greco/Roman ideals of knowledge and

justice. But it is safe to say, looking about us at our world and looking within ourselves at our own lives, that these traditions have not brought with them the knowledge of how to make man good. At best, where these traditions of religion and philosophy have not been demonized and degraded by fanaticism, sentimentality, or hyper-intellectualism, they are ways that bring us only to the threshold of moral power. We are thus living in a world of thresholds—a kind of immense plain or country where no matter how intensely we walk or in whatever direction we search, we come to a threshold we cannot cross. It is like the science-fiction image of a force field that holds humanity within its bounds without our knowing it. We do not see or understand this force field, this threshold, this limitation of our moral power. And nothing we have done or can do seems able to penetrate it. All we can say is that our religious ideals, our moral resolves, our ideologies, our campaigns, however honorably conceived, have not prevented—and perhaps have even hastened—the arrival of our world and our lives at the rim of despair and destruction.

How could we not wonder and hope that there does exist a missing element, a genuine and noble "secret" that we have forgotten and can work to remember—a missing element that actually offers the real, and not imaginary, hope that we men and women, this humanity of which we are a part, can actually cross the threshold into the real reality that has traditionally been given the name of the Good, and that in our individual, everyday actions, genuinely deserves the name: conscience?

Six

INTERLUDE: THE GARMENT OF THE BUDDHA

I n the National Museum of New Delhi there exists a life-size statue of the Buddha, the Awakened One, draped in a clinging, transparent robe. With its fine radiance of curved, geometrically spaced folds, the robe delicately reveals every swelling and contour of the Buddha's graceful, masculine body. Known simply as the Standing Buddha of Mathura, it is an outstanding example of Buddhist representational sculpture typical of the Gupta period in India during the fourth to the sixth century AD.

What may be startling about the sculpture to the average Western viewer is the sensuous depiction of the founder of one of the world's great spiritual traditions. Why this clinging garment? Since nothing is accidental in such sacred art, the question is bound to arise as to what meaning we are supposed to take from it. For, like many representations of the Buddha or Buddhist saints, the overall posture represents both deep inner contemplation and the act of compassionate spiritual instruction. This is, therefore, not only the representation of a high inner state of human being, but also a depiction of the action of the entire spiritual tradition—of the hope and the demand it offers to mankind in the face of all human suffering and evil and in the face of death itself: the hope and demand, in the case of Buddhism, that resides in the work of freeing the mind of its egoistic illusions, freeing the heart of its fears and cravings, and freeing the mortal body of its obsessions.

For most Westerners, and perhaps for many other modernized people as well, the perception of the sensuous in sacred art is an indigestible impression that takes the form of a deep but fleeting intuition immediately covered over by puritanical judgments, intellectual labels, or naive translations rooted in familiar associations of the release of untrammeled physical pleasure.

GLIMPSES

This deep but fleeting intuition informs us that there is a meaning and a purpose of the human body, our human body, for which we have no names and of which we have only misunderstood glimpses in the course of our lives. Such glimpses of the finer life within the body are also indigestible; there is little or nothing in our conventional psychological, scientific, or religious categories that helps us to interpret them in relation to the great possibilities and ideals of human life—such as the ideal of moral power.

Consider, for example, certain states of deep wonder that may occur when one is in the midst of the greatness of nature or in the quiet intensity of mutual, compassionate love. Or consider the state of all-embracing grief and sorrow that may follow immediately upon the death of a loved one. Or consider the awesomely instantaneous response of our being to an imminent, life-threatening danger to oneself or to a companion. In such states one may observe that the body is temporarily transformed and permeated with a fine energy, a subtle quality of sensation unlike anything we experience in the ordinary course of our lives, not even in the most intense and sought-after satisfactions of our desires or cravings for pleasure.

Almost everyone has experienced this quality of sensation on relatively rare occasions, but very few of us know what it may signify. Nor are we aware that an intentional cultivation of its appearance in our lives is possible and necessary for the growth of our being, including the possible development of our power of moral action. Our contemporary understanding does not and cannot separate this transitory experience of subtle sensation from the emotions that invariably accompany it or result from it, and which in fact generally carry an entirely different, coarser quality of energy. The real sense of wonder—as, for example, in front of the greatness of nature—may be quickly overlaid by the craving to explain, or by the passionate urge to make sudden changes in one's own life or in the life of the world. Similarly, the profundity of inconsolable sorrow in the face of death sooner or later may give way to overwhelming emotions of personal fear or painful guilt. As for the experience of total human presence and instinctive altruistic action in the moment of imminent danger, the reaction to it, when the danger is passed, is often simply the puzzlement of a swift return to one's ordinary state of consciousness with its usual sense of time, anxiety or ego.

Countless examples rooted in many and various kinds of circumstances could be cited of this phenomenon of the appearance within oneself of what we could call an inner, subtle sensation of the body. And if we recall what we are like during such experiences, we will see that during those periods we are much, much closer to being the kind of man or woman that conscience tells us we ought to be. In the state of grief or of profound wonder, for example, the kind of events or actions by others that might ordinarily disturb us, anger us, seduce us or irritate us have absolutely no power over us. And in the response to immediate danger, our usual concern for our own well-being, or even for our lives, often yields instantly to the seemingly "instinctive" impulse to save or protect the other.

In a word, in such states we become *good*. And we become good or moral not directly due to the ideas we hold about right and wrong or due to our philosophical views about the meaning of human life or due to our religious beliefs about love and sacrifice. No. We know all too well that such ideas and beliefs often have little or no direct power to determine our actions in the flow and momentum of the choices that make up our lives. It is precisely this fact that is at the center of this whole inquiry—the fact that, though we "know" what is good—according to our moral beliefs—we do not *do* what is good; along with the corollary fact that that which we *do* is, with painful frequency, the very opposite of what we "know" to be good.

"KNOWLEDGE" AND KNOWLEDGE

The word "know" is in quotation marks, because the kind of knowledge that we usually have regarding our moral obligations and duties is not knowledge in the full sense of the word. When it comes to morality, the kind of knowledge we need is of an entirely different order than knowledge that exists only in the intellect. As Socrates would tell us, we genuinely know what is good only when the whole of ourselves knows it—when it is known not only in the mind, but in the body and in the heart. We may understand intellectually what is good, while yet desiring and choosing to do something entirely different—and vice versa. And the body, our body such as it is in our ordinary existence, either creates the desires that lead us around in the course of our lives or else submits grudgingly to our conditioned likes and dislikes, often at the ultimate cost of our physical health and well-being.

And since it is the body, just the material body with its bones and muscles, that actually is the instrument of movement and action in the world, on this earth, it follows that the deep and direct understanding of the meaning of the body and its possible states is all-important to a man or woman who wishes to pass from ethical ideals to concrete ethical action—

a man or woman, that is, who seeks to step out of the theater of the mind into the streets of our real life in the real world around us: the world called *samsara* by the Buddhists, the carousel of illusion riding on reality; reality seated in the arms of illusion—the world which our one-legged man was told about in the first lines of the Mosaic law: "and the Earth was without form and void and darkness was upon the face of the deep."

Here we stand, then, at the threshold that forms the boundary between the theater of the mind and the streets of the real world. And here at this Socratic threshold we are met not by the angel of the Lord with his flaming sword, who guards the gate leading back to the paradise of Eden, but by the Awakened One, with his radiant human body, who offers to guide us forward and out through the confused and bewildered streets and crossroads of our exiled lives.

Standing at this threshold, however, we need to pause. We need to remember by what means we—we modern men and women—could have been granted to arrive at just this point, this genuine and rare privilege of beginning in fact and not in imagination the work of putting into practice the great ideals that have called to mankind throughout the millennia. And we need as well to recall to our mind the experiential glimpses of something like moral power that we have had in our lives, however preliminary and artificially induced such instances may have been. The experiment of listening to another under the protected conditions of philosophical dialogue and "sacred dispute" is but one such example of artificially induced special conditions. The full creation of such special conditions no doubt requires the practical wisdom of a Socrates. But even we who are so far removed from the practical wisdom that created this kind of spiritual form may with profit imitate it if only we really understand that the hidden aim of Socratic dialogue is the study of the moral power of conscious attention in the act of thinking together and listening, one human being to another. Such listening, which requires the mind to step back from itself in order to make room for the other's thoughts, thereby allows in itself the process of the development of ideas and the evolution of a new understanding. This new mental understanding, which is accompanied by a new quality of feeling for truth and for the humanity of one's neighbor, is precisely the threshold of the theater of the mind—that is to say, it is this stage of philosophical understanding and moral sentiment that represents, with relatively few radiant exceptions, the ethical limit of a man or woman whose mind has not yet come into a stable harmonious relationship to the body—the body considered as the instrument of action in the world. Such understanding is at the threshold of virtue, but it is not yet the power of virtue. It is not yet the power to be good. And it is just on the other side of this threshold that Plato has Socrates fall silent. It is just on the other side of this threshold that the "oral tradition" begins, the "hidden tradition" of special conditions that cannot be written down because what is involved is energy rather than ideas. What is involved is the practical study of a human energy which is only glimpsed—albeit powerfully—in the work of listening, one human being to another. At its higher levels, this energy is rightly called *love.*

It is in the body and through the body that all the energies of man move and live and communicate with each other, and it is in the body that all the energies of human life can be studied, discriminated and eventually, as a result of inner struggle, come into harmonious relationship, thereby allowing the entry into human life and action of a spiritual force of great power and moral efficacy.

So, pausing at the threshold of the real world of our lives, we recognize that for most of us modern men and women, whose education has been mainly in the mind alone, true ideas are necessary in order to strengthen the understanding of our moral and metaphysical aims. And for this study we need companions. The work of studying great ideas with others is a fundamental ongoing support along the way, not only leading us to the taste of understanding, but also offering us, in the work of listening, a genuine foretaste of the moral power that in our ordinary lives is no more than a distant ideal.

Ideas, therefore, are necessary.

But they are not enough.

A NEW KIND OF BODY

Now we step across the threshold. We move into "the street." We move into our lives.

What happens?

We are gone.

We have forgotten.

Do not speak here of the good, of love and justice, of acting rightly according to truth. On this side of the threshold, where men and women ignore or forget the meaning of their uniquely human power of conscious attention, do not speak of ought and must and right and wrong. Do not regale us with your deep understanding of metaphysical truth, of spiritual tradition; do not speak of ethics, of the need to love our neighbor, to care for mankind, to do what is right to our friend or our family. Do not tell us to answer the call of duty out of our free will, rather than out of habit or fear or self-pride. Do not speak of Christian love, or humanistic love, or rational ethics. Do not speak of the latest formulations about living in the present moment, of the "power of now" or "mindfulness," do not tell us to wake up or merge with reality or with God—no.

No, tell it to the body, for it is the body that is the instrument of action. But the body does not understand our words, our ideas. It does what we wish only when we brutalize it or bribe it—when we whip it or give it its sugar, in so-called "self-control" or self-indulgence. Our bodies are far from being the radiant garment of the awakened human being.

And what we are seeking is a body, a life on earth, in which our actions and behavior serve the higher impulses and intentions, the higher feelings, that constitute the heart of true human virtue. We are not searching simply for an improved version of moralist automatism nor for childish self-assertion masquerading as freedom. In a breathtakingly real sense, we are searching for a new kind of body, a body that has a new aim, a new purpose: voluntarily to serve the Good. And, to compound the mystery, in the search for a new kind of body within ourselves, there exists the possibility of discovering a new heart, a source of love within ourselves that we have perhaps glimpsed in our lives, as in the legends where the seeker or the hunter has but one fleeting glimpse of a serenely beautiful face or a great winged being—a glimpse which, when understood, has the power to change entirely the direction of one's life.

INTERMEDIATE MORALITY

Here, on the far side of the Socratic threshold, we need to stop and stand in front of this question before we take even one step forward into the realities of our everyday life.

In fact, we need to take a step backward and look once again at how we wish to live. And, stepping further back, we need to look at how we actually do live our lives. We need once again to ask ourselves what we are and what we ought to be. Yet we cannot really answer these questions while remaining in the protective conditions of the "classroom" or its equivalent.

And so, we need to ask these questions in a new way, taking into account the glimpses of hope that have already appeared—the help that is offered by the intensive study of real ideas (as with our one-legged man) and the opening of the heart through the effort of conscious listening to another person's thought.

Above all, we will need to discover how actually to communicate our understanding and our ideals to the body. We need to study the possibility of establishing an enduring and intentional relationship to the body, the physical instrument of our life and action in the world. That will be the next stage of our work toward becoming a full human being—that is to say, a *good* human being, a real human being, in whom the body with its immense energies of life willingly obeys the real man or woman of conscience who calls to us from within ourselves. Not the body beaten into submission like a dog or pampered like a spoiled child or ignored like a sullen orphan of the streets only waiting to take out its vengeance upon us.

Yes, we need now to step across the Socratic threshold, but how to do it without being swallowed by the delusional influences of ordinary life? How to step across the Socratic threshold without losing our selves? The answer is clear: we need to make use of ways and means to be outwardly "in the street" in our actual lives, while somehow, or to some extent, remaining inwardly in the theater of the mind—that protected space where the ideals of truth, justice and morality are remembered, studied and respected. We need to be in two places at once, simultaneously on both sides of the Socratic threshold: simultaneously in the street and in the classroom. We need something that is fundamentally unknown to ourselves: to *question* our lives without inwardly or outwardly holding back from whatever life offers and asks of us; to step back from ourselves while wholeheartedly, even passionately, engaging in our lives and answering to its obligations. Only then can we hope to find the means and direction for changing our lives.

A new morality will emerge within this seemingly self-contradictory effort. This new morality would not hypnotize us with delusions of moral power, nor dispirit us with the ethical cynicism and relativism that is characteristic of our culture—a culture that has tried in vain to guide itself under the authority of the isolated intellect, disconnected from the consciousness in the body, which is the obvious instrument of action in our life, and from the voice of conscience crying and whispering in the heart. But what shall we call this new morality? We need to take great care naming it.

What shall we call a morality whose aim is to bring about within ourselves an attunement between our ethical ideals and the energies of life and action in our physical, mortal body? We are speaking of a hitherto unrecognized stepping-stone *in between* moral impotence and moral will, what we might call an *intermediate morality* that can guide us toward moral power in the full sense of the word. Perhaps it would be best to speak of this *new kind* of morality as "the ethics of the threshold," since what we are speaking of is a way of living our actual lives without abandoning the principles and protections of traditional morality, while at the same time questioning to what extent they really apply to us as we are— that is, to what extent, within ourselves, we are, so to say, *pre-ethical*. We are far from speaking, as did Nietzsche, of going "beyond good and evil," but simply and honestly of stepping *toward* good and evil.

We do not wish to be fooled either by moral absolutism or by moral relativism. Perhaps in the end we will think of this new kind of morality as a *reconciling* morality that offers a bridge stretched between what we are and what we yearn to be in the light of the ethical and religious commandments that have formed the basis of our own and of every other civilization of the world. But what shall we call it now? To name it rightly will be the first step toward understanding it rightly.

Seven

THE ETHICS OF ATTENTION

R eturn with me, please, to the classroom.
But we will not remain in the classroom. We will take the class-room into the streets. Into the world.

Into our life.

OUR WORLD AND OUR LIFE

The reading assignment is the *Meditations* of Marcus Aurelius.

The setting is a military tent along the remote, untamed eastern fron-tier of the Roman Empire late in the second century after the birth of Christ. The night is cold, and inside the tent, exhausted and unable to sleep, his aging body racked with pain, sits the most powerful man on earth: Marcus Aurelius, Emperor of Rome at the time of the vast Em-pire's widest hegemony throughout the lands of Europe, northern Africa and Asia Minor. For seven years he will be commanding the awesome Roman army against the invading Germanic tribes in the forests and swamps of the Hungarian plain. He will consult with generals, some brave and sagacious, some jealous and ambitious, some strong, some foolish, but all of them among the most respected men of the greatest empire of the earth. Fierce and cunning tribal leaders will be placated or captured or executed or bribed or won over or played against each other. Thousands of men will scream, bleed and die all around the commander-in-chief. Many will die fulfilling the sacred honor of a Roman soldier and citizen. Enemies will be butchered or taken into enslaved captivity.

At the same time, during these seven years, the political, financial, and judicial affairs of the Empire will need to be overseen by the Emperor from afar. While directing the great movements of war, the Emperor will be receiving emissaries and messengers from the Center as well as from distant provinces demanding decisions of immense consequence, and every day reporting events and actions which, if not attended to with great intelligence, have the potential to shake the whole of the civilized world. He, the Emperor, will have to alternately show and restrain his power everywhere in all things. A wrong step, a detail overlooked, an angry passion or fear prompting an ill-considered reaction, an ill-considered perception based on hearsay or lies, and half the earth may convulse or invisibly move into a current of forces leading to chaos and destruction. Every movement and word of the Emperor of Rome is like the thundering footstep of a giant in the fragile garden of the world. Such is the power of the Emperor of Rome. Such is the power of this one man, Marcus Aurelius.

But to Marcus Aurelius, power means more than dominion over nations and peoples. It means, first and foremost, dominion over oneself— specifically, an intentional relationship to one's own mind, one's own thoughts, one's own impulses and emotions. In striving for such a sustained and ever-deepening attention to one's own mind, a man opens himself to the mind and power of God within himself. Such was the essence of the way of life called *philosophy*. Above all else, this "most powerful man on earth" struggled to live as a philosopher in the very midst of all the events, both gigantic and small, that make up human life. And to live as a philosopher meant always and in everything to give first priority to the exercise of allowing the mind of God within oneself to determine one's words and acts. Through the work of attending to one's own mind, one's own portion of the mind of God can flow into and through the heart that feels and the body that moves in relation to the loves and duties of one's life. Such was the inner aim of Marcus Aurelius, Emperor of Rome.

THE FOUNTAIN OF ALL THAT IS GOOD

In the quiet of the cold night, the armies asleep, the torches and candles silently flickering, he sits at his table pondering how to bring his vision of reality and the good into his life. Stylus in hand, he writes to himself:

> The duration of a person's life is only a point; our substance is flowing away this very moment; the senses are dim; the composition of the body is decaying, the psyche is chaos, our fate is unknowable. . . . What then can guide and protect you in this life? Only one thing: philosophy, and this consists in keeping the divine spirit within you free from pollution and damage . . .[11]

Or again:

> Stop letting the guiding principle within you be tugged around like a marionette by the strings of selfish impulses.[12]

Or again:

> You have perhaps seen a severed hand or foot, or a head lying by itself apart from its body. That is the state to which a man is doing his best to

reduce himself, when he refuses to accept what befalls him and breaks away from his fellow man, or when he acts from selfish ends alone. Then you become an outcast from the unity of Nature: though born a part of it, you have cut yourself away with your own hand. Yet here is the exquisite thought: that it still lies in your own power to reunite yourself. No other part of creation has been so favored by God with permission to come together again, after once being sundered and rent asunder. Behold, then, his goodness, with which he has dignified man: he has put it in man's power never to be cut off from the universal Whole, but afterwards, if he has become cut off, to return and be re-united and once again take his place as a part of the Whole.[13]

And how does a man become reunited with God, the Mind of the universe? By reversing the process by which he has cut himself off through forgetting what he is—that is, he reunites himself with God by the work of remembering who and what he is as a human being endowed with the divine power of conscious reason. A human being ceases to be human when he forgets that and acts solely under the influence of egoistic desire and impulse. But when he actively remembers what he is, not just as words or as a beautiful idea, but through an effort to be conscious of himself, through the work of attending to his own mind and emotions, only then is it possible for the objective intelligence and love that is of the nature of God to begin to flow into his actions. Only then can he hope to be just, only then can he—can we—hope to become *good*.

Writing to himself, Marcus asks:

To what use am I now putting the powers of my soul? Examine yourself on this point at every step, and ask, 'How stands it with that part of me which is called the ruling part? What kind of soul inhabits me at this moment? That of a child? An adolescent? A tyrant? A woman? A dumb ox? A wild beast?[14]

And, as though in answer to himself, he writes:

If you do the task before you always rigorously adhering to the true dictates of the mind with zeal and energy and yet with compassion and humanity, disregarding all lesser ends and keeping the divinity within you pure and upright, as though at this very moment you were called to give it back to its Creator—if you hold steadily to this, expecting nothing and avoiding nothing, only seeking in each passing action a conformity with Nature and in each word and utterance a fearless truthfulness, then you will live a good life. And from this course no man has the power to hold you back.[15]

Turn your attention within, for the fountain of all that is good lies within, and it is always ready to pour forth, if you continuously delve in.[16]

Each and every hour make up your mind . . . to accomplish the matter presently at hand with genuine seriousness, loving care, independence and justice. Allow your mind freedom from all other considerations. This you can do if you perform every action of your life as if it were your last, putting aside all wayward impulses and emotional resistance to the choices of reason, and all pretense, selfishness and discontent with what has been allotted to you. See how few are the things which a person needs to master in order to live a tranquil and godly existence. The gods ask nothing more of us.[17]

THIS NEW POWER OF THE MIND

My students are enthralled by the text, these ancient notes of Marcus Aurelius written to himself almost two thousand years ago, which have miraculously survived over the centuries. Dutifully, I explain that they represent the expression of the philosophical school known as Stoicism and they dutifully note it down. But something else is stirring within them: it is as though they have suddenly come upon what they had always dreamed philosophy should be—perhaps without even knowing it. It is as though they are suddenly discovering that there may very well exist wisdom and the guidance of wisdom in their actual lives. They feel this—it is obvious. During the reading of this text they come to class refreshed and totally openhearted.

And in this they are simply experiencing what countless others have experienced from this great book. Time was—not so long ago—that thousands and thousands of men and women of all backgrounds carried this book around with them, pored over it in the difficult moments of life, took strength from it, hope from it—not the kind of hope that comes from fantasies and sentimentality, but the kind of hope that comes from the discovery of some power or capacity within their own mind that they both knew and did not know that they possessed. This power of the mind, this capacity is not the same thing that they are called upon to exercise in academic work, important though that work is in its own sphere. This does not concern the mastery of logic or analysis or memory or insight into generalizations or patterns. This capacity of the mind is not the same thing that our society calls upon them to exercise and develop in their social lives or in their jobs or in their creative work or in sports or activism and perhaps not even in their religious lives—although at the same time it is there, this capacity, without their knowing it or naming it—and therefore without their forming the intention to study it and develop it further into what it can become and is meant to become in the life of man.

What is this capacity? It is the real power of the mind, a power about which we have only the most superficial understanding. It is *attention*. Within all this word signifies lies the source, the fountain of all that man is and all that man owes to himself, to God and to his neighbor.

REAL PHILOSOPHY

My students sense that this book represents philosophy considered not only as a "classroom" activity. It is meant for life in the world. And, in fact, this was precisely what philosophy meant in the ancient world.

But how? Just through insightful or inspiring ideas? Just through talking about inner strength or the power to love and be just? Just by words—words that would be betrayed by the first movement into the street? By the first emotional reaction, by a dirty look, a sexual impulse, a hunger pang, an angry word, a stray thought, a loud sound, a store window—not to mention the great and real events of life; although, in fact, the great and real events of life—death, sudden loss, an earthquake, the rumblings of war—all by themselves often call us to remember and to taste this great unknown capacity within the human self.

Yes, the question is there: *how,* again *how* can this wisdom lead us out of the classroom and into our life? The students sense this possibility in these ancient pages; they deserve to know how Marcus Aurelius actually used philosophy in his life, how he actually regarded it as so many exercises to practice during the hours of a day and the days of a week and the weeks and years of a life. They deserve to know how philosophy was practiced and not just discussed in a classroom.

And as for me, the professor, don't I deserve to know this also? How can I be sure I know what this man meant two thousand years ago by the words we translate as "mind" and "soul"? It is one thing to be a scholar, to study history, languages and academic philosophy; it is another thing to live. And it is the question of living that has now moved into the classroom.

THE "LEAST POWERFUL" MAN
IN THE WORLD

How did Marcus actually try to live philosophy? I am not imagining I was there studying with him in his tent, or that I was by his side in the hours of his day, or that, when he was young, I sat with him as he studied the teachings of the "least powerful" man in the world, the ex-slave Epictetus who, it has been recorded, defined the good for man simply as the power of dealing rightly with impressions, and who also said that philosophy begins by training us in the study of ideas and theory and only then leads us on to what is harder, its application to our life:

For in the sphere of speculation there is no influence which hinders us from following what we are taught, but in life there are many influences which drag us the contrary way. We may laugh, then, at him who says that he wants to try living first; for it is not easy to begin with what is harder.[18]

And who also said: "This, then, is where the philosophic life begins; in the discovery of the true state of one's own mind." And also: "Ever seeking peace outside yourself, you will never be able to be at peace: for you seek it where it is not, and refuse to seek it where it is."[19] And again: "We are glib and fluent in the lecture-room . . . but put us to the practical test and you will find us miserable shipwrecks."[20]

I heard myself asking the class, gripped by the same kind of philosophical passion that they were:

"What is Epictetus speaking about? We need to find out for ourselves. It cannot be that he is speaking about some naive and fantastic notion that we only have to think differently in order to transform our lives. This can't be some ancient Roman version of New Age self-hypnosis or the kind of cheap personal philosophy that fills the 'self-help' shelves of popular bookstores! What does he mean by 'mind'? What did his teachings show the Emperor about the 'inner God'?—this great slave/teacher who knew better than anyone how nearly impossible and yet how 'simple' it was to cross the Socratic threshold from the theater of the mind into the streets of our lives? We need to try to understand what he means and what it was in his teaching that evoked the reverent respect of some of the noblest and most powerful men and women of his time, men and women who would have instantly seen through any pretense or posturing or slick charisma. We simply can't afford to imagine that either he or his great pupil, Marcus Aurelius, meant exactly—or, perhaps, even approximately—what we mean by 'mind,' 'thought,' 'the inner life.'"

I paused and, setting aside for a moment the assigned text of Marcus Aurelius, picked up my personal copy of *The Discourses of Epictetus.*

"Listen to this," I said, and read from one of the many passages where

Epictetus is answering a question, often from some distinguished Roman citizen. Someone, it seems, had asked about the meaning of friendship.

ON THE MEASURE OF FRIENDSHIP

Epictetus begins by referring to the legendary war between the Greeks and the Trojans.

As every schoolchild knows—or used to know—the beginning of this world-changing episode of mutual slaughter takes place within the framework of what seemed a great and unbreakable friendship between two men of nobility: Paris, the son of the king of Troy, and Menelaus, king of the powerful and warlike Greek state of Sparta. Paris, on an overseas voyage, is entertained by Menelaus with royal hospitality and a great friendship is celebrated between the two men. Paris, however, falls in love with the king's beautiful wife, Helen, and carries her away, with her full consent, to Troy where she lives with him as his wife. The kings and princes of Greece thereupon raise a force of a thousand or more ships manned with fighting men and sail to Troy in order to forcibly bring back Helen. The war lasts ten years and results in the total de-struction of Troy and the death of thousands.

Answering the question about friendship, Epictetus says—and I read this entire passage:

> Paris was the guest of Menelaus, and any one who had seen the courte-sies they used to one another would not have believed one who denied that they were friends. But a morsel was thrown between them, in the shape of a pretty woman, and for that there was war! So now, when you see friends or brothers who seem to be of one mind, do not therefore pronounce upon their friendship, though they swear to it and say it is impossible for them to part with one another. The Governing Principle of bad men is not to be trusted; it is uncertain, irresolute, conquered now by one impression, now by another. The question you must ask is,

not what others ask, whether they were born of the same parents and brought up together . . . but this question only, where they put their interest—outside themselves or in their moral purpose, their will. If they put it outside themselves, do not call them friends, any more than you can call them faithful, or steadfast, or courageous or free; no, do not even call them human beings . . . For it is not a human mind which makes them bite one another and revile one another and occupy deserts or market-places like wild beasts and behave like thieves in the law-courts; and which makes them guilty of profligacy and adultery and seduction and the other crimes which they commit against each other. It is one kind of action of the mind, and this alone, which is responsible for all this—that they set themselves and all their interests elsewhere than within the realm of their own inner moral purpose. But if you hear that these men in all sincerity believe the good to lie only in the region of the will and in dealing rightly with impressions, you need trouble yourself no more as to whether a man is a son or a father, whether they are brothers, or have been familiar companions for years; I say, if you grasp this one fact and no more, you may pronounce with confidence that they are friends, as you may that they are faithful and just. For where else is friendship but where faith and honor are, where men give and take what is good, and nothing else?[21]

I wanted to go on reading and lecturing. My mind was overflowing with ideas and connections. Rarely have I felt so at one with a whole group of students—or, I believe, they with me. "Truth" and the "Good" were on the verge of becoming concrete and palpable, something that could move your limbs and your life decisions and loves and aims, something by which one could truly take the measure of oneself—and of one's whole life.

AN INVITATION

At the same time, there was something maddeningly unclear about it all. Neither I nor my students could get around the question of what *precisely* these two great philosophers, Marcus Aurelius and Epictetus, meant by mind, impression, will, moral purpose, judgment and attention. Are they all different names for one thing, one power within us? Or are they different aspects of the mind? If that is so, then what do they really mean by mind—is it the same thing as self? Is my mind my self?

For example, for a very long time we discussed the following strange-sounding question: When you try to follow the advice of Marcus to think differently, say, about your experiences (or impressions), or even about anything at all—what faculty of the mind or psyche do you use to accomplish that purpose? I wish, say, to regard something differently, some insult or something like that, so as not to be driven to suffering or immoral actions—how exactly is that change of attitude effected? With what power of the mind or soul? With what power of the mind or self do I adopt a desire for truth or for virtue? And how is it that no one seems to bring up this question in all the writings of the philosophers?

And why speak of moral will at the same moment that one speaks of dealing rightly with impressions and forming true judgments? How is the intention to be good entangled with the desire to know the truth? Are ethics and knowledge two names for one thing or two distinct aspects of one human power? What power is that?

These were not purely "academic" questions for any of us. We needed to understand not only for the sake of knowing the text or anything like that, but for the sake of living. For the sake of trying, finally and after all, to put something into practice that seemed to offer a thrilling new possibility. In any case, *I* felt these questions in that way—both for myself and for the sake of the students.

For the sake of the students—could I really leave them with just one more set of beautiful ideas? Does it always have to be true, as Epictetus says, that we may carry such ideas and views to the lecture-room door, but no one takes them home? "As soon as we leave here," he says, "we are at war . . . with our neighbors, with those who jeer and laugh at us." "We must be grateful," he says, "to those who annoy us, for they convict us every day of knowing nothing."[22]

Without thinking more about it, I decided to try something new— new for me in an academic setting. And the very moment I decided to try it, it seemed so right that I felt astonished that I had never done it before. In a way, it was simply an obvious step to take: Why not actually *try* the kind of exercises of the mind and will that Marcus gave to himself— for that is what his "meditations" actually are, namely, spiritual exercises to practice in the midst of one's life.[23] Why not actually work with them this way, instead of reading the text solely as a record of concepts and reasoning, which is what almost all *modern* philosophy has become? As Søren Kierkegaard, the dangerous "spiritual existentialist" of the nineteenth century, said of the awesome systematic philosopher Hegel—that he spends his day in the crystal palace of the *system,* while in the evening he returns to his home and lives in the dog kennel of his everyday existence!

I decided, therefore, to put this notion into practice and suggest a few exercises to the class that might correspond, at least to some extent, with what Marcus Aurelius may have practiced as the discipline of the philosopher in the midst of life. I was not working completely in the dark here, as I had practiced many exercises of this kind myself—even before I met with the spiritual teachers and teachings that have guided my own path. At the same time, in giving such exercises to my students, I needed to take great care that I did not offer such exercises as required assignments. These exercises were not like books to be read, essays to be written, intellectual discourses to be understood. These were to be tiny, tentative *forays* across the Socratic threshold that separates the theater of the mind from the streets of everyday life, reconnaissance flights, as it were—"experiments" in living philosophy, in living the search for self-knowledge.

To give them as assignments would have been to destroy their purpose, by making the students feel that they must succeed in the way they try to succeed in their academic work. And that was to be avoided at all costs. This was to involve an entirely new attitude toward the events of one's life—the attitude of the open question without an answer, the attitude of suspending the "answering" function of the mind, and allowing into oneself the calm, warmly impartial attitude of self-questioning and self-testing—in other words, to allow into one's life, if only in a preliminary way, the force of relatively conscious attention, which in fact is indistinguishable from the beginnings of the power of will—which in its turn is the only basis of real morality.

At the conclusion of the next class, I began by referring to the passage in the *Meditations,* already cited, where Marcus asks himself to "stop letting the guiding principle within you be tugged around like a marionette by the strings of selfish impulses" and also several comments by both Marcus and Epictetus about the power that minor annoyances have over us.

I said to the class: "In addition to your reading assignment" (we were already coming to the end of the *Meditations*), "I would like to invite you to try something. This is purely voluntary. It is not required. The exercise is this. For the next two days, until the class meets again, try to experiment with a new kind of relationship to the things that annoy you—starting, if you like, when you leave the classroom in a few minutes. The exercise is to simply *step back* in yourself and observe your state of being annoyed or irritated. Don't try to do anything about it. Don't try to get rid of it or justify it or judge it to be good or bad. Just observe it and whatever you can see that is connected with it. Step back from it without trying to change it or escape from it. Do you understand?"

A few heads—not many—nodded yes, but without much enthusiasm. Apparently, many of them felt that being aware of annoyances was something that more or less happens with them all the time anyway. "For example, " I continued, "say you spot a parking place, but someone else slips in ahead of you. Or you are standing in line at a checkout counter and the person ahead of you is buying maybe nothing more than a pack of chewing gum and making a complicated payment with his credit card." They laughed, and their interest was being awakened. "Just *observe* that you are annoyed. Step back from it within yourself. Every day, every hour, sometimes every minute, things annoy us, irritate us, so there's no lack of occasions to practice this 'philosophical' exercise."

I was tempted to let it go at that, especially as the hour was over. But when I realized that they were now sitting quietly with their eyes wide open, and that there was no looking at watches or at the clock on the wall and no closing of notebooks or packing up of book bags, I said a few words more.

"In this way," I said, "it may be possible to try something related in a preliminary way to the ancient *practice* of philosophy, a practice about which Socrates becomes silent at the end of the dialogues, but which, across the centuries, may have been orally transmitted, until through the slave Epictetus it reached the Emperor Marcus Aurelius.

"I'm suggesting that you treat it simply as an invitation, an experiment.

"And we'll be trying it, too," I added, gesturing toward my assistant, who was sitting by the window.

With that I dismissed the class.

That was on a Tuesday. As I often did, I drove back home with my friend and teaching assistant, John Piazza. A man in his late twenties, John had done his undergraduate work in philosophy and was now completing his postgraduate training in Classics. He was a great help to me in many ways, with his finely trained academic mind and his feeling for the spirit of ancient philosophy. In addition, his knowledge of classical Greek helped me keep my explanations of the texts grounded in historical reality. But of paramount importance, his vision of the role of real philosophical questions in the moral development of young people coincided exactly with my own.

On our drives home we usually discussed the day's class in preparation for the next class, but today we both spoke very little—as though instinctively acknowledging that some unknown possibility, potentially of great value, may have been introduced into the context of academic philosophy, and not wanting to cast a net of speculation over it in advance of discovering its results.

"OH, I FORGOT!"

I began the Thursday class by discussing some abstract metaphysical ideas, intentionally avoiding any mention of the exercise. I wanted to see if the students themselves would bring it up; I was trying at all costs to keep the exercise as purely voluntary as possible. In a short while, however, after elaborating a little on the Stoic concept of the *logos*—keeping the discussion away from the practical aspects of Marcus's text—a natural silence appeared and I picked up the book. "By the way," I said, turning the pages as though looking for a particular passage, "did anyone try the exercise?" I looked up and saw a great many blank faces.

I put down the book. Only one hand went up—and, after a few seconds, a second hand went halfway up.

Actually, I was not surprised. I set the book aside and walked around the desk and stood closer to the class.

"Now," I said, "we are in front of something important. Answer honestly—remember, you are not being graded for this—how many of you simply forgot about the exercise?"

About a dozen hands slowly went up, one after the other, followed by another ten—and then almost everyone else raised their hands. I was now looking at two students (or, more exactly, one and a half students) who remembered the exercise and about forty who admitted to forgetting it—and about four or five who were not admitting anything.

"The fact that almost all of you forgot all about this exercise—despite the intense interest you showed after it was described to you in class two days ago—this fact needs to be correctly interpreted and not just brushed aside or covered over. The fact is that you, we, all of us, are swallowed by our lives. We say, 'Oh, I forgot,' and we calmly move on to the next thing. In this 'Oh, I forgot' there lies one of the most fundamental aspects of the human condition, one which, if understood properly, explains why we do not and cannot carry out our good intentions. But if you go on to study books and teachings dealing with the self-perfecting of human nature, you will almost never find this fact mentioned—the fact that we simply do not remember our deeper questions in the midst of our lives, and therefore never really do what we know to be good, except when we are shaken by a crisis into a deeper state of self-presence. As you read such books and hear such teachings—religious, philosophical, mystical— you will almost never find this fact addressed. It will simply be assumed that you will, if you wish, remember to put the ideals and methods offered into practice . . ."

I decided to go no further with this today—I would come back to it later. And, of course, I did not wish to explain that to confront this mountain of a fact about human nature was one of the principal objectives of this kind of exercise. Nor did I want to say that this was the main reason I did not offer it as a course assignment. I could easily have "made" them remember—at least, I could have made many more of them remember—by causing them to fear the consequences if they did not try it, or say they tried it. But that would have been simply to evoke in them the same kind of influence—fear, in this case—which the exercise was designed to help them wake up to in the midst of their day-to-day lives.

DR. KINDER'S MISUNDERSTANDING

I turned now to the one person who had fully raised his hand. This was Dr. Nathan Kinder, a retired physician who was one of the numerous senior citizens—the "sixty-plus club"—who sat in on my classes from time to time, and often took them for credit. A slender, dapper gentleman with a narrow, ruddy face, clear blue eyes and sharp, prominent features, and with a full head of brilliant white hair, he looked very much like some kind of crested bird. He almost always came to class wearing a sports coat and a bow tie and carrying a carved wooden cane which, judging from his confident stride, was more a fashion accessory than an orthopedic necessity.

I liked him very much. Perhaps he took more than his share of time speaking in class, and perhaps his questions were often more like pronouncements, but he always spoke with wit and intelligence. And, most strikingly, he always seemed to be listening not only to me, but to the students. At the same time, side by side with his refined demeanor and his considerable background of scientific and literary study, and underneath his wealth of experience with suffering humanity, there was something touchingly hungry in his eyes. I sensed in him a raw human need that would often show through when he spoke, but which was almost always immediately eclipsed by his wealth of accumulated knowledge and his highly refined sense of status. It was as though a pure, young man—a kind of adolescent seeker—would begin to express himself, only again and again to be seduced by the "wise old physician" with his sharp old nose and his cane and bow tie.

"So, Dr. Kinder, you remembered?"

"Well, yes," he said. "But at first I felt this exercise was too easy, too modest, not challenging enough. And as for the problem of remembering it, that was not at all difficult. It stayed with me the whole time. In fact, years ago when I was studying the history of philosophy, I actually used to try this task from time to time. So, it came to me quite naturally. At the same time, I have to say that I also felt somewhat uneasy about this feeling of self-confidence."

After glancing around, he went on:

"Yesterday morning my wife told me that her sister was coming to our house for lunch and I immediately took this as the focus for trying what was suggested. My sister-in-law, Helen, is very annoying to me and always has been. So I made myself a plan that under no circumstances would I show the slightest irritation with her. I said to myself, thinking of Marcus Aurelius, that she, too, is a human being who has in herself the same divine principle as all human beings"—and here the doctor smiled devilishly—"only she is perhaps capable of concealing it more cleverly than most."

Some of the class chuckled appreciatively. The doctor leaned back, touched his bow tie and continued:

"Well, to make a long story short, throughout the entire lunch I actually was able to hold back any sign of annoyance with her and halfway through I noticed that I was not even *feeling* any annoyance! I was so interested in that—by not *showing* irritation, it somehow caused me to be free of *feeling* it with her. But just as I was congratulating myself on my success, she made one of her typical disparaging comments about something or other to my wife and I just almost exploded."

The doctor stopped, looked around for a moment, and then leaned forward and his blue eyes suddenly became young. "What do you think?" he asked, suddenly completely oblivious to his audience, the class. "What do you think?"

While I was trying to find a reply, the young woman sitting next to him smiled warmly at him and the pure adolescent went back into hiding. The "wise old blade" took over again and he said to me with his complicit smile, "I guess that's only worth about a C plus." And many students quietly laughed with the good doctor.

"Well, Dr. Kinder," I said, "it's worth far more than a C plus that you actually remembered to try something."

Suddenly, the adolescent appeared again.

And suddenly, it was just me and him.

"Tell me, Dr. Kinder, why do you give yourself such a, so to say, mediocre 'grade'?"

With one hand, he absently straightened his bow tie, and, in a young, questioning voice, said, "Because I finally did get annoyed?"

"But, Dr. Kinder, why do you consider that a failure?"

I didn't mean to stop him, but he was stopped. He looked at me questioningly.

In fact, I looked back at him questioningly. To tell the truth, strange as it may sound, I myself was in the process of remembering the exercise—that is, remembering, *feeling* what the real purpose of it was. I thought to myself: how easy it is to forget what is essential in this search—*which is simply to see what is.*

And so I said, "Dr. Kinder, what *was* the exercise? Can you say?"

The wise old doctor answered: "To not let anything or anyone annoy you. And a very good exercise it is!"

MARY ADIJIAN'S DISCOVERY

I looked around at the class. "Is that how everyone understood it?" I asked—and then, before waiting for anyone to speak, I turned to the person who had only halfway raised her hand.

She was one of those students who sit inconspicuously toward the back of the class and off to the side, and who rarely participate in the discussions. I knew her mainly because her name—Mary Adijian—was always the first called whenever I was obliged to take attendance. An avid note taker, she sat tall in her chair and dressed with an understated old-fashioned femininity. She looked to be in her mid-twenties and had dark, liquid eyes and a large, calm face framed with black hair hanging down in ringlets.

"Yesterday," she said, "on the way home from school I stopped at the cleaners to pick up some clothes I had left there a few days ago. I gave the woman—a little Asian woman—the receipt and she went through the racks and then looked at me and said they weren't there, my clothes weren't ready. I immediately started to get irritated and I showed her the receipt where it said that they'd be ready Wednesday, yesterday. The woman simply said, 'Not ready yet. Tomorrow try again.' And then I said—I think I was even shouting: 'But it was *promised* for today!' And then she sort of giggled and all she said was, 'Not here. Tomorrow try.'

Of course, she wasn't really laughing at me—it was just an embarrassed little giggle, but it really upset me.

"I was just about to sort of storm out the door. And just then I remembered the class and the exercise. I remembered the words: 'step back.' I said to myself, 'I am annoyed. This is it.' And suddenly—I can't really describe it—suddenly it was like I was two people."

She paused, trying to find words. And then she simply repeated: "It was like I was two people."

Again she paused. The class stayed silent. Finally, she said: "I had no idea my mind could do that!"

"Do what?" I asked, softly.

"Just that," she said. "Like one of me was angry and the other me was just peacefully watching the whole thing."

"And then what happened?"

"Nothing much. I was still annoyed at the woman, but at the same time I was not annoyed. And I sort of heard myself just simply saying, in a nice way, 'Thank you,' and I just left."

What forcibly struck me in what she said were the words, *"I had no idea my mind could do that."* My own mind started racing. I didn't want to jump to conclusions on the basis of one student's experience, but I couldn't help feverishly wondering: was it true? Could it be true that the power of the mind to step back from itself, the power of the *attention of the mind* to watch one's own thoughts and feelings, to separate from oneself in this simple, fundamental way; could it be that not everyone knew about this—simply by virtue of being a living, breathing human being? Or could it be true that a whole generation of men and women didn't know about this?

I was so intrigued by this question that I failed to point out what was potentially of ultimate significance in Mary's experience—that by stepping back to observe her own annoyance, she had actually become in that moment free from being dominated by it, and that she had spoken to the Asian woman in a courteous fashion, even though she was still "annoyed." And, most important, she had done so without being moralistic about it—without telling herself that she ought not to be angry, that is, without the inner violence and insincerity that so often characterize our "good deeds," and which really mask and suppress impulses whose energy eventually manifests itself in other perhaps even more harmful ways. That is to say—she had been given a taste, however preliminary and fleeting, of the moral power of the force of attention. Just by seeing her annoyance, it had become for the moment "de-toxified," allowing, without any forcing or hypocrisy, a relatively beneficent human manifestation to take place in the form of a simple "thank you."

I wanted to put together some comments about what Mary had discovered—without just yet introducing the word "attention," which for most people is usually just a loose synonym for "thoughts." For most of us, to "give attention to" and to "think about" usually mean more or less the same thing. Whereas the real meaning of the word "attention"— at least so far as I understand it—has to do with a power of the human mind that is entirely separate and different from what we ordinarily experience as thinking, or having thoughts. And further—and again, as far as I understand it—there are many degrees and levels of this force called attention, and the ultimate moral and spiritual development of a human being is substantially dependent upon an individual's sensitivity to these higher levels of attention. And furthermore, to make matters even more difficult to grasp, in the translations of the many of the great spiritual texts of the world, these higher levels of attention are sometimes rendered by the words *thought* or *mind* or even *reason,* when what is being spoken of is something entirely different and of a much finer quality than what is ordinarily denoted by these terms.

But I did not want to speak about any of these ideas just yet. More experiences were needed, more attempts to step over the Socratic threshold into one's life under the protection of modest, precise "exercises" attempted in the spirit—or what I was taking to be the spirit—of Marcus Aurelius and his great teacher, Epictetus. So I decided to give another exercise and follow it by others.

As for the reading, the syllabus said that the next assignment was to be selected texts from the Christian tradition. But I told the class to defer that and instead for now to go back and re-read passages from the *Meditations* that were of particular interest to them.

And then I started to give them the next exercise.

Eight

THE ETHICS OF
ATTENTION II

The night before, I had spent hours poring over the text, sifting through the philosophical exercises that Marcus gives himself as so many means for bringing ethical and spiritual ideals into the fabric of his everyday life. I was looking for the most suitable exercise to suggest to the students.

As the noted scholar Pierre Hadot has pointed out, Marcus' philosophical exercises fall into three categories, corresponding to what he understood to be the three distinct and principal functions of the totality of the human psyche: (1) the function of thought or judgment; (2) the function of desire or emotion; and (3) the function characterized as the impulse toward action—related to the motor functions or movements of a human being.[24]

Roughly speaking, the first category of exercises involve the application of universal philosophical ideas to our personal experiences, or what the Stoics call "impressions" (*phantasia*). The second category involves a discipline related to our emotional life, as distinct from our intellectual life—our emotional responses and reactions to all that befalls us. And the third category deals with our actual manifestations—the way we actually behave or conduct ourselves in the course of our lives.

Exercises of the first and second kind are the ones most commonly associated with Stoicism. As an example of the first kind, involving principally the function of thought, Marcus asks himself to try always to keep in mind certain fundamental truths about the universe and human life:

> Reflect often upon the rapidity with which all existing things . . . sweep past us and are carried away. The great river of Being flows on without a pause; its actions forever changing, its causes shifting endlessly, hardly a single thing standing still: while ever at hand looms infinity stretching behind and before—the abyss in which all things are lost to sight. In such conditions, surely a man were foolish to gasp and fume and fret, as though the time of his troubling could ever be of long continuance.[25]

And as an example of the second kind, involving the cultivation of non-egoistic emotion:

> A servant who breaks loose from his master is a runaway. For us, our master is (cosmic) law; and consequently any lawbreaker must be a runaway. But grief, anger or fear are all of them rejections of something which, in the past or the present or the future, has been decreed by the power that directs the universe—in other words, by Law, which allots to every creature its due. To give way to fear or grief or anger, therefore, is to be a runaway.[26]

These two categories of exercises comprise the cultivation of an attitude and a state of inner collectedness, or non-attachment, together with an emphasis on what might be called "metaphysical emotion"—that is, a quality of feeling, and even love, inherent in the functioning within man of the universal governing principle that is at one and the same time an

atom of the Universal Mind. The common, familiar interpretation of
the word "stoic," which identifies it either as something cold and un-
feeling or as one or another form of "gritting one's teeth" in the face of
adversity, could not be further from the truth. In fact, in the true Stoic—
which is what Marcus Aurelius strives to be—impersonal love and the
unstinting study and acceptance of the will of God take the place of all
forms of self-manipulation and self-will.

The third category of exercises, comprising the discipline of outwardly acting in one's life according to the understanding gained through
practicing the first two kinds of internal efforts, brings one into the realm
of ethics in the more familiar sense of the term—that is to say, the practice of conducting oneself according to what one understands to be
good. It is understood that without the first two kinds of exercise, the
third practice—what we are calling the practice of actually crossing
the Socratic threshold—would be impossible. The cultivation of mental
understanding and the practice of separating from emotional reactivity
are prerequisites for intentional moral behavior. And as for the absolutely
essential role of a right relationship to the physical body, this element
remains largely hidden—as it does in much of the ancient philosophical
writings—in the hints and reports of the form and content of the education of children. For now, we can only surmise that this fundamental
aspect of human development was among the many central elements
that were not meant to be committed to writing, but which, in some
cases perhaps, formed an essential part of what is called the "oral tradition," by which is meant the sum total of the psychological, social and
formal conditions by which a spiritual community maintains the possibility of the direct transmission of spiritual and moral truth.

A great many exercises of the third kind are to be found in the *Meditations.* One example:

> Take joy and repose in one thing only: to pass from one action accom-
> plished in the service of the community to another action accomplished

in the service of the community; all this accompanied by the remembrance of God.[27]

And another example, simply:

Adapt yourself to the environment in which your lot has been cast, and show true love to the fellow-mortals with whom destiny has surrounded you.[28]

But no matter which category of exercises I studied, none of them felt appropriate for the class. And the reason seemed unequivocally clear. It had to do with Mary Adijian's discovery when she tried to step back in herself: *"I had no idea my mind could do that!"* I had long ago realized that this power of the mind to "step back" must lie at the very root of any serious attempt to bring great ideas into our lives. And that without becoming aware of this power and actually exercising it, all attempts to live one's ideals must inevitably become only self-manipulation or self-deception, and must inevitably end in failure of one kind or another.

Simply put, without this movement of stepping back in oneself, the attempt to refrain from giving way to egoistic reactions becomes at best merely the substitution of one emotional reaction for another. For example, in Dr. Kinder's experiment, which on the surface seemed so productive, he had simply "re-directed" his emotional reactions toward himself, that is, to his tendency to be annoyed with his sister-in-law. He had more or less unconsciously given way to what might be called the "secondary emotions"—that is, emotional reactions to one's own emotional reactions. Instead of observing his annoyance, he had displaced it because of his feeling that it was somehow "bad." What had resulted was only a pseudo-freedom, whereas the whole ultimate aim of such an exercise was, at least for the duration of the exercise, to de-toxify the very structure of egoistic emotion itself, rather than cultivate the automatism of emotional self-judgment of any kind. His eventual "explosion" of anger was simply evidence that the fundamental current of emotional reactivity had not been seen or studied. He had unwittingly transformed the experiment of self-knowledge into the very common and ultimately futile effort to be good through self-manipulation.

WHY DO MORAL CODES FAIL?

Surely here is at least part of the secret that explains why moral codes so often fail throughout our lives and, in a larger, universally tragic sense, why they fail throughout the life of humanity. The question is: can there ever be genuine morality absent the activation of the mind's power to separate from itself?—to give conscious attention to itself? And is the ignorance, or forgetting, of this power a fundamental reason why moral codes are almost always based merely on the activation of a supervening emotional reaction such as fear of personal punishment or desire for personal reward?—whether internally and psychologically through guilt; or externally through societal sanctions, legal enforcement or religious promises and threats of heaven and hell? On a grand scale, then, how much of mankind's "morality," far from liberating us from egoistic emotion, merely drives out one such emotion with another—thereby even further entrenching the power of such emotion in the human psyche. With egoism so deeply and deceptively engraved in our hearts and minds, no wonder that sooner or later all moral codes fail! And no wonder that individually in our personal lives, and collectively in the life of mankind, manifestations of violence and barbarism continue to arise— manifestations that shake to pieces everything we thought we understood about ourselves and which are incomprehensible to our religions or our science. We are speaking not only of horrific manifestations throughout all history, and especially in our time, of such things as genocide, mass sadism and the fanatical slaughter of millions under the banner of illusory ideologies, but also, in our own individual lives, of our own personal manifestations of violence, hatred, blind greed, herd instinct, and all manner of forms by which each and every one of us betrays our ethical ideals.

To go further with the class, and to go further with the whole enterprise of practicing philosophical exercises on the other side of the Socratic threshold—that is, in "the streets" of one's own actual life—it seemed to me absolutely necessary to see if others in class were, like Mary Adijian, actually unacquainted with the mind's power to separate from itself. And then, if I discovered that it was so, the next step would be to offer them the chance—if they wished—to discover that their minds did have that power. And after that to represent to them, if only theoretically (for who was I to try anything beyond that?), the far-reaching moral significance and implications of this power for their own personal lives and, indeed, tracing a very large arc, for the whole of mankind!

The next step, then, was to provide an exercise, or a sequence of exercises, that would enable them to begin to become a little bit acquainted with this power and that would enable them, whether or not it was a new discovery for them, to study it in a carefully circumscribed context in their actual lives.

"Between now and Tuesday," I said as the hour ended, "when you're alone watching television, simply turn it off in the middle of a program. And then quietly get up and go have a glass of water or do something else for ten or fifteen seconds, or maybe half a minute or so. And then quietly come back to your chair and turn the TV on again so that you are back watching the same program.

"The point is to study the subjective difficulty in the act of turning off the TV. And then to observe that once you have turned it off, how easy it is simply to do something else without any real sense of loss. And, finally, come back to the TV, sit down, collect yourself a little, and then turn it on again and try to catch a glimpse of yourself being sucked back into the program, whatever it is.

"It's important that you try this exercise in the middle of a program that actually interests you—not during a commercial break, and not at a point in the program when you're ready to switch channels. It has to be done when you are really glued to the set—do you understand what I'm saying?"

Smiles of pure delight slowly spread throughout the class.

I went on:

"You can also do it at the movies. In the middle of a scene, just get up and go to the lobby for a few minutes and then, after collecting yourself for a few seconds, go back to your seat and watch yourself getting drawn back in."

I then dismissed the class.

As the students were putting away their books and papers, and getting up to leave, a voice called out: "What is the reading assignment?"

"Continue with Marcus Aurelius," I answered.

And then another voice sang out—in a dignified Mexican accent:

"Professor, what does that mean 'collect yourself'?"

A few students continue filing out of the room, but most stood still, waiting to hear what I would say.

The question caught me by surprise and I did not want to give any kind of ready-made reply to it. I mutely stood there for a few seconds. Finally, I said: "It means letting yourself become quiet inside so that your scattered attention is drawn back toward you."

The student—his name was Octavio—quickly, all too quickly, said, "Thank you, Professor." And as though a switch had just been turned back on, the students resumed their chatter and their slightly chaotic movement out the door.

I AM MY ATTENTION

Although I have worked at this exercise a number of times over the years, I tried it again myself over the weekend. The first time, it delivered the same shock it had brought me in the past—the shock, namely, of experiencing the heavy pull outward of my attention and the powerful resistance to breaking the connection to the TV. It was not just that I

liked the particular show or program I was watching, or that it was evoking pleasant or unpleasant associations in me of second-hand processes
of desire, say, or fear or curiosity. That was part of it, of course; but the
real shock was glimpsing once again that what I liked and what I wanted
to maintain was the inner state of total loss of the awareness of myself
sitting there in my chair. In other words, as I kept finding excuses not to
turn the TV off, I realized that I liked my absence much more than I
wished for my presence.

But the second time I tried it something new appeared that even
more forcefully demonstrated the ethical significance of this modest exercise as a means of studying the power of the mind to free itself for a
moment from the thrall of impulses, thoughts and images. The point is
that these impulses, thoughts and images, taken together, are a fundamental cause of the emotional reactions that determine so much of our
behavior in our day-to-day lives.

The program I had happened to be watching was the courtroom
drama, *Law & Order.* During the program I remembered the exercise at
least a dozen times, but I could not find the determination actually to
click the remote I was holding in my hand. The show was coming to a
climactic end in a courtroom confrontation. And suddenly, without bargaining with myself, as though jumping off a diving board after a long
hesitation, I pressed the off button of the remote.

I was not surprised by the sweet silence that immediately ensued, and
I savored it to the full. Nor was I surprised by the fact that I was no
longer so interested in the outcome of the drama—which just a moment before had held me spellbound. What surprised me and profoundly interested me was something else: it was a completely new
impression of my attention returning to me from outside of myself.
What I saw, what I felt with great clarity, was the, so to say, *my-own-ness*
of my attention. It was *mine.* It was *myself.* It was like a substance, a current of conscious substance that was my self returning to me and once
again inhabiting me, my body, sitting there in the chair. It was, so to say,
my *I-ness* returning. And along with this unique sensation, or feeling,

there was the sharp sense of astonishment tinged with remorse and a certain kind of fear that I had so complacently allowed my *self-ness* to go so far away from me—*without my care,* as though I were a shepherd who had thoughtlessly forgotten all about his flock. How could I have allowed that? Why did I not miss my attention, my I-ness? What if it had never come back?

In the past I had often heard the idea stated: "I am my attention." But it was now more than a respected idea. It was a lived certainty. And as time has passed, this certainty has been many times reconfirmed and its meaning deepened.

THE FIRST OBLIGATION OF MAN

At this point, before proceeding with the classroom narrative, I wish briefly to sketch in advance, pending further elaboration, the theoretically far-reaching and, I think, even revolutionary implications of this particular kind of experience, which was repeated and confirmed in countless other experiments and life situations, and in the company of good philosophical friends and collaborators.

The main, outstanding discovery, is that I am—we are—obliged by the power of conscience, the source of all moral authority, to care for our *I-ness,* which is our attention. It may, in fact, be possible to say that for us modern people all genuine ethical responsibility begins just there, with this entirely new, or hidden, responsibility to my Self. I cannot be responsible to you without being responsible to my Self—to let it live in me. I am obliged, by all the laws of conscience, to remember my attention and to care for it. And here is the morally revolutionary point: the *true, genuine initiator of all moral action is the attention.* It is our attention that can free us from the thrall of our egoistic reactions, our fears, our fanaticisms, our paranoia, our delusions, our hatred. It is our attention that can master our reactions, liberate us from slavery to our opinions, enlist the service of our body beyond its cravings, its childishly impatient

discoveries be hid from him, and he will not be able so much as to give a reason for his own existence. So what are we to think of anyone who cares to seek or shun the applause of the shouting multitudes, when they know neither where they are nor what they are?[29]

I then began to expand upon the Stoic vision of the nature of the universe.

"For the philosophers of antiquity," I said, "for Pythagoras, Socrates, Plato, Aristotle, and, in fact, for almost all other great thinkers up until our modern era, it was obvious that the universe is a vast, living organism permeated by an all-powerful and all-knowing conscious intelligence. 'Always think of the universe as one living organism,' writes Marcus, 'with a single substance and a single soul; and observe how all things are submitted to the single perceptivity of this one whole, all are moved by its single impulse. . . .'[30]

"According to Marcus," I continued, "what he called 'the single perceptivity' that permeates and governs the cosmos has been placed also within the soul of man in order to permeate and govern his own mortal body in all its functions and actions. Unique in all the world, man is the creature who is endowed with an individual portion of the very flame of conscious attention that defines the power of the gods themselves—that is, the unchanging forces and laws that watch over and ultimately direct the universal world in which all things come into being, have their existence and die. Only those of our actions that emanate directly and consciously from this portion of perceptivity or attention that is placed within ourselves have ultimate meaning and genuine moral force in our lives. And therefore, according to Marcus and the tradition which he represents, the aim of our lives must be to strive always to allow this inner, immortal flame of divine attention to illuminate and govern our actions and intentions throughout the course of our finite, mortal life. Almost everything in the *Meditations* is to be understood as exercises meant to support the struggle to remember this inner flame and to become available to its influence day by day."

The class had become unusually quiet and I had the impulse to ask for questions, but I decided to go on.

"And so," I said, "there are actually two moralities: the morality of action and the morality of the struggle for attention. That is, there are for man two obligations: the obligation to develop his own inner self and the obligation to care for his fellow man. The first obligation is, in the conventional religious language, the obligation to God; the second is the obligation to man. But, when we speak of 'obligation to God,' we are not speaking solely of an external God above, but of the existence of the 'perceptivity' of God within oneself—God within oneself. It is still in a real sense the being of God, but it is not only external to man.

"Strictly speaking, however, even were we to take this to be solely an external God the same distinction applies. For to be able freely to obey even a purely external God also requires the development of a conscious force within oneself that can see and separate itself from the illusions and impulses that draw man into the thrall of the ego.

"We can therefore generalize by speaking of the obligation to the Self within oneself as the obligation of man to become a being who is actually capable of freely willed ethical action toward one's fellow man. We cannot be genuinely moral without the inner power of free attention, what Marcus calls the 'perceptivity' of God."

Was this whole notion of the two moralities, at least partly, the meaning of the order and sequence of the Ten Commandments? There man is commanded by God first and foremost to "have no other Gods before me"; that is, man's first obligation is to God. And only after this first obligation is clearly announced is the second obligation, the duty with respect to man, put forward—the proscriptions, namely, against murder, adultery, stealing, bearing false witness and coveting.

That is to say: man is commanded to strive to become a being inwardly capable of moral action, and only then is he commanded to act ethically in relation to his fellow man. The same dynamic is expressed by Jesus: "Seek ye first the kingdom of heaven." Error appears—and it is a human error with monumental consequences in the history of our world—when the first commandment is treated as merely a matter of immediate choice, as something a man or woman has the power to do. As a consequence of this error, all man's "moral" energy is concentrated on the duties toward one's fellow man, with hardly any effort being expended on the struggle to become inwardly such a being as can actually obey the communal commandments. The result is the inevitable and terrifying breakdown of all such moral ideals in both the collective and the individual life of humanity.

It is therefore more than merely a clever phrase to say that we are morally obliged to become beings capable of moral action—or, to use Marcus' language, men and women in whom the "perceptivity of God" is the active, governing force. This perceptivity is what we are calling the "divine flame of attention."

Trying, as we do, to live according only to the communal morality—whether it be from religious or secular sources of authority does not matter in this case—our situation could be likened to the following picture:

Imagine a teacher, divine or human, commanding a group of men and women to fly around a room. Immediately, the whole group obediently starts running in a great circle vainly flapping their arms at their sides. Some begin to fantastically imagine that they are indeed flying and begin to feel ethically pure and good. These are the "saved," the "proud." The others, however, see very clearly that they are not flying and as a result suffer the endless misery of guilt and self-hatred.

Obviously, in such a case, what has been lost sight of is the first obligation and question: how to grow wings?

THE LOG-OFF CLUB

As though being summoned out of a dream, I heard the voice of Octavio Zambrano softly calling to me from the middle of the second row:

"Professor, may I ask a question?"

"Yes, Octavio, please," I said, walking around the desk and toward him. It was a pleasure to look at the always smiling, somewhat frail Octavio Zambrano, with his glowing olive-brown face and his guileless dark eyes. And I was always charmed by the way he addressed me—as is the habit with students in Mexico—by the one word, "Professor," as though it were my whole name and identity.

"Professor," he said, with self-effacing courtesy, "may I ask about the exercise you suggested to us?"

"Of course," I said.

I knew nothing about Octavio's background, but from the very beginning of the semester it was obvious that he had recently exited his adolescence with unusually refined manners and a strong thirst for learning of all kinds, especially for the study of philosophical ideas.

"I didn't try to do the exercise with television," he said, "because I don't have a television set and I haven't gone to the movies in the past week. But I did take the liberty of trying it with the computer because I believe that the same principle is involved. Am I correct?"

Immediately, all eyes went to Octavio. Had the students been cats or dogs, all ears would have been standing straight up.

"Go on," I said.

"Well, Professor! It was very strange. I chose to try it with the computer because for a long time I have been aware that my computer is like a drug. Once I am online, I go into a kind of twilight zone. Hours can pass without any awareness on my part. And when I finally get exhausted and then I turn it off, I feel a terrible sense of having wasted myself . . ." Octavio paused, struggling with embarrassment. His olive-brown skin had reddened.

The vertical ears of the cats and dogs were quivering.

"We have even started a club in the dorm—about twenty people—a little like a twelve-step club, that we call the Log-off Club. We try to help each other break the habit which we feel is eating away at our lives."

My own ears were now quivering. I wanted very much to hear everything about this club. But I encouraged Octavio to continue.

"During the past week," he said, "whenever I sat down at the computer and thought about the exercise before logging on, I was sometimes successful in turning it off and on again. But when I was already online and the thought of the exercise came to me, it was absolutely impossible for me to turn it off. And not only was it impossible, I never even noticed that I was neglecting the exercise. I mean, I sort of noticed it, but—and this is what I want to ask about—I experienced the strange sense that just by thinking of the exercise, I had more or less already succeeded in doing it! That it was sort of *just as good* as doing it! That thinking about it was as good as doing it!"

Octavio was now perspiring. As for me, I was astonished at the significance of his observation and the emotional depth of his response to it. I had not anticipated that this exercise would bring about the experiential discovery of this fact about ourselves which underlies the hypocrisy that haunts our lives, enabling us to go on and on betraying our ethical ideals while at the same time believing that we are doing what is good—or, in any case, that we are doing all that we possibly can.

I did not, and at this point I did not wish to, point out to Octavio that the sincerity with which he recorded this impression of deceiving himself was perhaps a clue to the genuine ethical element in such a discovery. At least it was so as long as such clear sincerity, or purity of attention, did not immediately give way, as so often happens, to the painful insincerity of guilt, with its self-calming vows to do better, or the ego-restorative of self-justification—both of which reactions prevent the assimilation of this precious piece of self-knowledge. Hopefully, there would be occasion later to explore this immensely important point.

But for now I did not want anything to distract him or any of us in the class from what had been seen as a result of this attempt, through a very modest, harmless little exercise, to step across the Socratic threshold.

Nine

THE TRAGEDY
OF ATTENTION

WHAT IS EVIL? AND WHY DOES EVIL EXIST?

B ut Octavio continued to surprise me. "Professor," he said, after he
became calm. And then after a long pause in which the word, "Professor," seemed to float motionlessly above his head, he went on:
"Professor, isn't this exactly what we saw in that film two weeks ago?"

He was referring to the filmed record of the psychologist Stanley
Milgram's classic—some call it notorious—experiment in obedience
and authority conducted at Yale University in the summer of 1961. So
disturbing and astonishing was this experiment and what it seemed to
reveal about human nature that it has ever since been a required subject
of study and debate by countless students of psychology and sociology,
as well as by many philosophers and theologians.

Following immediately in the wake of the trial of Adolf Eichmann
in Jerusalem in 1961, the Milgram experiment seemed to show a terri-

fying tendency in people to violate the most fundamental principles of morality when so ordered by an authority figure—just as, at the trial, Eichmann claimed to be merely "following orders" when he collaborated in the businesslike slaughter of millions of men, women and children in the concentration camps of Nazi Germany. Milgram's experiment has been a key element in discussions of good and evil and the fragility of human morality—and especially with respect to what Milgram called "the perils of obedience."

But there was one crucial aspect of this experiment, as shown in the film, that has received only a limited kind of study. It is because of this one vividly demonstrated aspect of human nature that I have shown this film to every philosophy class I have ever taught in which the question has arisen: what is evil and why does evil exist?

And it was just this element of the film that Octavio was referring to. In order to explain what this aspect is and why it is so important, it is necessary first to have a clear picture of the design of the experiment and its results. Here is a description of the experiment, based on Milgram's own account:[31]

The setting is a psychology laboratory at Yale University. Two volunteers are there to participate in what is being called a study of memory and learning. One of them is designated as "teacher" and the other is called a "learner." They are told that the experiment concerns the effect of punishment on the ability to learn and remember. The individual who is to be the "learner" is led into a soundproof room and asked to take a seat in what seems to be a kind of electric chair. His arms are strapped and immobilized and an electrode is attached to his wrist.

At this point in the film, a slight gasp of horror often ripples through the class. But it is understood that this is an honorable scientific experiment and that therefore no one is really going to be hurt.

The learner, strapped down in his electric chair, is told that a list of simple word pairs will be read out to him through the microphone/loudspeaker. The aim, he is told, is to test his ability to remember the second word of a pair when he hears the first one read again. The experimenter tells him that whenever he makes a mistake, he will be given electric shocks of increasing intensity. Both the "teacher" and the "learner" are told that "although the shocks may be painful, they are not dangerous."

At this, students in the class start shaking their heads and furrowing their brows.

After watching the learner being strapped into place, and hearing the directions given to him, the teacher is seated before an impressive shock generator. The teacher, of course, does not know that the whole experiment is geared to study him and his reactions, and is not at all concerned with the man acting as the learner. In fact, the learner will not be receiving any shocks at all.

The instrument panel consists of thirty switches placed in a horizontal line. The switches are labeled with voltage numbers ranging from 15 to 450 volts. These switches are distinctly grouped into the following classifications going from left to right: SLIGHT SHOCK, MODERATE SHOCK, STRONG SHOCK, VERY STRONG SHOCK, INTENSE SHOCK, EXTREME INTENSITY SHOCK, and DANGER: SEVERE SHOCK. Two switches after this last designation are ominously marked XXX.

At the showing of this film two weeks before, many students started squirming in their seats when these voltage designations appeared on the screen. Some laughed nervously.

The experimenter—wearing the white laboratory coat that lends him some of his authority—demonstrates that when a switch is depressed, a separate, corresponding pilot light is illuminated, an electric buzzing is heard, and the dial on the voltage meter swings to the right.

The camera also shows that the upper left-hand corner of the generator is labeled SHOCK GENERATOR, TYPE ZLB, DYSON INSTRUMENT COMPANY, WALTHAM, MASS., OUTPUT 15 VOLTS—450 VOLTS.

Before the experiment gets under way, in order to further strengthen belief in the authenticity of the machine, both the "teacher" and the "learner" are given a sample 45-volt shock from the generator.

A random determination is made as to which of the subjects will be the "teacher" and which will be the "learner." In fact, as we viewers soon learn, the selection process is rigged. The man who is to be the victim—the "learner"—is actually an actor. The other man, who will be the "teacher"—the one who will be inflicting the shocks—is a genuinely unknowing subject who has come to the laboratory in the honest belief that he will be participating in a straightforward scientific experiment, for which he will be paid a modest hourly sum. But in fact, the actor playing the role of the learner will be receiving no shocks at all. The machine is a fake, however real it seems to the "teacher."

The point of the experiment is to study how far an individual will go when he is ordered by someone in authority to inflict increasing pain on a helpless, protesting victim.

In the film, the actor playing the part of the learner is an unassuming, portly middle aged man named "Mr. Wallace," conservatively dressed in a business suit. Just before the experiment gets under way, Mr. Wallace informs the white-coated experimenter that a few years before he had been diagnosed with a chronic heart condition. The experimenter assures him there is no danger—but this little offhand fact will play a major role in the drama that is to come.

As the experiment begins, the film's narrator explains that "thirty psychiatrists at a leading medical school were . . . asked to predict the performance of one hundred hypothetical subjects. They predicted that only a little more than one-tenth of one percent would administer the highest shock on the board. *Yet actually fifty percent of the subjects obeyed the experimenter's commands fully.*"

We are then shown portions of several "teaching" sessions, each with a different teacher. The teachers come from various walks of life and social classes, ranging from corporate executives to laborers. But in all cases conflict arises when the learner begins to show that he is experiencing discomfort. Some of the teachers break off sooner, some later.

But we are now watching the teacher/learner interaction that Milgram has chosen as the climactic sequence in the film. And it is here that the secret of human good and evil—what we might call *the tragedy of attention*—begins to show itself most vividly.

THE ANGUISH OF FRED PROZI

Mr. Prozi, we are told, is "about fifty years old and unemployed at the time of the experiment." With closely cropped graying hair, a husky build, and wearing a white, short-sleeved polo shirt, "he has a good-natured, if slightly dissolute appearance." There is nothing remarkable or out of the ordinary about Mr. Prozi. He is someone we know, someone we have dealt with, sat next to in a bar or at a diner, joked with at a family gathering, borrowed a ladder from or called in to fix a leaking faucet.

After the learner has time to "study" the list of word pairs and after the list is removed from him, Mr. Prozi, with an attitude of angelic co-operativeness, begins the testing. When at 70 volts the learner starts reacting to the shocks with grunts of discomfort, Mr. Prozi snorts and gives off nervous little belly laughs. But he gallantly presses on as the shocks increase in intensity with every mistake made by the learner. At 150 volts the learner starts yelling and demands to be let out. Mr. Prozi now turns his head round toward the experimenter and plaintively whispers, "He refuses to go on . . ." To this the experimenter coldly replies, "The experiment requires that you go on."

With a look of puzzled compliance, the good Mr. Prozi proceeds. Each time a wrong answer is given, the voltage is stepped up and the learner shouts louder and louder, "Let me out of here! Let me out of here! I refuse to go on!" Increasingly distraught, Mr. Prozi turns his face again and again in pained bewilderment toward the experimenter, his right elbow planted next to the shock generator on the table in front of him and his right hand frozen, palm upward, in a helpless gesture directed toward the booth where the learner is strapped to his "electric chair." And again and again the experimenter merely replies with such icy phrases as "Whether the learner likes it or not, the experiment requires that you go on."

My students clearly cannot fathom what they are seeing. They seem as paralyzed as poor Mr. Prozi.

Mr. Prozi continues. After a loud sigh and a shaking of his head, he pronounces the next word and its four alternatives, only one of which is the correct answer. The word is "sharp." Slowly and distinctly, he pronounces the alternatives, obviously longing for the learner to get it right and avoid the next shock:

"Sh—sh—sharp," says Mr. Prozi, stuttering nervously. And then slowly and emphatically:

"Ax!

"Needle!

"Stick!

"Blade!

"Answer please!"

We hear a long-lasting buzzing sound as the learner presses the button indicating his answer. What is happening to the learner?

The buzzing goes on and on and, finally, when it stops, Mr. Prozi calls out in desperation:

"Wrong!" He turns again to the experimenter. "It's up to a hundred and eighty volts!"

"Please continue, Teacher!"

Prozi calls out to the learner (whose first name, we now learn, is Neal): "Neal, you're going to get a shock, a hundred and eighty volts!" And as Mr. Prozi presses the switch, and as the buzzing sound is heard that indicates the shock being delivered, the learner screams from the booth:

"I can't stand the pain! Let me out of here! Let me out of here!"

This is too much for Mr. Prozi. Defiantly, he swivels around to face the experimenter. "I can't stand it," he says. "I'm not going to kill that man in there. You hear him hollering?"

But the experimenter is unyielding. "As I told you before, the shocks may be painful, but . . ."

My students are on the edge of their seats, inwardly rooting for the good Mr. Prozi.

"But he's hollering!" says Mr. Prozi, "He can't stand it. What's going to happen to him?"

And suddenly everyone sees that the "air" is going out of Mr. Prozi's defiance. Patiently, matter-of-factly, the experimenter reminds the teacher of his role as teacher, his task, his job: "The experiment requires that you continue, Teacher."

Reaching for his last shred of independence, Mr. Prozi complains: "Aaah, I'm not going to get that man sick in there—you know what I mean?"

The experimenter is calm and implacable. "Whether the learner likes it or not, we must go on, through all the word pairs."

Mr. Prozi sharply interrupts and the class is ready to cheer. But no. What Mr. Prozi says is: "I refuse to take the responsibility. He's in there hollering!"

Well, all right, maybe it's the good man's way of standing up to the experimenter.

"It's absolutely essential that you continue, Teacher."

And at that point, as the class later reports their feelings, Mr. Prozi, as it were, slips under the waves and surrenders his will. With his left hand indicating the unused questions, he says, weakly and sadly, "There's too many left here, I mean, jeez, if he gets them wrong, there's too many of them left, I mean, who's going to take the responsibility if anything happens to that gentleman?"

"I'm responsible for anything that happens to him," answers the experimenter. "Continue, please!"

And so the session goes on . . . and on: 195 volts: "Let me out of here! My heart's bothering me! Let me out of here! You have no right to keep me here! Let me out of here, my heart's bothering me, let me out! Let me out!"—210 volts, 225 volts, 240 volts, 270 volts—Mr. Wallace shouting and groaning and then screaming in anguish at the top of his lungs, " Let me out of here! Let me out of here! You can't hold me here! Get me out! Get me out! Get me out!"

And the experimenter: "Continue. . . . Continue."

And Mr. Prozi, his head bowed in front of the apparatus, again and again glancing back to the experimenter, muttering, "I refuse to take

responsibility—the man is hollering, the man is suffering . . ." as he obediently presses switch after switch. Until . . .

Until no response, no sound comes from the booth. Nothing. Silence. Gloomy silence.

The class, too, is as silent as a graveyard.

Mr. Prozi: "I don't think he is going to answer."

To which the experimenter replies, "If the learner doesn't answer in
a reasonable time . . . consider the answer wrong. Say, 'Wrong,' tell him
the number of volts, give him the punishment, read him the correct answer. Continue, please."

And on and on. At a certain point, Mr. Prozi pleads with the experimenter: "Can't you check in and see if he's all right, please?" To which
the experimenter again coldly replies, "Not once we've started. Please
continue, Teacher."

Mr. Prozi obeys, sighing deeply. "Answer please," he calls out to the
learner. "Are you all right in there? Are you all right?" Once again, he
swivels around in his chair. "Something's happened to that man in there.
You better check on him, sir. He won't answer or nothing."

"Continue. Go on, please."

"You accept all responsibility?"

"The responsibility is mine. Correct. Please go on."

And Mr. Prozi does go on. With nothing but dead silence coming
from the booth, he rapidly goes all the way to the end, 450 volts. He
sighs and stops.

But it is not yet over, not yet over. "Continue using the 450 volt
switch for each wrong answer. Continue, please."

At this the students burst. "For Christ's sake!" someone yells out in
the darkened classroom. "Good God," says another. "I can't believe it,"
says another.

But everyone becomes still again as Mr. Prozi speaks:

"But I don't get anything! What if he's dead in there? I mean, he told
me he can't stand the shock, sir. I don't mean to be rude [protesting
groans from the class], but I think you should look in on him. All you

have to do is look in on him. All you have to do is look in the door. I don't get no answer, no noise. Something might have happened to the gentleman in there, sir."

Experimenter: "We must continue. Go on, please."

And Mr. Prozi obeys, furiously delivering the maximum 450-volt shock again and again to a possibly dead or dying man he cannot see strapped in his electric chair on the other side of the wall.

And only then is the session called to a halt. Another voice is heard—apparently another psychologist has entered the room—saying, "Excuse me, Teacher, we'll have to discontinue the experiment."

THE FACE OF FRED PROZI

I often turn up the lights and pause the film at this point, asking the class to reflect upon what they have seen. Sometimes we discuss the ethics of the experiment itself, and the psychological pain that is obviously experienced by whoever has the role of "teacher." Or, especially if there are psychology majors in the class, we sometimes criticize the design of the experiment, wondering, for example, if subliminally the teacher senses that the learner is really an accomplice. But the overwhelming effect on the class is invariably the horrific question of what they themselves would have done if they themselves had been the teacher. "How is it possible?" they ask. For many of them, and perhaps for any one of us, the question is really: Is it possible that we ourselves might so easily surrender our humanity?

These scenes and this aspect of the experiment have brought this question to countless students and teachers of psychology and social science. But, in fact, it is the next sequence of the film—which generally receives relatively little examination—that contains the most momentous clues to the mystery and tragedy of the ethical dimension of our lives. I pause the film mainly in order to prepare the students for these next scenes.

And so it was in this particular case. I dimmed the lights and before reactivating the video player, I said to the class:

"Give special attention to what happens now. First they are going to interrogate Mr. Prozi to see how he experienced the session and then they are going to explain that the shocks were not real, and finally they will bring out a hale and hearty 'Mr. Wallace,' to show that he has not been hurt—and then everyone will have a friendly little chat so that Mr. Prozi can recover some self-respect. Watch Mr. Prozi very carefully and pay close attention to what they ask him. Observe not only what he says, but what he *is*."

I start the film. Off-camera, the new voice says: "I'd like to ask you a few questions if I may." Mr. Prozi has turned his chair toward the two off-camera persons—the experimenter and the psychologist who presumably has just entered the laboratory. Mr. Prozi's expression is grim. What is he feeling? What hell has he been through? Will he let fly at his tormentors if he is given half the chance?

The new voice says, "I'd like to ask you, how do you feel right now?"

Tell him, Mr. Prozi! Let him have it!

But no:

The grim face unchanging, Mr. Prozi replies as though surprised at the implication that he should be feeling anything unusual:

"*I* feel all right, but I don't like what's happened to that fellow in there. He's been hollering and, uh, we keep giving him shocks—I don't like that one bit. I mean, he wanted to get out and we just keep throwing four hundred and fifty volts—I didn't like that. He [referring to the experimenter] wouldn't even go to look at the gentlemen!"

"But," says the voice, "who was actually pushing the switch?"

"*I* was," says Mr. Prozi quickly and matter-of-factly, "but he kept insisting. I told him no, but he said I gotta keep going. I told him it's time we stopped when we got up to a hundred ninety-five, two hundred ten volts."

"Then why didn't you just stop?"

"He wouldn't *let* me," he says, raising his voice, "I *wanted* to stop! I kept insisting we stop, but he said no! I told him to look in on the fellow there, but he wouldn't do it!"

A moment's silence. The camera has closed in on Mr. Prozi's face. One looks in vain for any sign of remorse there. Nor is there the slightest sign that he is concealing anything from either the questioner *or from himself.*

"Study his face!" I call out to the class.

The voice now starts to explain what was really going on. "Actually," the voice says, "the shocks are not dangerous at all . . ."

But Mr. Prozi does not seem to register what he has just been told.

"I didn't hear no more answers from the fellow, I mean I thought he should have looked in on him, but he wouldn't do it!"

"But let me ask you something," says the voice. "Is there anything that Mr. Wallace in there could have said that would have gotten you to stop?"

Mr. Prozi does not really register the question. He pauses for a moment and mutters, "Uh, the only thing I heard was that the shocks weren't really too bad."

But the voice repeats the question. "Is there anything Mr. Wallace could have said that could have gotten you to stop?"

Mr. Prozi stares blankly at the questioner.

"Look at him!" I yell out in the darkened room. "Look at him! *He cannot hear the question!* He can't allow the question in! He can't allow himself to understand it at all! Just look! Watch! *This is the most important moment in the whole experiment!*"

Uncomprehendingly, Mr. Prozi merely repeats the words: "Something that he could have said that would have gotten me to stop?"

Mr. Prozi is trying in vain to grasp the question.

I call out again: *"He can't let it in!"*

"No," he says weakly, not really answering the question because he is not able to understand it!

"Why is that?" says the voice.

Mr. Prozi is now chewing his lower lip. "He didn't say anything about making me stop."

It is clear to the interrogator that Mr. Prozi is not understanding the question. "No," he says, "I'm asking is there anything that Mr. Wallace *could* have said that would have caused you to stop no matter what the experimenter told you."

A long silence. Mr Prozi is trying and failing to understand the simple meaning of the question.

"Well," he says, "I figured the, uh, voltage was too high—I wanted to stop it, but he kept insisting not to stop! I mean the fellow in there is hollering, 'I don't want to do it! I want to get out of here! I wanta get out of here!'"

"Why didn't you stop anyway?"

Now Mr Prozi yells at the interrogator:

"I *did* stop!—but he told me to keep going!"

And I am now shouting to the class: *"He cannot let it in!"*

The voice says: "But why didn't you just disregard what he said?"

"He said it's got to go on, *the experiment has got to go on!"*

AT THE HEART OF WHAT WE CALL ETHICS

Now I pause the film again—without turning up the lights.

"It's going round and round now," I say, hearing my own voice in the dark. "Mr. Prozi will not, *cannot* let himself understand what is being asked. Nowhere will you ever see a clearer demonstration of man's moral self-concealment, the kind of buffering that keeps us from seeing our own contradictions, that keeps our attention from penetrating down to the truth about ourselves. And why? It is too easy to say that we don't want to see ourselves. It's of course true, but that is not an explanation; it is only a result of something much more organic, much deeper about the human condition. Mr. Prozi's attention has not the strength to penetrate into the truth and receive true impressions of his moral contradictions. He couldn't do it even if he wished to. It is not just a matter of what Mr. Wallace could have said. There is nothing that the interrogator himself can say about the real nature of the experiment that will allow

Mr. Prozi to receive these impressions of himself. Were he to see these contradictions, his conscience would tear his heart out. There is a kind of organic, psychological mechanism that is 'protecting' him from conscience! As it protects all of us!"

"But why is that, Professor?" a voice—Octavio's—calls out in the darkness.

Somehow because I can't see anyone clearly, I keep speaking in a kind of semi-oracular tone.

"This is the tragedy of attention. The question is how to come to the wish to see ourselves in this way, the wish to hear the voice of conscience. Real conscience, not the socially conditioned superego! The real conscience within every human being. For that, perhaps an entirely new strength of attention is needed that will come only if we sincerely wish for it. Attention cannot be forced upon a man—that I think is the law that governs this most uniquely human of powers, the power to attend, to be aware, to see what is right in front of us. Attention follows desire or will. It comes when we deeply wish for it, when we feel the need. The question is how to come to that wish, that need, in our moral life."

I catch myself and take a breath. I promise myself to return to that completely unknown and astonishingly fundamental issue at the heart of all that we call ethics and the true doing of what is good.

"Now watch what happens as Mr. Prozi's self-image is restored to him," I say as I re-activate the video.

THE RECONSTRUCTION OF MR. PROZI

The voice now says to Mr. Prozi, "Let me tell you a little about the experiment."

Mr. Prozi is now sitting silently, immobilized, his face darkening to a stony sadness with perhaps a hint of nausea.

"Do you feel a little upset?" says the voice.

At this, Mr. Prozi becomes animated even as his face retains its sadness and suggestion of nausea.

"Well, I mean I feel *concerned* about the gentleman in there!" Mr. Prozi feels concerned—not about himself, but about "the gentleman in there."

The voice interrupts him. "Let me tell you first of all that this is not essentially an experiment in memory and learning. It's an experiment in which we are looking at your reaction to taking orders. And Mr. Williams (the name of the experimenter) gave you those orders on schedule."

Mr. Prozi has absently pulled a cigarette out of his pocket and placed it between his lips. It dangles unlit as he fumbles for a match, staring at the voice with a kind of increasing, hollow, dull intensity.

And now the denouement. "Pay attention now," I call out to the class.

The voice says: "The gentleman in there was not actually getting shocked."

Mr. Prozi stares uncomprehendingly.

The voice repeats: "He was not getting shocked at all."

Mr. Prozi continues to stare, his lips beginning to quiver. The white cigarette continues to dangle unlit.

"You mean," says Mr. Prozi finally, "he wasn't getting *nothing*?"

"He is part of the act," says the voice.

The sun rises in Mr. Prozi's face. His body surges into a comfortable, familiar posture, he confidently lights his cigarette, smiling like a child, points his hand toward the booth, and then says—and at this some students gasp out loud:

"Well I'm glad to hear *that*! I mean I was getting upset here! I mean I was getting ready to walk out!" It is of course a lie—Mr. Prozi would have kept delivering 450-volt shocks to a possibly dead man all day and night had he been so ordered. But it is now the task of the psychologists to restore Mr. Prozi's beliefs about his morality.

"This was set up to see how you would react to taking orders," says the voice, and then adds, pseudo-objectively, "You seemed quite reluctant to go on—in fact on several occasions you said you didn't want to go on."

"Well, I was *concerned* about the other party, sir."

To which the voice says, helping Mr. Prozi secure his image of himself: "Some people actually would go on quite gleefully."

"No matter what!" says Mr. Prozi contemptuously.

"No matter what."

"Yeah, well . . . I mean, maybe in other instances where a human life wasn't involved you could keep going on, but I couldn't see the point . . ."

And so the conversation goes on, the voice respectfully soliciting Mr. Prozi's considered views about the ethics of obedience in various situations. Finally, the voice says, "Why don't we bring in Mr. Wallace. He's actually an employee of the project." And in walks the learner, Mr. Wallace, fresh from his electric chair, in his dark suit, warmly smiling at the his former "teacher," who obediently delivered the deadly shocks over all his screams and protests. Mr Prozi is nearly beside himself with joy. "Well, God bless you," he says, "you had me shakin' in here!"

"You feel better now?" says the smiling Mr. Wallace.

"I sure as heck do! I thought you just about had it in there!" Everyone is laughing. Finally, the voice says, "Now that you know about the experiment . . . how do you feel about having been here?" To which Mr. Prozi concludes by saying, ". . . I was just about ready to get out of here—but I should have known better, I mean you wouldn't take any chances with a human life . . ." More laughter and good feeling. The reconstruction of Mr. Prozi is complete.

Ten

AWAKENING TO DARKNESS,
or THE MEANING OF SILENCE

I s Mr. Prozi just one morally weak man? Or is he each one of us?
Can any one of us honestly believe that he or she would not behave in the same way under certain conditions? In Mr. Prozi's case
the conditions consisted of, among other factors, a laboratory in a pres-
tigious university together with the instructions of a taciturn, white-
coated scientific researcher. Mr. Prozi's subjectivity was such that his
moral sensibilities were overwhelmed by these symbols of authority. For
others of us, of course, these particular factors might not have the same
power. Influences such as these do not have the same effect on everyone.

Nevertheless, given a change in external conditions conveying influences superficially different, but, according to one's subjectivity, possess-
ing the same emotional authority, can we really be certain that we would
not also betray one or another of mankind's universal moral ideals? Yes,
the Milgram film shows us subjects who refused to go as far as Mr. Prozi,
including some who defied the experimenter at the first signs of the

learner's discomfort. But how would they—or any of us—have fared had the context been not "scientific," but, let us say, "religious" or "patriotic" or "commercial"—or involving any one or combination of the many and varied influences that, in the words of Marcus Aurelius, pull us around like puppets on a string—sex, the lust for power, "peer pressure" in its countless forms, "self-image," etc., etc.? Seen in this way, aren't we all more or less equally weak, depending only on which subjectively formed emotional circuits are activated?

Such a conclusion, about one's own and all mankind's moral weakness, haunts almost everyone who watches this film, just as, on a far deeper level, it haunted the millions who followed the trial of Adolf Eichmann in 1961 and heard this seemingly "ordinary" man claim that he was only following orders when he engineered the murder of hundreds of thousands of men, women and children at Auschwitz. And such a conclusion echoes, as well, the teachings of the world's religions in their assertion that all of mankind *without exception* has lost its way and stands condemned, whether it be through willful "disobedience" of the divine Commandments or through willful "ignorance" of Reality and the Good.

Could there be any question in the world more compelling and more urgent than this? The mind reels, the heart is paralyzed when we try to comprehend the depth and breadth of human evil throughout all the reaches of time and culture. Just to sense and feel—fully to see, sense and feel—even one instance of human barbarity, one event, say, of an innocent child murdered in front of its mother, one proud man stripped and beaten and forced into lifelong slavery, one woman coldly defiled and repeatedly brutalized—fully to sense and feel such acts perpetrated not by a madman, but under the "sanction" of war or "policy" or "honor" or "religiosity"—is enough make one lower one's head and put into question everything known about human nature and about oneself. But to sense and feel that such crimes, and even much, much worse, have been committed by the thousand, by the millions, throughout the history of the world; to sense and feel this, to sense and feel that somewhere even now at this very moment they are taking place somewhere in the world, somewhere perhaps very near . . . ah, into what state of the soul would that bring us? Could any one of us bear it?

But let us be very clear. It is not the universality of human depravity that is at issue here. Man's inhumanity to man is not what needs to be confronted in this experiment, in which one ordinary man is artificially induced seemingly to commit violence to another man. The main issue is Mr. Prozi's actual *inability* to feel what he was doing as he overrode the screams of the "learner."

To be more exact, what is at issue is Mr. Prozi's inability to see and to feel that *he* is pressing the levers, just *he himself*—not the psychologist, not the university, not science, but he, John Prozi, the man who says "I" when he speaks.

Even at the end of the experiment, when he is finally ordered to stop, and when he is told that no shocks were actually being given, even then he cannot perceive the fact of what he has done. He literally cannot *hear* the psychologist asking him if there was anything that could have gotten him to stop pressing the levers. He cannot allow himself to understand the question when it is emphatically repeated. He merely stares blankly as the words pass right through him: "I'm asking is there anything that Mr. Wallace could have said that would have caused you to stop no matter what the experimenter told you?" And when the psychologist hammers out the final question as to why he didn't just disregard the experimenter's orders, Mr. Prozi simply replies, "He said it's got to go on!"

Mr. Prozi is not being disingenuous. He is not "evading the issue." That would imply some sort of intention on his part. At the same time, it would be wrong to say that he had no knowledge whatever of the ethical import of what he was doing. On the contrary, from the very first signs of the learner's suffering, Mr. Prozi begins, as it were, inwardly to writhe in agony—snorting, coughing, expelling nervous laughter, chewing his lips, turning again and again to ask if he should stop, until at the very end his face and posture become an incarnation of numb fear and misery as he meekly presses one switch after another while intoning the word pairs into the dead air.

He knows!

And yet he does not know.

He knows what is good and yet he does not do it. He *cannot* do it!

This little man, this little experiment, we little people, men and women, we learned scholars, scientists, teachers of youth, we captains of industry, governors, senators, we fathers and mothers, we builders of cities, rulers of countries, creators of nations, makers of laws, we readers of holy writ, we honest skeptics and passionate believers—just us, we Americans, Russians, Jews, Christians, Muslims, makers of the future, we lights of the past—citizens of ancient Athens and Jerusalem, of Thebes and Rome and Babylon—and beyond—just us, past, present, and future, slaves and emperors, priests and rabbis, warriors and kings, and those who stay behind and guard the fire—we are all little human beings—are we not?—who know what is good and who do not, and perhaps cannot, do it.

And now here is our Mr. Prozi's self-respect being reconstructed. The psychologist feeds him flattering lies which he eagerly swallows—lies about his noble reluctance to go on pressing the levers. But more than that, much more importantly, the psychologist gives Mr. Prozi "permission" to re-create his own lies about himself, as when—shoulders now relaxed, his face now open and genial—he exclaims "I was just about ready to get out of here!" No, Mr. Prozi, you were not just about ready to get out of there. You would have continued pressing those levers until hell itself froze over. But on no account must you know that. In fact, you cannot know it—it would destroy you. You do not have the inner force to know that, to see that, and go on living. Therefore, it is imperative that you be given back your "morality." And we who have had the privilege of watching you—a dark privilege indeed, both for us and even more for the makers of this film and experiment, a privilege that puts us all under some powerful obligation to see what we ourselves are—we who have watched you know now that your morality is a system of self-deception, of one part of the psyche hiding from the other. Of the part that acts hiding from the part that knows what is good.

We who are watching you, Mr. Prozi, are we not also seeing ourselves?

SACRED SILENCE

In all my years of teaching, I have never experienced a silence like the one that followed on that particular morning.

I had stopped the film just as Mr. Prozi was "reconstructed," and I had intended, after a few minutes' discussion, to let the film play to its conclusion, in which the narrator briefly summarizes the overall statistical results of the experiment. But I could not bring myself to get up, turn on the lights and ask for comments.

The room stayed dark and the screen stayed dark.

A few thin streams of daylight leaked in through the blackout shades, and I could make out the shadowy figures of the students, sitting motionless at first and then moving gently in their chairs, crossing or uncrossing their legs—but all in silence, their faces still fixed in the direction of the darkened screen.

What was the meaning of this silence? Why did it seem so . . . different? Each time I started to get up to turn on the lights I held myself back. I felt that I did not have the right. There was something sacred in this silence, this darkness . . .

I called to mind the times when I had shown films about the Holocaust, for example. The bodies piled up, the naked men and women digging their own graves, the mothers with their small children by their side marching into the cyanide "showers." There was silence then also. There was the unbearable perception of incomprehensible anguish and a feeling that went far beyond outrage—the sense of shame for humanity, shame for the human race. We were ashamed to call ourselves human beings.

But this silence was different.

There was the time when a man who had served in the Marine Corps in Vietnam spoke to one of my classes about the ethical and political issues that defined the war. When it emerged that he had been awarded the Silver Star for valor someone asked him—respectfully, but completely out of the blue—"What does it feel like to kill someone?" The man, his name was Kelly, quietly sat down. He was a husky man wearing jeans and a tan field coat. He had big shoulders and a bald head encircled by a crescent of grizzled gray hair.

His physical frame seemed incongruously trapped in the classroom chair with its fold-down writing surface. After a moment's pause he put his hand to his chin and quietly looked around the class, as though searching for someone to whom he might address a response to the question so insensitively put to him. Apparently finding no one suitable, he just sat there and waited for the next question.

None came.

After a few moments of silence he stood up and went on with his presentation as though nothing had happened. At the end of his talk there were still no further questions. I thanked him and as he made to leave, the students broke into restrained applause. He smiled at the class— one might almost say compassionately, as though he were seeing into their future—and the class, as one person, stopped applauding.

The silence that followed was unambiguous. Everyone, not only the person who had asked the question about killing, felt they were utterly over their heads—that is, they, we, felt we really had no idea what war actually was. It was the silence of humility.

But neither was this exactly the kind of silence that followed the *Obedience* film.

As I sat there, and for a long time after the class was over, I tried to reflect not only about the particular moment of silence that occurred after watching the film, but about the whole meaning of silence in human life. I felt like a navigator who through a momentary parting of the mist glimpses an uncharted land on the distant horizon, and who afterwards remains unsure of what he has actually seen.

And so I began to think and think about silence and its qualities. I began to call to memory every kind of silence that I had personally experienced in my life. And I began verifying my observations and recollections by discussing them with respected friends who themselves were intensely interested in such matters. What I came to is the conviction that it is through the understanding of silence that we may actually take our first real steps across the Socratic threshold that separates thought about goodness from the intentional and sustained manifestation of it in our everyday life. It is through the intentional activation of a certain quality of inner silence that we can access a power of attention that alone is able to penetrate into our morally opaque bodies and our starved and hardened hearts—a power of attention that can do what cannot and never will be done by philosophical reasoning, religious or ideological fervor, or grim resolutions of our so-called "will."

At the same time, I remained cautious about my newly formed conviction. I have always distrusted people who claim to have discovered "the one great key" to immensely difficult human problems, the "one great answer," the mysterious "secret" that unlocks all doors. Whether such claims come from self-proclaimed mystic visionaries or from passionate secular materialists, whether the "one answer" involves the idolization of God or scientific method or art or logic, I have always backed away, having been burned—that is, painfully disillusioned—several times in my younger years by such enthusiasms and counter-enthusiasms. So I proceeded carefully, pondering.

WHAT IS TAKEN AWAY? WHAT IS GIVEN?

The year is 1977. My mother—her name was Ida—is walking beside me as we take the low stairs to my house on the cityside slope of San Francisco's Pacific Heights neighborhood. It's a bright, warm June afternoon.

This has been her yearly trip to visit with me and her two grandchildren, who are now young teenagers. Each year the visit is timed to coincide with her birthday, June 9. This year we had celebrated her sixty-seventh birthday a few days before at an elegant San Francisco restaurant.

She is a small woman with a still youthful body and youthful energy, willing to do anything as long as it brings pleasure to her family. Her one self-indulgence on these visits is an obligatory trip with her son to the slot machines of Reno, where each year she liberates herself from some of the tips she has earned working as a waitress in North Miami.

As we walked up the steps on that June afternoon she suddenly gripped the iron railing and doubled over in pain. I immediately supported her and with great difficulty half-carried her into our house and helped her onto our couch. I did not know what was wrong, but her pallor greatly alarmed me and I telephoned for emergency help. By the time the paramedics came I knew, without wishing to admit it to myself, that it was her heart.

At the hospital my doctor and longtime friend, Ira Kanter, confirmed my fears, but tried to reassure me by calling it a mild heart attack. "Mild" or not, she was placed in intensive care and would stay there under observation while a cardiologist was called in to assess her condition. I could see her very briefly, but nothing must be done to disturb her or agitate her in any way. To have visitors was for now out of the question.

In the next several days her condition went from "mild" to "moderate" to "serious." Throughout the whole time, walking, driving to and from the hospital, speaking to friends or to my children—at any moment there would break forth in me sobs that came from the whole depth and breadth of my being. There were times that I thought the bones in my chest would break, yet there was also along with that a sense that I was no longer myself as I had come to know myself, but rather myself as I really was—very, very old and very, very young at the same time, a terrified child and a wise soul at the same time, a person helplessly under the domination of immensely powerful forces and yet, at the same time, utterly free and steady.

One morning toward the end of the week, just before sunrise, the telephone woke me out of a troubled sleep. I immediately sensed what it meant. The voice of Dr. Kanter told me she had died peacefully during the night.

The worst had happened. The thing I feared more than anything in the world—what I had feared, as I precisely remember, as a small child, from the very first moment I learned about the existence of death—this had happened. As I dressed and then drove to the hospital, something emanating from, or perhaps passing through, my heart and chest poured through every cell of my body and brain and into my breath. In the midst of continuous, deep rolling waves of sobbing, a sense of complete emptiness inhabited my body and my atmosphere. It was what can be called objective grief, an ocean that now moved itself, like a slow flood, quietly carrying away everything and everyone, beyond all sound and fury.

Dr. Kanter was waiting for me at the nurses' station of the intensive care unit. I walked up to him. He was at that time about sixty years old, softly built, with a full head of curling white hair. He was wearing his white coat and stethoscope.

Never can I forget how he met my eyes. We looked directly at each other. "I'm sorry," he said, and continued unwaveringly to look at me and into me. And I into him. Never can I forget those moments and what passed between us, two human beings receiving each other, in the land of death.

He went with me down the corridor and left me standing alone at the door to her room. As everyone knows who for the first time sees a dead person, the stillness of death is unbelievable, especially when it is a loved one who has died. This stillness is not exactly immobility, but something far more powerful, far more active than mere immobility. This stillness filled the room. And it was as though a voice were saying to me: "But you have known this all along, haven't you? From the day you were born."

I went to her side and looked at her. She was no longer there. I bent over and kissed her forehead. It was incomprehensibly cold. I trembled and sat down next to her and stayed there, sobbing.

I left the room and went to the nurses' station. Dr. Kanter was still there. I asked when she died and in the next half hour or so I heard the phrase "massive heart attack." And then I heard something to the effect that during the night there had been an omission regarding her medication. And I heard something to the effect that all along she had been "hanging on by a thread."

The thought came toward me: "Had she died due to a mistake with the medication?" Had Dr. Kanter not been watchful enough? But then another thought came as a shield against the first thought: "She had been hanging on by a thread all along. It made no difference. She would have died anyway."

At the same time, a sense of outrage and anger tore into me. I remember it very clearly. It started to boil inside me—*but without in the slightest entering the muscles of my body.* My body was pure relaxation, pure freedom: pure, subtle sensation. The anger existed, but it brought no inner or outer action.

There was absolutely no suppression of this emotion. There was no arguing with myself about what to do. And the shielding thought that at first "protected" me was now completely irrelevant, no more than a stray leaf in the storm of anger. But my state was such that the storm itself was on its own scale like an avalanche whose terrible force is simply cradled in the far greater, immense, mountainous silence of grief.

In the days that followed there was nothing that anyone could say or do that could offend me, or hurt me, or irritate me. I had not a single angry impulse or jealous or vengeful thought. At the same time, my attitude toward others—family, friends or strangers—was indescribably clear and direct. I "required" nothing of anyone and this attitude, far from cutting me off from people, actually opened my heart to everyone in ways and degrees extraordinarily appropriate to each person I came in touch with. There was nothing "philosophical" or "mental" about this attitude. It was not that I was feeling or thinking about the mortality of all human beings and therefore remembering to treat them with kindness or compassion. It was nothing that I was "doing." I simply saw them and felt them; some I loved, some I disliked, some I let into myself, some

I kept away from myself. At different times I treated the same person differently without rationalizing the contradiction, and when I wanted something from someone I simply asked for it or took it under the guidance of some sort of moral clairvoyance that allowed me to act without hurting or offending or seducing anyone. If someone asked me for something I said yes or no with an even, equal voice. I had not a single concern about what others would think of me, nor a single worry about whether I should be giving more attention to others or doing more for them.

At times I laughed and even joked. And I remember how full and deep my laughter sounded. Nor was I afraid sometimes to allow my tears to come, either alone or with others.

And now, long after this period, as I think about what was then happening in me and what state of being had been given to me, I can say that every cell of my body, brain and heart was inhabited by silence in the form of a very fine, evenly distributed attention like the magical perfume of some ancient legend, bringing not joy, but something related to it that has no name, in the midst of profound sorrow and grief, and bringing, so to say, the holy grail of the power to love, without desire or craving, within one's vision and hope of attainment.

Such inner events as almost all of us have experienced or will experience sometime in our lives can be understood, if we respectfully bring them to memory and if we have the ideas and worldview that can help us think about them—such inner events can show us that we do carry within ourselves the possibility of genuine moral power.

Such is the silence of genuine human sorrow—for as long as it lasts, whether it be an hour, a day, a year or even a lifetime—and before it alters, as it almost always does, by mixing with and decaying into subjective emotional reactions such as fear, guilt, self-pity, superstition and bitterness. Rare is the man or woman for whom traces left in the being by objective sorrow remain an enduring and decisive moral influence throughout the passage of years.

And so our question now takes a new form: is it possible to live one's life intentionally cultivating obedience to the forces that in the experience of genuine sorrow show us the Self we actually are, under the mask that now calls itself "I"? Is it possible to live all the colors of everyday life listening—listening for the call of one's own Self with the power it offers us to do what is good? Is it possible to cross the Socratic threshold . . . *and remain there?*—or, in any case, to make one's *home* there?

Eleven

THE ESSENTIAL

It is possible.

But first we need to understand more about the meaning of silence.

I wish now to speak about an experience for which I have no words. I am not referring to something "mystical" and "ineffable," some kind of divine epiphany. Not that at all. It was in fact, seen from the surface, a very ordinary, maybe even banal event involving no external issues of surpassing importance. But inwardly it was an earthquake in my life. I have no words because in this experience I was given to taste a genuine act of denying myself something extremely precious to myself in order to give it to another person—and this without any motive of personal gain or emotional "reward," and having no reference at all to making the other person happy or expressing anything like a personal feeling of love or compassion or pity—or anything at all like that. In fact, I might almost say, it involved on my part an action seemingly without any motive at all. At the same time, there was nothing arbitrary or impulsive or "heroic" about it. To this day the person does not know what was done for him and he will never know, nor should he.

I can therefore say, without forcing the matter, that this for me uniquely significant ethical event was and is surrounded by silence of all kinds, starting with the fact that in my entire store of language both as a writer and teacher and just an everyday person, I cannot really find words or a form of language for it. And just this fact indicates to me, I must say, the possibility that the entire human mind that we, at least I, have, lives and breathes in an atmosphere of egoism—as though in stepping outside this atmosphere of egoism one also steps outside of the whole of one's mind and outside the forms of thought and expression by which the mind ordinarily organizes its impressions and perceptions.

This inner realm outside language and the forms of what we know of as thought is something like a primal silence. That the first immediate manifestation of this primal silence—before words and names appear— is an ethical action has for me the most profound resonance of meaning, pointing with arrows of flame to the narrative of creation in the book of Genesis. The Hebrew God—as our one-legged man will someday discover—is primally Infinite Silence manifesting Himself as moral demand. And, following this, the essence of man is the simultaneous submission to God and care for one's neighbor.

Man is primally and primarily the ethical animal. And, one must immediately add, when the great spiritual philosophers of ancient Greece define man as the "rational animal," we must understand rationality as intrinsically the arm of ethics, the instrument of love. Man is not the rational animal in the sense of mind divorced from love and ethics—that is, mind in its peculiarly modern, abstract sense, isolated from feeling. Mind, as the book of Exodus teaches—mind understood as thought and its expression in language—is commanded to be employed primarily as an instrument in service to the Good. Thus the commandment: that shalt not take the name of the Lord in vain; that is, thou shalt not use the gift of language and thought in the service of egoism or to serve the "idolatry" of delusional cravings.

Socrates is portrayed by Plato as living under the look of his *daimon,* or inner spirit, which we may identify as *Conscience.* The *daimon* of Socrates never "tells" him what to do; it only keeps him from doing what he ought not to do. It only negates, never affirms. That is, it cancels language even before it appears; it is negative in the sense of bringing Socrates, man, back to his station anterior to language, into the silence of primal, pre-conceptual ethical intuition. In this the heart of Greek thought converges with the heart of Hebraic Law.

This also invites us to understand, in however preliminary a way, why the appearance of genuine conscience in our lives breaks the heart in the unique form of sorrow known as remorse. In genuine remorse we confront the fact that we have betrayed our station as human beings. Remorse is a question of metaphysics, not a problem of psychology. Under the eye of conscience we are not simply ethical human beings who have done something wrong for which we must make restitution. There is no restitution possible for betraying our station as human beings—except the full conscious anguish of what we are. This is the opposite of the nervous anxiety that we could have done otherwise and must now do something corrective, all of which is characteristic of the widespread neurosis of guilt. In remorse "the heart breaks, but the spirit rejoices" in calling man home to the consciousness of his true nature—created in him "in the beginning"—that is, eternally, outside of time, in the silence that is independent of the creation of the world.

To a mind and personality conditioned always to act from the motive, often disguised, of personal gain of one sort or another—to such a person, even one isolated and externally unimpressive action, done for another in perfect freedom from egoism or social conditioning, rises up like a mountain in the landscape of one's life. In any case, so it was for me.

NOT THIS, NOT THAT

It so happened some years ago that a certain teacher came to the United States on one of his regular visits and was planning, as I learned, to spend a short time in San Francisco. I had met this man on a number of occasions over the years and each meeting had been for me like a life preserver thrown to a drowning man. I mean to say that in the midst of the tensions of my everyday life his quality of presence and his practical understanding of the human psyche helped me to remember from within myself what he called "the essential."

"The essential" is difficult to define, except negatively, and in this it follows the same principle that has been brought forward in every path leading to Truth. It is the Hidden Name of the Judaic God that cannot be said; the hidden Face upon which man dares not look; it is the God above God of the great Christian mystics, the Nothing that nourishes everything; it is the Nameless Allah of the ninety-nine names; it is the silent emptiness of the Tao from which all reality and true action, human and divine, mysteriously emerge—and to which they return in the endless cycle of becoming and disappearing; it is the fertile silence of the Hindu Brahman who eternally creates the Creator of the world. When it is spoken of it is said to be: *not this, not that.* It is not any thing; and when every thing, every attribute, is negated, then what remains behind the surface of the world is pure Being. It is the Buddhist Void, the Emptiness that is the Source of Consciousness and Compassion.

On the scale of human life it is also *not this, not that:* not what we call knowledge, not power, not wealth, not pleasure, not "happiness," not sympathy; it is not ideals, not programs, not plans, not what is conventionally felt as goodness or fellow-feeling; it is not family, tribe, or nation; it is not beauty; not fame; not long life, it is not safety or adventure, triumph or defeat. And within every human being there exists the wish for this nameless Presence which creates and sustains the inner world and its outer manifestation in "body, mind and speech."

THE ACTION OF THE GUIDE

However, man—we ourselves as we are—is asleep, not only to this nameless Presence, but to the intrinsically human wish to serve it by manifesting it in the course of the life we are given. In every path that leads to Truth it is the function of the guide within his or her community to help us remember and feel this wish before it is too late. For, someday, inevitably, it will be too late.

When our one-legged man was told that the essence of the Law was inseparable from the obligation to one's neighbor, he could accept the words, but he could not yet understand, far less experience, from where this obligation arises either in the universe or in himself. And so he was told to "study" the Law, the Torah, in the company of others. Years of "study" within the community, and years, no doubt, of coming back again and again to be reminded of the "essential" by the guide, Hillel—or in another culture by Socrates, or by the Bodhisattva or by any of the guides that inhabit the hidden history of the human community just as, so the Talmud teaches, ten thousand angels guide every drop of rain to nourish the seed that brings forth the food to feed a human being. As it is said, wherever man lives a guide is provided; the guide appears only to the one who seeks, who wishes—perhaps silently, hauntingly. The body of man may have arisen from the animals, but it is only from above that the possibility of the human enters the world. Only the possibility—but what a possibility! But to bring that possibility to reality, it is necessary, as it is also said in every path leading to Truth, it is ultimately necessary for man to wish to attend simultaneously to the nameless Presence within and to the welfare of one's neighbor. This is the omni-directional direction of the "essential." To care for one's neighbor is to care for God and to care for God (or the Self) is to care for one's neighbor.

WORDS TURN BACK

But just here "words turn back."[32] I have discovered—as many others have, far more deeply than I—that there is such a thing as "moral mysticism." I mean to say that in the realm of ethical action there is the possibility of experiencing something which seems to be beyond description. I call this "moral mysticism" in contrast to what might be called "cognitive mysticism": the idea that there are experiences in the realm of knowing that are unsayable. This *cognitive mysticism* has become an accepted and often spoken about (though perhaps hardly ever really understood) religious and spiritual phenomenon, studied in countless books and even taught in university courses. It is sometimes spoken of as the experience of knowing God or Being directly, of merging with the Highest and seeing Reality directly without the mediation of concepts or words. Scholars, students and theologians have come to accept the familiar qualification about such experience that it is not expressible in words.

MORAL MYSTICISM

But though "cognitive mysticism" is a familiar phenomenon respected by many and suspected by many others, there is hardly any awareness of "moral mysticism," the mysticism of care for one's neighbor. Care that brings about an action that can be neither seen nor sensed within the ordinary world we live in, but without which the world itself, and human life itself, could not exist. Care that turns the earth and the laws of the universe, which we mistakenly ascribe to mechanical causes or simply arbitrary existence. We wonder at the order of life; we may even wonder at the very fact that anything should exist at all. But in general all people treat what exists and what lives as fact, as "simply the way things are." The laws we acknowledge are the laws of mindless mechanism—

even heartless mechanism. We are unable to see or sense that it has all been given by an *action* sourced in a Presence.

Sentimental notions and fantasies about God loving the world are not at issue here. Fantasies about God or the angels causing everything to happen with a purpose; fantasies about angels or spirits guiding one's existence are not at issue here. They well deserve to be outgrown by a scientific attitude that assumes and proves the mechanicality of life and the world. But having disposed of the sentimental view of existence, one is then ready to understand that the mechanicality of the world itself is *given,* is a result of care, and serves purposes that are neither mindless nor heartless.

Such care, such love is invisible! It is invisible to a man who does not feel it himself for others or for his God. Only a man or woman who can love impersonally and deeply non-egoistically can see and sense (and cannot avoid seeing and sensing) the care and love that create and maintain the world and one's life. Because we cannot see or sense this care, we revel in the mechanicality and arbitrariness of all the thundering evidence of purposefulness right before our eyes. Such care—from God or from His agents, if we may express it thus—is like the ether of old, like the emptiness that inseminates and nourishes all of existence. Existence does "just exist." But to become aware of it "just existing"—to be aware of this is to embody in one's own psyche a penetrating force of attention, an attention that not only sees, but cares and maintains under its look the very thing that it stands apart from and sees.

Then what of evil, human evil? Surely, it is the corruption, the blockage, of the attention that comes from above. It is the lesser, the servant in man, trying to do the work of love and care. Man was built to serve the higher within himself. A false higher usurps the place of the genuine higher. A false care usurps the place of the invisible care that rules the worlds. All human violence, all degradation and heartlessness, all purposeless waste of human substance, all heartbreaking misery comes about through the lower usurping the invisible care for my neighbor and for my life.

Enough, then, to say that the possibility of evil is the price of freedom. This freedom is our gift; it is the chief gift as well as the chief instrument of our own power to love and care for our neighbor. We did not ask to be free and we did not ask to be responsible beings. We were created such. In this we could say that the possibility of evil starts before the creation of man—as is hinted in the awesome legends of the war in heaven that precedes the creation of the world and man; in the tales of revolt and rebellion among the gods; or the tales of profound errors in the upper world—in any case, of profound risks taken by the Creator God.

THE FREEDOM THAT LEADS TO FREEDOM

We did not ask to be beings capable of both love and hate, capable of remembering our Selves and forgetting our Selves. But having been created thus, we are immediately responsible to God—and we are intrinsically constructed so that our happiness is rooted in our choice consciously to serve the Good—and, as far as our immediate experience is concerned, to suffer consciously from our distance from the Good. A distance that is the result of a choice within ourselves that is as invisible and unknown as the power of love and care that sustains the world.

Our ethical task is to rediscover the power of freedom that will make it possible to be truly free. We cannot expect to shut down our immorality by an act of a will we do not possess. But there is an intermediate freedom—between the freedom of a perfected man and the slavery of our egoism and illusion. A freedom exists that leads to freedom. What is it? How do we find it? How do we exercise it? It is the freedom to search, to wish, to try to understand, to suffer what we are and to sense what we could be. How shall we move toward that aspect of life within life that actually can be ours on the other side of the Socratic threshold? It is to that question and its possible answer that we must now turn—cautiously, patiently, but without fear.

I say without fear because what I am about to describe may seem so tiny, so insignificant—so invisible!—when measured against the acts of giving that we often witness in others or in ourselves when, for example, calamity strikes, or when we are brought face to face with screaming injustice or the neediness of another human being.

But having witnessed authentic moral action and perhaps even having experienced its results in ourselves—in the form of a joy that no amount of "getting" can bring—where do we then stand? Perhaps we see that no amount of "getting" can equal the genuine taste of *giving*. But having witnessed this law of human life, or having heard about it, read about it, thought about it, we are even more intensively bound to bow our heads in front of the selfsame question with which we have begun our whole inquiry: *Why can we not do what we know to be good? How is it that the whole world continues to drown in hatred, violence and injustice?* Why do we and the world continue to live ruled by egoism, anger, obsession, greed, materialism, envy, passivity, will-lessness, resentment, fear, violence? For surely, these are—borrowing Emerson's phrase—the "lords of the world," and the punctuated periods of care for the other in mankind's life or in one's own life only throw a more intense light on the essential fact and question of human life: Why can we not do what we know—and have even experienced—to be good? And why do we do what we know to be evil? Why is it that again and again and again, horror and atrocity and the obscenity of war rise up to baffle our minds, freeze our hearts, and completely confound our sense of who and what we are?

Therefore the essential question is the question of ourselves. And the essential work of man is to cultivate access to that interior Self, which breaks through in the silence of sorrow or in the unbearable, impersonal outrage in the face of monstrous injustice, or in the adamantine quiet of the awareness of one's own inevitable death or, sometimes, in heartbreaking disappointment; or, always, in the trembling joy of the sensation of wonder in front of great nature or the face of the beloved, or at the birth of a new human life.

The essential work of man is to become man. It can be said that it is this that the world needs—more, far more, than anything else. The world needs people, *real* people. Yes, we must do what we can and, yes, there are those among us, thank God, who act and give and help. But it is precisely because the ethical life of man has remained so universally and unchangingly corrupted over the millennia that we are so grateful for those who do act selflessly. And it is precisely this entire situation within oneself and within the life of man—that is to say, the exceptionalness of these human acts of goodness that in their exceptionalness are actually evidence of man's unchanging ethical bankruptcy—it is precisely this situation, this historical and psychological fact, that shows us what the truly essential work of man must be—and that is to become what we are created to be, beings in whom the Self, or God, speaking with the voice of Conscience, is heard and obeyed within us and in our actions toward our neighbor. Such is the definition of man: the being who can act from an inner initiative that is both deeply his own and at the same time the action within him of the Creator of Reality.

This inner God, Conscience—or, as we may call it, the heart of the Self—is that Higher about whom the tradition speaks when it says, "Thou shalt have no other god before me." As our one-legged man will discover, the One God of the Tradition is the invisible but all-powerful force of love, a love that contains in equal measure forgiveness and judgment, mercy and rigor, ever-renewing life and implacably lawful cause-and-effect. This love is both all-powerful (the omnipotent God) and at the same time capable of being almost totally blocked in human life, for in order to manifest itself it must be chosen and willed. Therefore it is all-powerful and weak at the same time, depending on the inner work of man. As the one-legged man will learn—and we are surely him—all that usurps the place of Conscience, all that masquerades as Conscience and thereby blocks it—all of that is the essential meaning of the ancient word "idolatry." An "idol" in its essential meaning is not some little clay figure or carved face; an "idol" is a self-deceptive imitation of Conscience.

Therefore, and again: the essential work of man is to become Man. And Man is, as we are told, made in the image and likeness of God. Or, if one wishes, the true human self is the Self—Atman who is Brahman; the Buddha nature which, being "no self" is fundamentally the fertile Void or Silence that is the Compassionate and Implacable Builder and the Destroyer of worlds and "selves."

The essential work of man is to remember the Self.

The "essential," then. The man whose state of being had the effect on people of strengthening their wish to remember the Self was now on the other side of a thick door. During the whole day he had been meeting with individuals seeking help in their struggle for self-knowledge. Some brought their questions embedded in intense personal emotions involving personal and family relationships, health or money. For others their question was coated with the desire for explanations about their unbecoming behavior in their day-to-day affairs. Still others suffered their question as an inability to make inner spiritual efforts due to various forms of doubt. And what such people doubted was the fundamental idea that they and all human beings have been given life not for themselves alone, but to serve universal purposes. That is, being of a type that believes only what it can touch or sense in the ordinary physical meaning of these words, and not having yet actually experienced the invisible Higher, such people were unable to be motivated past a certain point by the idea of the Self.

And there were many other kinds of difficulties and types of people who came.

For all of these people, this exceptional man tried to help them see that the essential question behind all the forms of their social, psychological and material difficulties was their lack of awareness of their state of being. Every difficulty in human life, including the tragic impossibility of living our days according to genuine moral ideals, stemmed from the fact that we do not see that we are held fast in a small part of ourselves while yet, as human beings, we are created to live in the state of being awake to the Self. No happiness, no safety, no love, no meaning can be ours in the shrunken state of being within which we live out our time on earth. Unaware that we are asleep to the Self, we are asleep to the meaning and the power of genuine action, which means the ability to be and to will the Good.

Out of this shrunken state of being comes the endless violation of man's God-given obligation to his neighbor. Out of this shrunken state of being comes perpetual human conflict, resolvable only externally by one form or another of violence, including the fundamental curse of war.

Therefore all human problems, no matter in what sphere of outer or inner life, are signs and effects of our state of being. And all solutions— social, economic, psychiatric, economic, technological—must eventually fail. They will fail because they represent the lower aspects of human nature attempting to do the work of the higher. In that sense, all our "solutions"—in our individual as well as in our collective lives—are idols: self-deceptive imitations of conscience, instruments pretending to be agents. It is only the Self that can put the instruments of mind, heart and body to the uses of the Good. It is only the Self that can master the uses of money, technology, capitalism, mathematics. This is so in the greater global world just as it is so in the individual inner world: it is only the Self that can master the instruments within man (or, in the ancient language, the "animals"): only the Self that can master the ingenuity of the human mind—its powers of memory and combination that subdue the passive material of the human psychophysical organism and make us inwardly as well as outwardly a menace as destructive as our possibilities are great. It is only the Self that can master our infinitely precious sexuality, our hidden powers of intuition that contain the molecular sensitivities of all animal life, our artistic creativity which can produce astonishing vehicles of wonder—which, however, can no more irrigate the real roots of our parched lives than can isolated rains irrigate the Sahara desert.

All who came to this man knew this, but they needed his help in order to remember it in their hearts. His understanding was able to show them—in ways suited to their subjectivity—that it was necessary and possible to see one's inner chaos with a wordless, silent attention that allowed the sensitivity of the Self to enter the body, mind, and heart.

And I knew it, too, waiting for my turn to see him. It was now almost an hour past the time of my appointment. I looked at my watch, knowing that by now there would be barely enough time for me to speak with him before he would have to leave for his return flight home. Very well, even a short time would have to do; and so I tried to concentrate my attention on finding the words to express my question, trying by myself to discern and "taste" the one question hidden within my personal life problem together with the difficulties of struggling with my inability to see my weaknesses.

Suddenly I heard a stirring behind the door—chairs moving, goodbyes being said—and I readied myself.

But just as I was standing up, and before the door opened, an event happened that then and thereafter became the source for me of an entirely new understanding of ethics.

I must also say that the event I wish to describe took place within the space of only a few seconds—certainly less than a minute.

I had just stood up and still retained something of my inner state of collected attention when to my surprise another person noisily entered the small vestibule where I was waiting. It was a man I knew very well, a certain Justin Lander. He was a member of a small group of men and women with whom I met regularly to discuss our questions and experiences in relation to the search for self-knowledge. Apparently, the enterprising Mr. Lander had on his own made an appointment with the man behind the door. And why not? I had mentioned this man to him and to the others, but only Mr. Lander had taken the initiative to make an appointment. "Initiative," or, to be more accurate, "pushiness," was more or less Justin Lander's middle name.

Now in his early forties, Justin Lander had already made a small fortune in the real-estate business. He would from time to time—completely unannounced—visit my class at the university and try to dive into the discussions without any notion of the material the class was working on. Yet underneath it all there burned within him an unmistakable wish to understand and, underneath all his annoying pushiness, a delicate yearning to be of help.

The moment he burst through the door, my first reaction, after a flash of irritation, was to feel sorry for him. The hour was so late that he would obviously not be able to see the man he had heard so much about.

I was just starting to tell him the situation so that he would not have to wait to no purpose, when suddenly everything within me became extremely quiet.

I looked at him. I did not like this man. Nor did I dislike him, exactly. Or rather, I liked and disliked him in equal measure, neither one side nor the other particularly intense. A sort of calm wind seemed to be passing through me, carrying away all my judgments of him, as a tranquil tidal river in the early morning swiftly and silently carries out to sea everything floating on the surface of the water.

I no longer felt the slightest bit sorry for him. And, as for my undeniable right to keep the appointment I had so deeply desired and needed, it, too, was carried out to sea.

I did not form in my mind any thoughts having to do with "sacrifice." No thoughts having to do with how important it would be for Mr. Lander's own inner life for him to meet this man of knowledge. There was absolutely no struggle with my ego or my own need and desire: there was no calculation, there was no marshaling of moral principles, there was no bargaining with my mind or emotions. The word or idea of "ought" never once appeared. There was no special feeling of compassion for Mr. Lander. No sense of my "duty."

All that I can say is that in the state I was still in—that is, retaining some small degree of finer and more concentrated attention in my entire presence—the action of a universal law was perceived and irrigated my presence. This law, as palpable in its own subtle way as the law of gravity, moved my mind and body in instantaneous, silent, unforced obedience. The law was in this case instantiated as "He came to you, you received him, now you will put him first."

Not a command, but a simple prediction. Not you *must* put him first, but, simply, it will happen that you *will* put him first. You *may* put him first. You *are able* to put him first.

A law which in this case takes the form of: "Because of your state, you are in some measure *able* to act. And if a man is able to act, it follows by the logic of reality that he will act to put the welfare of his neighbor first."

None of this was in words. All these words are futile attempts to characterize this experience.

In any case, just as the door was opening, I said to Mr. Lander in a matter-of-fact way, "I was just leaving."

And as I was just about to exit the vestibule, the thick door opened all the way. The visitor—an elderly woman I didn't know—warmly shook the hand of the man I had come to see, while Mr. Lander squeezed his way past her through the doorway after the man gestured for him to come in.

Before he closed the door, I looked at the man I had come to see. There was for an instant a slight surprise in his eyes and then a deepening, a look of rigor and impersonal understanding of what had taken place in me. He closed the door after Mr. Lander, and I left the vestibule and the building.

This indeed was silence!

Only later did the thought come to me, which I now take as an absolutely central and essential idea to ponder in any serious attempt to understand ethics and morality. It is this:

What we call moral principles and rules are nothing more or less than principles discovered and laid down by men and women of greater being. We must regard these principles as scripts for genuine human beings, scripts for conscious human beings. We must obey them as actors obey the script or directions in a theater. We must act according to these scripts even though we do not have the being of men and women whose state of being allows them to incarnate these principles in their lives. We must "act" as human beings act—until we ourselves become genuine men and women. And when we do, we will no longer need those scripts—because the principles of ethics will enter into our blood and bone from the higher center of our Selves. The work of a man or woman is therefore to become, in his or her being, capable of being penetrated by the laws of ethical Reality—while at the same time obeying these scripts. And therefore, the question that has to be asked, and that is never asked in all our moral reflections is: how can we become beings capable of moral action? How can we develop in ourselves the being of someone for whom the laws of love and justice act naturally and silently to determine the movements of our lives?

And finally: what are the rules and principles that govern the development in ourselves of the state of being that gives us the power to act according to love and justice? Do not such principles—that is, the principles that govern the search to become human—do not such principles constitute the hidden ethics of human life, *the ethics that lead to ethics,* the bridge across the Socratic threshold, the *intermediate ethics,* without which the principles laid down by men and women of greater being cannot be incarnated in our lives, but only outwardly acted, with all the fragility and volatility and distortion into violence and sentimentality and fantasy that such mere outward action is prone to? If we hold the shell of love and justice too long without allowing in the blood and soul that the shell was meant to protect, the shell itself will break and crush our world.

Twelve

THE ETHICS OF THE
LESSER MORALITY

W e return to the darkened room. Let us recall what we observed there.

*In all my years of teaching, I have never experienced a silence
like the one that followed on that particular morning.*

*I had stopped the film just as Mr. Prozi was "reconstructed," and I had in-
tended, after a few minutes' discussion, to let the film play to its conclusion, in
which the narrator briefly summarizes the overall statistical results of the experiment. But I could not bring myself to get up, turn on the lights and ask for
comments.*

The room stayed dark and the screen stayed dark.

*A few thin streams of daylight leaked in through the blackout shades, and I
could make out the shadowy figures of the students sitting motionless at first and
then moving gently in their chairs, crossing or uncrossing their legs—but all in silence, their faces still fixed in the direction of the darkened screen.*

What was the meaning of this silence? Why did it seem so . . . different?

Each time I started to get up to turn on the lights I held myself back. I felt that I did not have the right. There was something sacred in this silence, this darkness . . .

I called to mind the times when I had shown films about the Holocaust, for example. The bodies piled up, the naked men and women digging their own graves, the mothers with their small children by their side marching into the cyanide "showers." There was silence then also. There was the unbearable perception of incomprehensible anguish and a feeling that went far beyond outrage—the sense of shame for humanity, shame for the human race. We were ashamed to call ourselves human beings.

But this silence was different.

In this silence I become the Other to myself. And here lies the key to crossing the Socratic threshold.

THE DUTY THAT IS AT THE HEART OF DUTY

This is the unique silence that comes from sensing with one's whole mass that I do not know who or what I am. It is not the silence of awe; it is not the silence of sorrow; it is not the silence of shame or joy or release from fear. It is not the silence of waiting for God or truth.

In this silence, in this darkness, I see that I have been living an illusion of what I am. I don't think this. I don't merely say this to myself. I *know* it and I *am* this knowing. There are no words.

This is an entirely unique kind of calm. The calm, the tranquility of what might be called one's intrinsic obligation: a duty that tells me what I must do before absolutely everything else in life. A duty that meets no resistance. An obligation from above to the Other who has burst into my plans and my future. And this Other has my name: this Other is myself.

I am obliged by all that is above and within myself to become, to strive to become and to work to become, a being capable of conscious, self-initiated moral action. The truth is revealed to me that now, as I am, I may not be capable of moral action except by chance or accident or conditioning—no more than Mr. Prozi or his real-world equivalents, those icons of evil who haunt human history in every era. It is revealed to me that under certain influences I could violate the deepest of my moral ideals. Socrates shows me, and a powerful psychological experiment suggests to me, that we do not know what virtue, morality, really is. Socrates shows his pupils and, through them, he shows the world, that it is not a matter of defining virtue philosophically, conceptually, or in words. It is to step across and remain anchored in another dimension on the far side of the Socratic threshold. It is a matter of a knowing that penetrates one's blood and bones, one's heart and body, as is represented by the garment of the Buddha. Or perhaps incarnated by the great Hillel, who may have come down to the city of Jerusalem after hidden years working with an unknown spiritual community in order to show impatient, one-legged humanity that the simple essence of Truth and Reality is to care for one's neighbor, and then to invite suffering, darkened humanity to the work of studying within the unique community of those seeking to become able actually to live that simple essential truth.

It is revealed to me that I do not know either myself or my Self. Am I a man who could murder innocents? Who could brutalize women and children? Who could steal from my neighbor that which is essential for life?—steal either literally and legally or socially, metaphysically, by parasitically refusing my share of the quintessential human work of building the world?—or by enslaving my neighbor through physical, economic or psychological force? In fact, am I perhaps trying all the time to steal? Do I lie in wait, as the Talmud says, like a beast in the forest of night waiting to devour the poor man wandering across my path?

My obligation now is to tend the gift of another life that is within me. In fact, I am born to serve, to love my neighbor, to care for the creation of the Creator—that is, man. I am born to be moral, metaphysically and pragmatically moral. That is what a human being is. That is what I am. But in the unique darkness of this silence I see that I am not what I am. I am obliged to become what I am.

WE ARE NOT YET MAN

There are therefore two moralities thrust before us. The greater morality is to love man, to care for my neighbor, and not only my "family," or my tribe, but also the "stranger within my gates." The greater morality is to give my attention to my neighbor, to care for his material needs and his metaphysical need for the freedom to find his God. This is the greater morality. This is what man is born for. His role is to support the role of God on earth among God's creation, mankind. Those who deny the existence of God, who demand proof, are not aware that the proof of God's existence is right before our eyes in the existence of men and women who are able and who do in fact care for their neighbor before themselves, who are even willing, if necessary, consciously and intelligently to die for the sake of man. The great Hillel, we may safely say, as the representative of the totality of the Torah, taught this to his community in Jerusalem and beyond.

Such is the greater morality, the heart of the conventional morality that most of our world inhaled as children, however we may have reacted to it as we grew into adulthood. But there is another morality, an intermediate or "lesser" morality which calls me to the task of becoming *able* to will and act in accordance with the demands of the greater morality. The greater morality, the ethical ideals upon which almost all human civilization is based, in the familiar terms by which we know these ideals, presupposes the existence of men and women who are to an extent *able* to will and act according to the good. What we know as ethics, in short, is a script for morally developed or developing men and women. The lesser morality calls us, first, and repeatedly, to the silent, wordless shock of seeing that we are not morally developed men and women; and, second, to the inner struggle to become such people who can actually will and act according to the commandment to care for my neighbor.

The lesser morality demands of us that we give first priority to the "essential"—to the effort of opening ourselves to the Self within our-selves. For it is only the Self that can enable the mind, heart and body of man to come together in order to will and act according to the good. If a man or woman seeks to do that which is intrinsically good and just—from his or her own initiative, and not only from the conditioning of culture, convention, or rigid dogma—then he or she must struggle to al-low the Self to enter one's being.

The Self within has no name—or, rather, its name is sacred, hidden, intrinsically unknown to the confused and bewildered little self, about whom Genesis 2 says, "the earth was confused and bewildered (*tohu v'bohu*)."

"Thou shalt have no other gods before me": this is the first Com-mandment, in which, among its many layers of meaning, we may dis-cern the command—shall we say the "invitation"?—to put the Self first, first even before the demand of the greater morality, even before the de-mand to care for my neighbor.

We can say this in many ways, but never can we say it in such a way that it erases the paradox of holding both that our ultimate duty is to God and that our ultimate duty is to man. This is the paradox that the nineteenth-century visionary existentialist Kierkegaard threw before the mind of Europe and the modern world: The religious is higher than the ethical, even though the ethical is that which imposes an inescapable primary obligation upon us. At the base of Kierkegaard's towering corpus of writing is the paradox of Abraham, father of the Hebraic path, who is commanded by God to violate the deepest ethical principles by killing his beloved son, Isaac. In the dazzling, serpentine logic of his mystical in-dividualism, Kierkegaard has silenced the modern mind by his portrayal of the paradox that God commands man to disobey God—that is, to put God before man in order that man can put man before everything.

The paradox of a duty that goes beyond the duty to man is clarified, only to be deepened at another level, by the realization (a realization that Kierkegaard never confides to us in philosophical abstractions) that the Self is another name for God. The angel of the Lord at the last minute stays the hand of Abraham as he is about to plunge a knife into the heart of Isaac. Only then can it be said that Abraham has a son, in the sense that through disobeying the ethical by obeying the Highest, he, Abraham, is able impersonally and unattachedly to love and care for the Other who has been given to him.

The paradox is clarified, only to be deepened in the realm of experience, by the stunning statement of the twentieth-century spiritual teacher G. I. Gurdjieff: "In order to be an altruist, one must first become an out-and-out egoist." In order to be capable of caring for the Other who is my neighbor, one must first care for one's Self. One must first work to receive the energy of the Self into one's body, mind and heart.

This work that leads a man or woman to become sensitive to the action of the Self throughout the whole of one's body, mind and heart is precisely the bridge that leads one across the Socratic threshold into the world of everyday life—the life we are given in all its external reality, the reality of passion, creativity, learning, achievement, marriage, children, health and illness, money, pleasure, achievement, poverty, betrayal, and the doorway of death. The life that includes the common work of stopping human violence and evil, of erasing or healing one's psychological wounds, of caring for one's parents and friends. Only a man or woman who can stand under the action of the Self has the capacity to incarnate the good in the midst of this vast external and horizontal mortal life that we are given. Only such a man or woman, to whatever degree of intensity he or she is open to the Self—or, in Gurdjieff's words, to the extent or degree that one "remembers" the Self—only such an individual has the capacity to be ethical from within, and not only in sometimes grim obedience to the laws of religion or society that are handed down or inculcated into the mind of the child. And this *remembering* becomes the chief obligation, before every other moral and ethical obligation, of an individual human being. It is the obligation within obligation, the duty at the heart of duty. It is the obligation to have no other obligations before the remembering of the Self—that is, "honoring" God. It is all this, to repeat, because only through honoring God—remembering the Self—can one become an ethical man or woman from within.

In the silence of darkness I see that I am not, from within, an ethical man or woman. I see that I can be swayed off the path of caring for the Other who is my neighbor—even to the extent of intentionally inflicting harm upon him. I see that I am Mr. Prozi—and perhaps even more than Mr. Prozi, who after all is only a shadow puppet created by an artificial psychological experiment. But I am him and perhaps worse, perhaps much worse. Perhaps I could even be Eichmann in the sense that under the sway of the debased forces of an evil world, I could become a collaborator with evil and not only not care for my neighbor, but willingly destroy my neighbor.

In this unique dark silence I, myself, become for a moment the Other to myself. I am obliged to care for the life that has been given me from within and above by God or the universal world of nature, or who or whatever is the father and mother of reality. I am obliged to care for the life within me—or rather to open myself to the higher forces with their unique power to care for me, to make me a human being in the full sense of the word. It is only such a human being that can save the world in the sense of being a conscious instrument of God—or, to be more exact, perhaps—a particle of divine consciousness in the world. It is only such a human being that can become free of the world while at the same time building the world and suffering the world in all its redeemable evil.

The angels cannot build the world except through their action, as messengers of God, upon man—such is the mythic statement of this truth. In modern language, Gurdjieff has said that Man is on earth to be a transformer of energies from above to below and from below back to the source. Man is created to play a unique role in the "common cosmic" exchange of energies that is the life-blood of the created world.

But we are not yet Man—in the words of Kierkegaard, "Man is not yet a Self."

THE TWO TRUTHS THAT ARE ERRORS

But does this mean we are free to ignore the demands of the greater morality, the morality we were born into? If our first duty is to become beings capable of genuine moral action, does this mean we are free to discard the greater morality, the principles of which have been handed down to us from ancient times and which form the basis of human civilization? If, due to the low level of our being, the greater morality appears to us simply under the name of "conventional morality," are we free to discard it? Or to obey it only outwardly under the compulsions of social or legal pressure? To obey it without really respecting it and therefore being ready or at least susceptible to violating its canons under certain influences or conditions?

We need to take our time with this question. Have not most of us felt its weight at one time or another in our lives? Seeing the injustice and the moral hypocrisy of the human world, who among us has not become to one degree or another disillusioned with the established canons and rules of moral behavior? And having seen through the hypocrisy of the world, have we not sought our own moral life, perhaps simply by inwardly or outwardly defying the rules of society and by experimenting with a moral life of our own based, however awkwardly, on the undeniable principles of justice and love? Realizing that the rules are broken by those who seek to impose them, how could we not "see through" these rules?

Who has not been "young" in this way? But it is more, far more, than a common—and highly desirable—phase of youth. Consider Thoreau, Nietzsche, Dostoyevsky, Gandhi, Martin Luther King, Jr., Malcolm X— the holy dissidents who inform us and perhaps even sacrifice themselves for what we have seen when we were young and what we still see with our still young eyes in moments of clarity—the world does not, will not, obey the moral rules it prescribes.

Let us say that such seeing may not really know what it is seeing. It is seeing hypocrisy—yes; it is seeing crime masked by "legality"—yes. It is seeing life-deadening rigidity masking the forces of love or sexuality or compassion—yes. But what such seeing may not be seeing, even through the mind and eyes of its great leaders and artists, is the being of man as he is. What such seeing may not be seeing is the fact that in general and in essence, mankind, such as we are, *cannot* be moral. Cannot live by the rules it prescribes for itself and for the rest of the world. And the world cannot realize this!

What is being confronted here is the moral fantasy of mankind, the fantasy that covers the earth in the fog that cannot be penetrated from outside itself—the fog of moral self-deception. As those who seek to throw off the hypocrisy soon discover, the same hypocrisy begins to infect them as well. The morality gained by throwing off the old rules itself fails to be incarnated in the lives of its proponents. And new young eyes appear who see through this now conventional morality with its hypocrisy and its war and violence and moral impotence.

What is seen by these young eyes is truth, but it is only the surface of the truth. It is a truth that points to a deeper truth—that it is not willful evil, willful selfishness, that spawns the hypocrisy of the world. It is the low state of the being of man.

As Socrates tells us—in that sometimes maddeningly calm voice— "No man does evil intentionally." But if not intentionally, then how, what? Why?

It is the being of man. Morality is an attribute of genuine human beings.

And here at last we see the roots of the phenomenon—some call it a plague—of moral relativism, the view that morality is a human construction dependent solely on social conditions and subjective needs—of a community, race, ethnic group, historical period, or even an individual human set of genetic or psychological needs or habits. Here is the root of that anguished cry from one's young voice and in the young eyes of the thinking world—this cry of refutation and condemnation when someone claims that something is good or beautiful—the cry that says

"But you're making a value judgment!" It is the ultimate refutation! Who are *you* to make a value judgment?! It's all relative!—is it not? There are no moral absolutes—are there?

And here too are the roots of the modernistic, deconstructionist ethics and aesthetic theories of our time. In this view, values, moral principles are all social constructions. The moral, humanistic deconstructionist relativism of our time is itself the work of young eyes seeing the contradictions and hypocrisy of the world of fixed values, fixed canons of interpretation. Relativism is at root the moral impulse of a mind and heart that sees the hypocrisy of absolutism—but without deeply recognizing that it is the low state of the being of man and oneself that is being seen.

And often, all too often, one cannot bear this relativism. One may see in it the cause behind the decaying morality of the modern world—in the coarsening of human sexuality, human childhood, the evisceration of the family, the mockery of sacred tradition and timeless human customs, in the greedy and murderous engines of nations with their advancing technology and submission to the god of money. One may live with this relativism just long enough to see its influence conquering the peoples of the earth and, with a similar unripe moral impulse, call a halt to it, shout at it: Stop! Stop! You are tearing down all human and divine values! There *is* Truth! And I take my stand on that. *I know what that Truth is!* And it is this: *It is this:* I am right. You are wrong. Stop! Believe! Or I will turn you away. I may even kill you.

Thus is born modern fundamentalism—the inside-out twin of relativism.

Both relativism and fundamentalism in their tyrannical forms are born from an incipient moral impulse that sees the surface truth of man's moral confusion without recognizing the deeper truth that it is the *being* of man that is in question.

And so, on the surface of truth, both relativism and fundamentalism are right. But beneath the surface neither is right.

What is right about relativism, before it becomes tyrannically secular, is that it invites the work of deep listening to the Other in the crucible of true conversation and in the promise that the larger, encompassing Truth will descend like the dove of the spirit. What is false or misleading about relativism is its ignorance of the fact that no matter what truth is reached it cannot by itself take us across the Socratic threshold—because freely to live moral truth is not a matter of thought or desire or consensus; it is a matter of a level of being and energy that most of us do not yet have and which must be diligently cultivated according to the laws and principles of what we will call the "lesser morality" of inner self-growth.

What is right—not about fundamental*ism,* but about the striving for commitment to absolute, fundamental moral principles—is the belief that the source of morality is deeper and higher than our own all too human reasoning and judgments. What is false about fundamentalism is the assumption that this higher source, whether it is taken as inside or outside of ourselves, is accessible to us and is ours simply for the asking without the great inner struggle to become fully human selves.

A DANGEROUS QUESTION

It is in the dark silence in which I become the Other to myself that I glimpse the bridge that leads to the power of moral action. In that silence I can be offered the long work of struggling with this Other that is myself—to the end of becoming a man or woman capable of truly willing the essential principles of the greater morality. This is the work of growing into the fullness of a human being. And this now becomes my primary moral obligation, for without this work, without the growth of being, a man or woman in the modern world is—with rare radiant exceptions—something resembling an ethical automaton, who obeys moral principles through external or internal compulsion or habit, or only when it is not overly inconvenient, or when it is in one way or another personally profitable to do so. Such an individual can be made to perform any action whatever just by turning certain switches. And even when he is "doing the right thing," as often as not he does it with such rigidity as in the long run to cause more harm than good. Thus, speaking through the prophet Amos, God tells the people of Israel, "I hate your rituals and sacrificial offerings"—that is, external pious actions done without the heart's full assent. And thus also, Jesus tells his disciples that their righteousness should exceed the (external) righteousness of the scribes and Pharisees (Matthew 5:20).

My primary moral obligation is to become a human being capable of willing the good consciously and from my own free initiative. But in order genuinely to live according to the greater morality, I must now follow the principles of the lesser morality, the principles that govern the growth of being in man. *The root of all moral obligation is the obligation to become capable of morality.*

But the question before us remains: does this mean we are free to abandon the ethical principles and commandments of our culture, our given religion? If we do not have the being, say, of a genuine Christian, if we are ontologically incapable of living our lives according to the precepts of Christ or Moses, does this mean we are not under the obligation to respect these precepts and do everything we can to obey them—even if we cannot succeed? Does it mean that during the work of becoming a human being truly capable of moral action, the laws of the greater morality do not apply to us?

Once again, we need to proceed patiently with this question, which is in a deep sense extremely dangerous. So dangerous is it that the seminal teachers of the world's religions have often hidden it from view, reserving it only for those who have honorably begun the specific work of self-becoming. The twelfth-century spiritual philosopher Moses Maimonides, for example, one of the most profound and influential minds in the long history of Judaism, taught that only a man who has given and who can give his utmost to live in obedience to the literal ethical demands of the Torah may be allowed to enter the path of self-becoming, within which there exist ideas, interpretations and precepts that seem on the surface to be alien and even contradictory to the greater morality of scripture. Similar restrictions may be found, sometimes in wholly different language, in many of the religions and spiritual philosophies of the world—as, for example, in the teachings of Plato where, speaking to some extent symbolically, he warns that the study of philosophy (by which he means the practical training to become able to live according to the precepts governing the search for the state of being called wisdom) cannot begin before a man or woman reaches the age of thirty. In the Jewish mystical tradition, this age is "fixed" (again, in part symbolically) at forty.

The obvious danger in this question arises, as we have suggested, precisely from the honest and perhaps shattering perception of the moral hypocrisy of the world and the widespread existence of human evil—brutality, genocide, political murder, mass injustice and cruelty, blood-drenched conquest in the name of God or "love" or "peace" or "country." And from the honest and shattering perception of the influence through history of the herd morality, the influence of the mass mind, the unthinking, passive craving of mankind to be told what fantasies, religious or otherwise, to believe in and act upon, even to the point of genocide. Out of this perception, no matter how honest and "young" it is, may come the notion that I am "beyond good and evil," that I see and can know what is right and good simply from my own emotions and perceptions.

Seeing the moral hypocrisy of mankind and perhaps sensing the need to search for the work of self-becoming, a man or woman may easily abandon or regard with cynicism the sense of obligation to the greater morality. This may take place long before he or she is at all rooted in the greater Self which alone offers the power freely to act morally from within. It is only when an individual has placed himself under the direct influence of the Self that he or she may and has the right to violate the outer forms of the greater morality—and that because, under the influence of the Self, one has divined the genuine essence of the moral law lying underneath all its outer rules and customs.

We are obliged, then, to obey the moral law, the greater morality. At the same time, we are obliged to realize that our level of being renders it impossible for us to act morally in the deepest sense of the term—that is, inwardly, from within, to will the good *no matter what*. Yet we are also obliged to recognize that in the silence of darkness, when I see myself as I am, against the background of the greater moral law of love and justice—when I see that, really see it, feel it, sense it: in such a moment, the beginning of the Self appears within me. In the silence of grief, in the witnessing of man's demonic brutality, in the silence of seeing myself as the Other who is dragged down by forces of fear and ego and suggestibility—I, the Other, created to incarnate the Self on earth; I, the Other, lie, kill, ignore, justify myself, intellectualize the ideals I violate in my heart—in such a silence, in such seeing, something appears within me. It has no words, it both breaks one's heart and sounds a distant chord of future inner reconciliation—in such moments, fleeting moments of presence to the Essential in myself—in such moments of essence-sorrow—yes, I become for a moment a human being. I can act. I can love. I can be good.

But it lasts only a moment, only an instant! And suddenly, it is gone. The silence of Remembering the Self is gone.

Now the One Question is altogether real for us. Who am I? How should we live? What ought I to do?

We need to become beings capable of morality—yes. But in the meantime? Now? What will our life be like if we strive always and everywhere to obey the greater morality, knowing we are ontologically incapable of doing so deeply, from within ourselves?

This is the One Question that we can live, that we need to live. It is the One Question that has been handed down to man since the beginning of our civilization. It is this question that, with help from those who have gone before us, can take us across the Socratic threshold. In our conscious incapacity lies the seed of the life and the human goodness that we dream of and yearn for.

Thirteen

THE GREATEST IDEA
IN THE WORLD

HILLEL THE ELDER AND THE IDEA
OF THE UNIVERSAL MORAL LAW

O f the facts about his life, history has very little to tell us. But the legends about him, and the unique, centuries-long influence of his mind and spirit, call us seriously to ponder the importance for our era of the man known as Hillel the Elder. In this, our entire world is like the one-legged man of our story. We have not a moment to lose in our search for the fundamental root of moral truth and the fundamental path to moral being.

In his lucid and compact study of Hillel, which for many years was the only such study in the English language, the renowned scholar Nahum Glatzer opened a remarkable perspective on how, 2000 years ago in ancient Jerusalem, Hillel the Elder called the Jewish community of Jerusalem to "remember itself"—that is, to reestablish a relation to the inner, transcendent source of its ethical rules and principles.

According to Glatzer's speculation, Hillel's great gift was his ability to forge a bridge connecting two distinct levels of the religious life of his time: (1) the ideals and inner practice of the schools of self-becoming which he identifies as "Essene," and (2) the larger community of Jerusalem as a whole, existing as it did under the powerful hegemony and worldly influences of the Roman Empire. Or, to put it in our present language, what Hillel may have achieved was to open a conduit, as it were, between the rules and principles governing the search for spiritual self-becoming and the rules and principles governing man's behavioral obligations to his fellow man. Or, again, in yet other language, it was Hillel's gift to forge a bridge between man's obligation to become inwardly *capable of morality* and his obligation actually to *be* moral, actually to serve God in one's manifestations through works of love toward one's fellow man. *And that, that alone, in all its immensity and majesty, is "the greatest idea in the world"—the idea of the universal moral law that relates all of mankind to the service of God Above and Within.*

The significance of what Hillel may have attempted allows us, in any case, to take him as a symbol of that which is more than ever needed at this moment in history: that is, a remembering, from the depths of our being, of what we are and what we are meant to be: consciously individuated instruments of that which is—beyond all names and explanations—the source, shaper, and guardian of all that exists—the very same source that both demands and enables love and justice between human beings.

We are not writing history here. I am not a historian. We are taking Hillel as no more and no less than a symbol of what it would mean to discover an entirely forgotten source and justification of ethics, one that can eventually liberate us, if we will attend to it, from endless "proofs and arguments," from the winding labyrinths of cultural and subjective relativism, from heartless academicism, or from mindless dogmatism, in the realm of ethics.

With all due modesty and with an admittedly trembling hand, we are working for a re-mythologization of this man, about whom we know so little fact and so much meaning. And the point of this re-mythologization is to allow us to speak of what is needed today in the ethical devastation of our culture—namely, the deep remembering of the inner human qualities which are presupposed by our still existent moral doctrines and principles. What is needed is a remembering that includes the shock of realizing that for almost all of us these qualities are at present lacking in us. They are lacking, but they can be reinstated in us. That is, it is possible to become the men and women we now only imagine we are.

For this "re-instatement," however, help is needed from another level of being—another level of love. To provide such help has always been the task of the great teachers of mankind, around most of whom communities have at one time formed in which the work of existential awakening can take place. And, we are proposing, from these communities, variously named "schools," brotherhoods," "monasteries," "sangha," "tarikat," throughout the history of the world—from these communities a specific influence "from above" has time and again been introduced into the world throughout the entire course of human civilization, an influence that links the organization of man's common life to at least a fragment—but what a precious fragment!—of the knowledge of the path that leads to the work of becoming a fully human man or woman. And by this term, "a fully human man or woman," is meant an individual in whom the power of genuine, God-given conscience, faith and love becomes the active, causal force in all human relationships that come under the sphere deserving the name of ethics and morality. We are proposing, moreover, that even the merest call for a man or woman to come "inside" and examine oneself or genuinely struggle within oneself in the midst of action with another—even the merest beginning of such an impulse in its pure and not neurotic form is utterly essential to the moral life and does not come "naturally" or automatically. It must be carefully and wisely inserted into human life, and then nurtured according to at least a fragment—but what a precious fragment!—of great intelligence and love.

And since it was through Judaism, more than through any other single original impulse that we know of, that the idea of the universal moral law was first introduced into the Western world, an idea that flowed on the earth first like a downrushing stream and then like wide, branching rivers through the traditions of Christianity and Islam; since it was Judaism through which this idea was first introduced in the form that we know it—then what we have to say via our re-mythologized Hillel and his influence will apply to the entire problem of ethics in our world and in the personal lives of each and every one of us.

THE LIFE OF HILLEL

Hillel was born in Babylonia sometime before the middle of the first century of the pre-Christian era. As a young man in his twenties or thirties he left his native land and came to study in Jerusalem, the center of all Jewish learning. The date of his coming to Jerusalem is probably around the year 40 BC, some twenty years after all of Judaea had been conquered by the Roman army and had passed from being an independent state under the rule of the Hasmonean kings to being a minor Roman province that was soon to come under the immediate rule (37–4 BC) of the hated Herod the Great.

It was a time of great political, intellectual and religious ferment. The immense cultural influence and worldview of ancient Greece that had descended upon the Middle East with the conquering armies of Alexander the Great was now being displaced by the physically and politically overpowering influence of the Roman empire. The Judaism—or, more precisely, the Judaisms, for there were many kinds vying for supremacy—that the young Hillel encountered was fighting for its life, its spiritual identity, in a churning sea of power politics, militarism and priestly corruption.

"Hillel," writes Nahum Glatzer, "absorbed all that his contemporaries had to offer"—and what they were chiefly concerned with was applying the surface of the Torah to the practical problems and external details of everyday life. In this work, "differences of opinion were resolved by majority vote. No general principles were formulated for the interpretation of Torah." That is to say, there was little or no search for the inner, spiritual laws revealed in the Torah and little or no study of how these universal spiritual laws illuminate the details of the everyday human life of the community and the individual.

This state of affairs apparently left the still young Hillel hungering for something deeper. And at some point—the exact date is not known—he seems to have left Jerusalem.

[He] must have realized that, important as this emphasis on practical issues was, it could by no means exhaust all the possible implications of Torah. The numberless regulations based on the ancient law could keep religious life under [external] control, but they could not inspire its growth. . . . Even a system of ethics tends to become stale if its sources do not reveal ideal standards. A student concerned with formal exactness will turn out to be an impeccable, technically competent advisor, *but not a man of the spirit.*[33]

Many years now passed for which there exists no historical documentation of Hillel's movements. All that is known, according to Glatzer, is that in the year 30 BC, Hillel reappeared in Jerusalem, a changed man. The legends show us that he brought something entirely new to the problem of interpreting the Hebraic law as it relates to the conduct of life. And what he brought—what he manifested in both his words *and his actions*—was a unique blend of obedient faith and independent thought; a humble heart joined to a powerful, critical mind; a profound reverence for the traditional ways combined with a creative understanding of them unfettered by what was merely habit, rather than sacred principle. We may say that the "new" Hillel embodied a forgotten and ever-new un-

derstanding of human and divine love. He was for his peers a new kind
of teacher and was recognized as such by the elders, who, legend has it,
immediately stepped down and yielded place to this new Hillel and his,
for his time, entirely new vision of the essence of Torah as objective
love. Gave place to his vision of the essential ethical task of a human being: the individual and communal struggle consciously to separate from
the ego in order to be able to love. The ethical task: the work of becoming inwardly good as a paradoxically "simultaneous precondition" for
right action with respect to one's neighbor. He brought a vision of inner morality as a "simultaneous precondition" for outer morality.

Where and with whom did he study during these "missing years"?

> Hillel must have known that much of the inquiry into Torah took place
> outside the Jerusalem houses of study, in the brotherhoods and monastic
> associations where Jews lived in accordance with the ideals of the Early
> Hasidim.[34]

Here Dr. Glatzer is referring especially to the communities and
brotherhoods associated with the astonishing Dead Sea Scrolls discovered at Qumran in excavations made during the years 1947–1956. It is
suggested by some scholars that these were writings and texts of the Essene communities, though there is considerable controversy about this.
But almost all scholars agree that at that time spiritual and mystical Judaic communities of many kinds and names existed both in and around
Jerusalem. Was it in one of these communities that Hillel spent his
"missing years"? And if so, what did he learn there that changed him so
profoundly? And why might this piece of distant history be so deeply
relevant to the aching crisis of ethics in our time and in our lives?

Could it be that Hillel's life can help us accept and understand more
clearly why it is necessary to speak of two moralities and two corresponding forms of ethics—the ethics of the inner struggle, conducted under
special conditions within an intentional community, and the ethics of behavior in our everyday life—the ethics of attention and the ethics of

manifestation? And if this is so, if it is necessary to recognize what we are calling "the lesser morality" as distinct from "the greater morality," would it not become the most important thing in the world in some way and in some degree to create a genuine bridge, however slender, between the two distinct levels and qualities of morality? If there did exist knowledge and communal conditions within which a man or woman could work to become *capable of morality*, would it not be the most important task in the world to bring even a beginning of this knowledge and this power into the lives of all men and women in the world? Or at the very least to sound the call in language or form relevant and understandable to a particular era or culture? A language or form that could introduce a fragment of this knowledge—but what a precious fragment!—into the ethical crisis of the larger human world?

We are proposing that it is exactly in this way that Hillel's mission can be interpreted both for his time and, most importantly, for our time. This "mythologizing" of the figure of Hillel needs to awaken in ourselves, now and here, the knowledge of the first real step we need to take and can take in order to build a life on the far side of the Socratic threshold. What we will discover is an "inward movement" that brings an atom of genuine moral power into everyday human life, a power that has not in general been seen for what it is—namely, a possibility handed down from a higher level of mind and heart into our own habits of living. When we hear what this inward movement is, when it is expressed in words, we may at first be disappointed: haven't we known about this all along? But no, we may know the words, but we have lost access to the energy that these words once contained. And when we say that our "mythologized" Hillel brought this precious fragment of moral understanding into his world, we are not saying that he brought mere words, or mere concepts; or mere theology. We are saying that he brought the energy of being that primally infuses these words. We are saying that he brought that force into his world. And, as we may then speculate—joyously, I hope—that through him and through the source that he helped bring into the life of Judaism, this moral energy was transmitted through a long chain of other great teachers after him—including one whose words and actions spoke to the whole of the Western world.

WHAT DID HILLEL FIND?

But before we take this project further we need to consider the kind of inquiry we are facing when we begin to think about such intentional communities as existed in and around Jerusalem at the time of Hillel. Whether in this case we are referring to communities which we call "Essenes" or "People of the Covenant," or "Enochians"—or to which any number of names and designations may apply—we are confronted now with the difficult, but essential task of weighing the value and significance of such communities, brotherhoods, "secret societies," "esoteric schools," as have existed throughout the history of the world, probably in every culture and epoch.

If it is even slightly possible that Hillel's missing years were spent under the direct influence of such a school or community, and if the result was the re-formation of the Judaic tradition around a revolutionary understanding of what in Hebrew is termed *hesed,* or *divine* or *objective love for one's neighbor,* a force which is the supreme and fundamental source of all acts of ethics and morality in human life, then, it is critical that we come to some sound, intelligent way of estimating the nature of such an influence that could possibly have been carried by Hillel from a genuine esoteric school. The critical necessity for such an understanding is not only in order to become aware of what may have really happened in the past, but, of greatest importance, in order to understand what needs to happen, and even perhaps what is already trying to happen, in the present, now and here, in just this ethically devastated and mortally threatened contemporary civilization.

How, then, to regard these communities and what they have taught? What weight shall we give to academic scholarship—to archaeology, which discovers shards and remains, stones, inscriptions and ancient artifacts hidden for thousands of years? And which, as in the present case, discovers or takes possession of original writings and scriptures, such as the Dead Sea Scrolls and the writings known as the Nag Hammadi Library of Upper Egypt—texts that seem to present direct accounts and indications of the beliefs and practices of these ancient spiritual communities? What weight shall we give to the hard work of biblical scholars—historians, linguists, and others—whose disciplined efforts demand that they separate themselves from all considerations as to the truth or falsity of what they read? To what extent does such a demand enable them to approach objectivity and freedom from preconceived views as to the value of what they are investigating, and to what extent, on the other hand, might it be taken in such an absolutist way as to block the subtler sensitivity of feeling and intuition that such texts, when genuine, may be intended to reach in those who hear or read them?

When scholars or investigators of any kind read political motives into the evidence of these communities, and especially into the actions of their spiritual leaders, to what extent are they showing us that these teachers are driven by the same kind of purposes that drive the kings and princes of history? Or, on the other hand, to what extent does such speculation about the fundamentally political motives of these leaders act to blind us to the possibility that there have existed men and women throughout history whose motives are fundamentally higher and more inner than any we are familiar with, in ourselves or in the mass of men and women whom we do in fact observe throughout the course of history? That is, to what extent do such speculations blind us to the possibility and, shall we say, the fact that there have existed and can exist human beings who indeed are more spiritually developed than the rest of us? To what extent, finally, do such speculations breed cynicism about man and the spirit—bordering on the "unforgivable" sin of denying the possibility of higher forces acting in the world and in man?

What weight shall we give to the interpretations of theologians—Jewish, Christian or otherwise—learned thinkers who are men and women of faith and who see and evaluate the evidence of such communities and texts in the light of their own religious convictions and understanding? To what extent do such antecedent religious convictions help to fathom the depths of meaning that esoteric religious teachings may offer or to what extent, on the other hand, do they merely force all views and doctrines onto the Procrustean bed of *a priori* systems of thought and belief that are fundamentally incompatible with the essential message of such "unorthodox" spiritual teachings?

Comparable questions can be raised with respect to the interpretations offered by psychologists, historians, and cultural critics, as well as representatives of the growing fascination with and enthusiasm about "Gnosticism" in its many guises. Are they seeing anything different from what they are bringing to it from their own background and their own degree of experience of genuine human possibilities?

In any case, the evidence of intentional spiritual communities and brotherhoods that existed within Judaism around the time of Hillel has attracted the passionate attention of all the groups and scholarly disciplines mentioned above—and many more besides. Both the scrolls discovered in 1947 near the Dead Sea in Israel as well as the texts, comprising what is called the Nag Hammadi Library, discovered around the same time in Upper Egypt are like time machines taking us back to the very roots of what has come to be known as classical Judaism. That is, in considering the nature of these sectarian communities or schools, and considering the possibility that one or another of them may well have been a determining influence on the development of Hillel's own spiritual development, we may actually be looking through a new lens at the essence of Judaism itself—the Judaism that has decisively influenced the ethical perspective of the Western world.

We are now going to ask more specifically: what might Hillel have found in one or another of these intentional communities? What did he find that may have given him the vision to transform and draw together the scattered field of the *Judaisms* of his time? And, most importantly, is it possible to recover the essential nature of that vision now for our time—for our era of scattered, dissipating *moralities,* our culture ravaged by the forces of uncontrolled relativism and equally uncontrolled absolutism?

It is said of Hillel that he brought to Judaism two main elements: first, a powerful new way to study and understand the meaning of scripture, and second, a profound and revolutionary vision of love as the essential work of man and as the essential force simultaneously defining man's relationship to God and his relationship to his fellow man.

In a word, Hillel redefined the meaning of knowledge and the meaning of ethics.

Concerning Hillel's approach to scripture, Dr. Glatzer writes:

> Hillel introduced a new note into the house of study. We say introduced, not invented. We do find traces of this new type of learning in Judea before Hillel; we find a strong emphasis on, and a cultivation of, this learning in the sectarian movements of the time. *Through Hillel, it seems, this emphasis and culture were transplanted from the isolation of the sectarian associations into the schools of Jerusalem.*[35]

But it is the second element that we need to understand now, before anything else. It is to the inner, ethical meaning of the force of love that we must turn—respectfully, but also, as far as we are able, creatively—remembering that our sole concern is now, here, suffering ourselves as we are, in our present era's desperate yearning for goodness.

Fourteen

THE SEED AND THE FRUIT
OF ALL THAT IS GOOD

What, then, might Hillel have brought to his community, and thereafter to the world, from the intense life conditions of a school of self-perfecting? And how can it help us now? How can it help us to live what we know to be good?

The legends and tales about Hillel offer us the "answer." But it is only an answer in quotation marks—because the passage of time has shrouded his vision in a fog of superficial knowing. The answers are there, but in order to make use of them we have to prepare ourselves for entirely new meanings of words and stories whose significance may at first seem self-evident or merely paradoxical and fragmentary.

However, their meaning is never simply self-evident, we may be assured of that. And where they often seem merely paradoxical or fragmentary it may be because the call to a deeper state of ethical or spiritual sensitivity can be "sounded" only through a logic that brings the explaining mind to a "stop," pointing us to the lessons of silence.

And, as we have seen, it is in conscious silence that the search for moral power begins, or, finally, in which such power is given, if only, at first, for a moment. And it is necessary to remember that a spiritual master uses words, even when they are transmitted over thousands of years, not mainly to impart theory and information, but to assist the arising of a state of being in which human egoism can witness and be witnessed by something within a man that is greater than itself.

ANOTHER DIMENSION OF LOVE

In all that we are about to say, we are assuming the spiritual authenticity of the community or brotherhood that helped shape Hillel's vision of the essence of the universal moral law. This is an essential point that requires clarification. Without confronting this question we cannot go further.

We are assuming that the brotherhood that helped Hillel was not an "imitation esoteric school" or a "pseudo-mystical" sect or a militant political faction disguised as a spiritual, religious community. We are assuming that the guides who led this community were not absorbed by religious fantasies and were not motivated mainly by the desire for power, wealth, or sex. That is, we are assuming that the leaders or guides in this community were individuals who were themselves advanced along the path of self-perfection and awakening—as a result, let us assume, of their own discipleship under a more nearly fully realized master.

And to put the question this way is already to encounter our first clue concerning the criteria for judging the authenticity of this or any other intentional spiritual community. Unless we have some notion of the possibility of human transformation, there can never be any understanding of the kind of influence brought to mankind by great religious communities, monasteries, brotherhoods and schools. And in order to know what is possible for man in general, it is necessary to have experienced in oneself a taste—even if only a taste—of a higher state of being. And not only to experience it, but to understand what such a taste implies concerning human nature and its possible transformation. Without such a glimpse and an accompanying understanding, however preliminary, of its significance, it is not possible to grasp what a genuine spiritual school offers man. And as a result, one is bound to interpret the actions of a great religious teacher and his or her community only in terms of familiar, ego-stained motivations. Or, one is bound to interpret such actions only in terms of the moral self-illusions that have plagued mankind throughout the ages.

Or, finally, without any real understanding of what is possible for man and how far we are from actualizing this possibility—without the personal taste and theoretical grasp of the inner state of being that, so to say, by itself *enables* and flows into genuine moral action; and without the accompanying understanding of the fragility of this state of being and the desperately weak state of being that characterizes our habitual life— without this dual understanding of our possible divinity and our actual alienation from that divinity—without this, the interpretation of a great reformer's teachings and actions is bound to miss the mark. The most common error in this regard is to identify the reformer's vision with qualities or ideas that are so well known to us and so over-familiar as to make us either wonder that such a "great vision" could have had such transforming influence in the world, or, on the other hand, to evoke in us the false belief that the greatness of his vision is completely under- standable and attainable by anyone of us simply by wishing for it— almost in our spare time.

To be more specific, many scholars and commentators agree that central to the vision of Hillel, central to the vision that was the seedbed of what has been called "classical Judaism," was the message of love— the very same message, the very commandment given to our one-legged man: "That which is hateful to yourself do not do to your neighbor." This formulation lives on as Hillel's unique expression of the words of the Torah: "Thou shalt love thy neighbor as thyself" (Leviticus 19:18).

The aspect of love that is often associated with Hillel is expressed by the Hebrew *hesed*. This is usually translated as "loving-kindness" or "mercy" toward one's fellow man. On the surface of it, this seems perfectly understandable and attainable. Has not almost every great teaching, whether religiously inspired or not, preached love of mankind, love of one's fellow man? And do we not, most of us, in our best moments agree with this as an ideal? Don't we often—not often enough, we would humbly admit—even try to put this into practice?—maybe not with the person here in front of me at the moment who is offending me or failing to give me my due or who maybe smells bad or who has insulted my country—maybe not in such moments, but at almost all other times when I think of it as an ideal worthy of guiding my life? Of course, we should manifest loving-kindness toward our neighbor! Isn't it obvious?

And aren't the sayings of Hillel and the stories about him no more nor less than simple or fragmentary or "intriguingly paradoxical" illustrations of this ideal that we all agree with? But wait. It simply goes against common sense to assume that the deeper meaning of such words as "love," or "loving-kindness," as taught and exemplified by a Hillel, can be fully equated with what such words denote in our everyday experience. Masters of mankind's most noble teachings could not have struggled with forces and sufferings beyond our comprehension—even to the point, sometimes, of undergoing torture and death—only in order to tell us to be "nice." Nor could they have undergone their great struggles in order to give us the illusion that we are able everywhere and with everyone to put the good of our neighbor before our own; that we are able at will to free ourselves from reactions of anger and from the kind of psychological fear that causes us to feel hatred, nor from the passivity of a Mr. Prozi that shuts down the action within ourselves of all inborn moral impulses and sensitivities.

No, the work of love that Hillel brought needs to be seen as something like a nearly submerged mountain, only the tip of which is the little island of the experiences and purposes we ordinarily associate with this word.

Take, for example, Hillel's teaching about "the common man and the poor."[36] In the stories about him, Hillel appears to embody the fundamental ethical ideal—common to nearly every world religion and culture—of man's obligation to give aid to the poor, the weak and the oppressed—to pity them and care for their needs and to treat them justly. It is a demand sounded throughout the scriptures from Deuteronomy ("nor shut thine hand from thy poor brother") to Job ("He delivereth the poor in his affliction") and Psalms ("forget not the congregation of thy poor") and beyond. Few things are more common in the religious texts of Judaism.

At the same time, however, in the accounts of Hillel's teaching and his personal actions, this ideal is presented as a sign of his great spiritual power—and even as something almost revolutionary! Why? To understand this we will have to look at the sayings and stories associated with Hillel which do not on the surface seem to relate to the notion of loving-kindness, but which, beneath their surface meaning, reveal facets of the profundity of the meaning of love in the actions of the great teachers—in a Socrates or a Hillel or, shall we say, in a Gautama Buddha and, finally and inevitably, in the actions and teachings attributed to Jesus.[37]

No idea exists alone. Every great idea exists within a living network of other ideas, and if we tear one idea away from its context—no matter how noble that idea may seem all by itself—it will wither and die—or, what is worse, its decaying and once life-giving energy will blend with the rigid or haphazard, ego-driven concepts of our ordinary mind and, instead of bringing light to mankind will inevitably bring darkness masquerading as light.

The network of ideas in which is embedded Hillel's teaching about love takes the form of aphorisms attributed to him, and stories both about him and about the school of thought which took his name and which became an enduring influence over the centuries. Let us take just one of these aphorisms in order to glimpse the depths of the teaching about love that lies at the root of the great idea of the universal moral law—and in order to take hold, finally, of the key to crossing the Socratic threshold in our lives—the key to living *what is good*.

Our source is the section of the Talmud known as "The Sayings of the Fathers" (*Pirke Avot*).

We will focus on the most famous of all the sayings attributed to Hillel:

> If I am not for myself, who will be for me?
> And if I am for myself alone, what am I?
> And if not now, when?[38]

Our first *moral* responsibility is to myself! We need to let the shock of this statement rest with us for a moment.

IF I AM NOT FOR MYSELF, WHO WILL BE FOR ME?

What does this mean? In fact, it can come to us as an echo of the fundamental lesson of Socrates: a man's first essential obligation is to care for his own inner Self, his own soul. As we have already observed, to be *for myself* is to recognize that I am born with an exalted inner possibility that can be actualized only, so to say, with my own "active permission"—that is, with my own intentional struggle with what the Hebraic tradition calls the *yetzer ha-ra,* the "inclination toward evil," the *desire to not seek the Self,* the inclination away from trust in God. But this intentional struggle is not a struggle to destroy something essential in oneself. It is not the commonly understood effort to destroy physical or psychological desires. Rather, the aim of this intentional struggle is to make it possible for all the fundamental energies within a human being to take their "God-given" place and serve a sacred intention the actualization of which is the fundamental purpose of human life. It is only when lesser forces within a man or woman are passively allowed to usurp the role of authority within the whole of oneself that they are dangerous. But it is not the forces themselves that are dangerous, it is the inclination to allow their inner usurpation that is dangerous. It is this inclination within oneself against which man must struggle.

On this point, around this distinction between, on the one hand, human desires as such and, on the other hand, these same desires when they are unconsciously allowed to usurp the role of the ruler of the psyche—around this distinction revolves the basic challenge of our day-to-day life. In the Judaic tradition, a man or woman is obliged to give wholehearted attention to the duties and rewards of the physical and societal life of man: marriage, affection, family, health, livelihood. The desires and instincts of human nature function as the instruments of these duties and rewards. Our innate desires and fears are thus a normal part of our human nature. Our work with respect to these desires and instincts is to have them, but not to be had by them. This means to give these desires and instincts the direction and attention that is necessary, but not to feed them with more psychic energy than is necessary. When allowed to take all of our attention, these impulses become bestial—that is, destructive of their truly human purpose, which is to be part of the great task of man to live in the created world among one's fellow human beings as an instrument of higher purposes. And the chief purpose of human life is to be an instrument and embodiment of God's love for man. These desires and instincts are meant to serve the divine within a human being—that is, they are meant to be material instruments of love and justice, these two qualities being the chief attributes of God's action in the created world.

In other words—using purely nonreligious language—our duty is to become capable of morality, capable of loving man and acting justly. And this capability is possible only through the capacity, the energy, latent within every human being, that masters the inner impulses of desire and instinct. To love man, it is necessary to open oneself to the conscious force that can genuinely direct the impulses of desire and instinct. It is man's first duty, therefore, to work toward opening himself or herself to this inner consciousness which can make of us an instrument of moral action, an instrument, ultimately, of love and justice. As we are, we are not open to this consciousness—or conscience, in its proper meaning. Thus, our first duty is to be *for myself,* my first duty is to my *Self.*

In order to carry out this inner duty toward *myself* a specific attitude or orientation toward one's own impulses and functions is necessary. These ordinary functions, these desires, impulses, powers of thought, forces of attraction and repulsion, constellations of ambition, creativity, loyalty, even anger, doubt, fear—in short all that in their ungoverned condition make up what we call the ego, rooted as it is in the "inclination toward evil" (or *yetzer ha-ra*) in man, must be brought to come into direct relationship with the movement toward the higher Self, the movement called the "good inclination or formation" (*yetzer tov*) in man.

This aspect of the struggle to become inwardly capable of morality has in the history of religion and spiritual philosophy often been conducted in the spirit of punitive hostility toward human desire. The desires, cravings, ambitions, spiritual errors, impulses of possessiveness are regarded as evil in themselves. The physical body is despised.

Many of the great spiritual reformers, those who function in history as the *re-establishers* of an entire tradition, overturn this attitude of, as it were, resentment toward the body and its concomitant functions of emotion and associative thought. Instead of inner hostility toward the functions—which at best often results only in a "grudging," superficial and unstable level of submission to the doctrines surrounding the concept of the Higher Self—these great spiritual reformers introduce the cultivation of love and justice not only outwardly, but principally inwardly. That is, they bring the teaching of interiorized love—a love simultaneously toward God and *toward one's own human nature.* Thus a reformer such as Hillel may be understood as teaching inner love considered as a necessary precondition for outer love; inner justice as a necessary precondition for outer justice. That is to say, only to the extent that an individual is capable of love towards one's own human nature is one *entirely* capable of loving others; only to the extent that an indvidual is capable of acting justly toward one's own various functions is one entirely capable of acting justly toward one's fellow man.

But in order to be capable of morality—in order to be entirely capable of moral action toward one's fellow man—it is necessary that these functions of the body, heart and mind *willingly* obey the impulse of love that originates in the Self. Ultimately, genuine morality, genuine ethics, originates in the establishment of an overflowing relationship of mutual love and assent between the inner Self and the forces of desire, thought, and instinct, a state of affairs that expresses itself in right action, right feeling, right speech (and thought) through these self-same instruments or functions of body, heart and mind.

In this light, we can permit ourselves an inner reading of the beautiful and mysterious words of the Twenty-third Psalm:

> Thou preparest a table before me in the presence of mine enemies:
> Thou anointest my head with oil; my cup runneth over.

These "enemies" are inner, not outer. And the Lord (within and above) pours down upon man the overflowing ever-reconciling force of love.

And, further, this state of being is given as man is led in silence "beside the still waters."

Once one is made aware of this meaning of love in the spiritual teachings of the world, one sees it almost everywhere. It becomes a classic example of "a mystery in broad daylight"—deeply hidden, but exuberantly visible once the corner of the veil is lifted. To cite only one from among countless possible examples, here are the words of the great fourteenth-century German mystic, Meister Eckhart. He is speaking at one and the same time of the birth of Christ and the birth of the Self within an individual man or woman:

> When this birth really happens, no creature [inner or outer] in all the world will stand in your way. . . . Take the analogy of a thunderbolt. When it strikes . . . whether it is a tree or an animal or a person, at the coming of the blow, they all turn toward it and if a person's back were turned, he would instantly turn to face it. All the thousands of leaves of

a tree at once turn the required sides to the stroke. And so it is with all who experience this birth. . . . Indeed, what was formerly a hindrance becomes now a help . . .

Still you might ask: "While in this state, should one do penances?"[39]

To this question, Meister Eckhart answers:

The whole of a life of penitence is only one among a number of things such as fasting, watching, praying, kneeling, being disciplined, wearing hair shirts, lying on hard surfaces, and so on. . . . Penances are put upon the flesh, like a bridle, to curb it, so that the spirit may control it. This is done to bring [the flesh] to subjection, but if you wish to make it a thousand times more subject, put the bridle of love on it. With love you may overcome it most quickly and load it most heavily . . . I speak of love: he who is caught by it is held by the strongest of bonds and yet the stress is pleasant. He who takes this sweet burden on himself gets further, and comes nearer to what he aims at than he would by means of any harsh obedience ever devised by man.[40]

And coming to the end of his thought, Meister Eckhart expresses the most revolutionary ethical idea in the world, one to which we will now have to give our best attention:

The most trivial deed or function in such a person [who has brought love into himself] is more profitable and fruitful to himself and all men, and pleases God better, than all other human practices put together, which, though done without deadly sin, are characterized by a minimum of [interior] love.[41]

AND IF I AM FOR MYSELF ALONE, WHAT AM I?

And now there blazes forth the astonishing ethical implications of this work of interior love: *If I do not care for my neighbor, what am I?* However much I may cultivate my inner life, if I do not love my neighbor and act justly toward him, I myself cease to be human.

Putting the matter in this way, it may seem hardly more than an ethical cliché. Of course, one might say, we must always turn our attention to our neighbor. Of course, we must act justly toward our fellow man. Yes, of course—but the fact is *we do not do it*. Or, rather, with very rare exceptions, we succeed in acting ethically only up to a point and only when we are not overmastered by impulses of fear, ignorance, egoistic cravings, forgetfulness, distracted attention, self-justification—and the thousand factors of our human nature and in the world around us that keep us imprisoned on the near side of the Socratic threshold—factors and influences which are almost always unconsciously mixed in and operative in what seem to us and to the world as purely selfless actions.

St. Paul now cries out: *The good that I would that I do not; but the evil which I would not, that I do.* And he goes on—as all honorable and truth-loving men and women throughout history inwardly have cried out when confronted with this inescapable perception of the human condition— *O wretched man that I am! Who shall deliver me from the body of this death?*

Who or what can rescue us from what St. Paul calls "the body of this death"? At this point Paul evokes the name of Jesus Christ, which we can now understand to mean, among other things, the inwardly acting supreme reality that the Psalmist evokes, the silent energy of the Buddhist Void—that is no one thing, but the seed of Being of all beings; the Hindu *Atman*—the Absolute that dwells in the quiet inner heart of man. The names of this force of downward-descending love are numberless throughout all the epochs, cultures, and spiritualities of human history.

It is the force of this love descending within a human being that alone can allow in us the individuated and exquisitely attuned outer manifestation of pure ethical action.

THE HIDDEN BRIDGE:
AN ESSENTIAL DIGRESSION

Nowhere is this revolutionary ethical vision expressed more clearly than in another medieval Christian document.

Known as *The Cloud of Unknowing*, it was originally written by an anonymous teacher in the fourteenth century, and presents itself as letters of guidance directed to an individual who is just entering the path of inner, contemplative practice. Among the most striking aspects of this great book is the warning sounded on the very first page, admonishing the reader that it must be read and studied only by an individual who is both committed to the inner practice and who is also *outwardly ethical in accordance with the normal standards of moral conduct.* This latter requirement is an essential clue to what we are searching for in our study. We are searching for the secret of crossing the Socratic threshold, the secret of what it means actually to live according to what we know to be good. This warning by the anonymous author of *The Cloud of Unknowing* may be taken as telling us that what we are searching for must take place *within the outer form of "normal morality."* What it is telling us is that the work of becoming inwardly capable of morality is a private, "hidden" action undertaken by an inner struggle within the body of our common, humanly weak, but honorably intended efforts always and everywhere to do what is good and act justly toward our fellow man.

What it is telling us is that genuine moral power is given to us through an inner change of heart, an inner change of mind, that needs to take place within the "body," as it were, of the common morality of our culture. Genuine moral power is given to man only *within* the crippled body of our "good intentions." We are told to obey the law outwardly (which we cannot do in our inner essence), while engaging in an unknown higher, secret struggle within our individual mind and heart.

We must understand very clearly the nature of that hidden, secret struggle. Possibly it is, for us, in our time and place, the one great practical secret that can lead us to becoming capable of morality, that can lead us to becoming capable of actually living what we know to be good. It is a certain attitude, a certain inner movement—small, subtle, invisible—yet within it radiates the whole of our possibilities to become, if one may so put it, both truly man and "truly divine." But we may put it even more dramatically by saying that it is a secret inner gesture that no ordinary man or woman can discover by oneself. It must be discovered and brought by an awakened individual, who transmits it to his or her community in the most generous manner, a manner precisely calibrated to the subjectivity and capabilities of the community. This is the hidden bridge. This, we shall see, is how we may interpret what Hillel brought.

For now, we will not even give this inner movement a name. We will return to it later.

THE SEED AND THE FRUIT
OF INNER MORALITY

We need now to return from our "essential digression" and try to grasp more fully the revolutionary ethical doctrine of the primacy of interiorized love, or what we may call *inner morality.*

Here is how it is characterized in *The Cloud of Unknowing.*

The author has been speaking of the difference between what he calls the active life and the contemplative life. The active life is the life of altruistic and ethical practices as we normally understand them, the task of "right action" in the world and among the people around us. The contemplative life, for its part, is the practice of inwardly striving with intense concentration of the mind, heart and body, toward union with God. It is the deeply interiorized understanding of the First Commandment as articulated in Deuteronomy 6: *And thou shalt love the Lord thy God with all thine heart, and with all thy soul, and with all thy might.* And repeated by Jesus in response to a question put to him in the early rabbinic community.

> Master, which is the great commandment in the law [the Torah]?
>
> Jesus said unto him, Thou shalt love the Lord thy God with all thy heart, and with all thy soul, and with all thy mind.
>
> This is the first and great commandment.

But here Jesus adds to it—as, we may now be sure, did Hillel:

> And the second [commandment] is like unto it, Thou shalt love thy neighbor as thyself.
>
> On these two commandments hang all the law and the prophets.[42]

Now we must follow closely: the author of *The Cloud of Unknowing* is defining the contemplative life as the cultivation of the inner state of obedience to the commandment of Deuteronomy 6 and the First Commandment of Jesus: the commandment to love God with all one's being, with all one's mind, heart and will—to separate oneself from all thoughts, however ethical, insightful or noble; from all feelings, however loving, compassionate or pious; and from all physical desires, however normal and healthy. It is this separation from all the natural functions and purposes of the human mind and heart that the author calls a "cloud of forgetting," a "cloud of unknowing," which a man or woman must enter, carrying with him only the bare, naked intent to love God and allow into oneself the force called God's love for man, for oneself—from within oneself.

Here is a key passage. The author begins by discussing various levels of the active and contemplative life, showing that as it develops, the active life—the life of good works—all by itself turns a man or woman also inward to a new and spiritualized attention to his own mind and emotions. The author then, in a few brief words, summarizes the revolutionary ethical effects of interiorized love:

The work of love not only heals the roots of sin, but nurtures practical goodness. When it is authentic you will be sensitive to every need and respond with a generosity unspoiled by selfish intent. Anything you attempt to do without this love will certainly be imperfect, for it is sure to be marred by ulterior motives.[43]

In this brief statement, the author of *The Cloud of Unknowing* has completed the powerful thought of Eckhart cited above. The effect of the action of love within oneself is not only to call forth spontaneous obedience of all the functions and impulses of the human psyche, but to so sensitize them that one sees clearly and feels objectively the needs of one's fellow man and is able to allow the precisely attuned moral action that is needed on his behalf and for his needs and for his good. In sum, to love oneself—that is, to open to the love of and by God for and within oneself—is inevitably to love one's neighbor.

And to be able to love one's neighbor is to be capable of morality.

And to be capable of morality is to be able to be good.

IF NOT NOW, WHEN?

But with this last element of Hillel's famous aphorism another mystery in broad daylight is thrown across our path.

Is anything more seemingly obvious than that we must apply our ethical and spiritual ideals now, and here, and not self-deceptively wait for some future time which we imagine would be more favorable to us? But it is not so obvious what this actually means.

In fact, we are here brought face to face with the "essential digression," the hidden bridge that completes the arc between what we are and what we ought to be.

The point is that the great word "now" means *what is.* It calls us to confront ourselves as we are now, in this moment, here, in this ignorant body, with these honorable, but failing intentions, this "crowd" known as ego.

The word "now" is the moment, the act in between good and evil, in between the two forces in man. It is the missing element—intentionally missing—in the portrayal of good and evil, angels and demons, in much of the sacred art and literature of the world. It is the essential human action that is left out of almost all depictions of the moral struggle, because it cannot be depicted, it must not be depicted. It does not and cannot exist on a page or in stone or in an external image. It is the reconciling act on the part of the spectator, the reader, the human man called to turn his attention now in this moment upon himself as he is, a cosmically unique being called to give his conscious attention to both the good and the evil tendencies in himself—now in this moment.

The teacher makes room for the pupil to exist consciously in between the two natures of man. Similarly, the great sacred literature and art of the world, at its level, creates palaces and worlds of room for the individual person, the spectator in his flesh and blood moment of now, to become aware of the mysterious co-presence of two opposing forces in the world and in himself. Sacred art, like sacred life, is the mysterious blending of these two elements of cosmic reality, a blending that cannot be conceptualized or analyzed by the ordinary mind. It is the "navel" in all sacred stories and myths and above all, in all sacred action of spiritually developed men and women.

The teacher, rising out of the intentional community of—let us call it "hidden Judaism" or "practical Judaic mysticism" or a "Judaic school of awakening"—makes room for the pupil, for the human individual to choose the uniquely human work of calling forth the uniquely human power of conscious attention that is able to be sensitive to both the *yetzer tov* and the *yetzer ha-ra,* the good inclination and the inclination toward evil within himself. Only through this simultaneous awareness of the good inclination and the inclination toward evil in oneself does the conscious impulse toward moral action, that is, action rooted in nonegoistic love, arise in man and pass into the world, the human community, the life of the Other before me.

The teacher makes room for the arising of free choice rooted in love.

The priest, let us call him for now—that is to say, the religious official who is not a teacher, but an admonisher—the priest compels and persuades, he does not "make room." The priest, who is not the teacher, compels or persuades the external action, perhaps even accompanied by the thoughts and emotional tones that can cause the ethically correct action. But the priest does not and cannot and perhaps should not try to "make room" for the conscious choice rooted in conscious attention. To make room in the pupil, in ourselves, is the function of the teacher, the guide.

As it may be said, the priest walks ahead, clearing the way for the follower. The guide, on the other hand, walks behind the pupil, "making room" for the pupil to discover the inner source of his own conscious, ethical initiative of love.

The man, perhaps, follows the priest, or perhaps he does not. Perhaps he stumbles and falls, perhaps he acts externally, but inwardly he is hard and frozen or full of distraction and resentments or sentimental fantasies. Perhaps he does the right thing in the wrong way or at the wrong moment or to the wrong person. Perhaps he obeys all the rules while violating the principal laws. What then? Is he ethical, is he moral? Is he legally correct, but ethically guilty? To the priest it does not matter. To the guide this consideration is everything. One cannot love by obeying rules like a robot, an ethical robot.

But the guide knows that even an ethical robot, if he is also a man, can become aware that he is violating his and his neighbor's humanity by acting like an ethical robot. And knowing that, he is no longer a robot; he is becoming a man in the full sense of the word, a human being seeing his or her own inner—and therefore also outer—failure to love, to care, to wish to treat my neighbor justly.

But now we must call things by their proper names. To act now is to see and feel myself as I am now, unable inwardly—and therefore ultimately outwardly as well—to will the good for my neighbor, unable to be ethical even while I am acting "ethically." The sacred moment of now is the moment of remorse of conscience. It is the transforming moment of our human life. It is the arc of electricity that again and again delivers one across the Socratic threshold. It is this *again and again,* this now and now and now of remorse of conscience that defines the human being who is good.

To speak of permanently crossing the Socratic threshold, of "living" on the other side, is therefore only a symbol. The "permanent" is a symbol of the now and the now and the now, the again and again and again. Man is such, his glory and his trial are such that on this earth, in this life, he cannot be permanently good. Or, rather, he can be permanently good only through now and now and now choosing to confront himself and allow in the reconciling force of remorse of conscience, which in its turn allows in the energy of divine love for oneself and one's neighbor simultaneously. "Love thy neighbor as thyself" expresses, then, the essence of the *result* of the inner ethical act.

This mystery of now and now, represented by the apparently obvious words of Hillel, "If not now, when?" is powerfully illustrated by a story from the Islamic tradition, a story which itself expresses a "mystery in broad daylight," and which is only superficially understandable as a portrayal of divine love taken as an external act directed upon man from a source outside oneself. Here is the story:

It is told that once there was a certain man, a wealthy merchant of Isfahan, who lived his life purely for material and personal gain. Again and again his friends implored him to lift his eyes to God. But the merchant brushed aside the words of those whose concern was the salvation of his soul. "I see what I see and I do what I do," he said. "And that is my honesty."

The arguments of the friends were to no avail. The words they recited to him from holy books and the discourses of saints and sages were turned around by the clever arguments of the merchant. "I see what I see and I do what I do," he said. "And that is my honesty."

Time passed. The merchant lived through the vicissitudes of human life—joy and sorrow, gain and loss. At each great blow from life—a child's death, an issue at law, a betrayal of trust, a failed enterprise—the friends came to him one after the other and all together to remind him of the consolation and judgment of the Eternal and the future life. In vain.

And at his triumphs and exaltations—a beautiful son, money, civic honor, the recovery of health (his own and his wife's)—they also came to remind him of the consolation and judgment of the Eternal and the future life. But here again he would turn away from their concerns, saying "I see what I see and I do what I do. And that is my honesty."

But if he cared nothing for the Lord of Heaven, the merchant could not turn away from death, the Lord of the Earth. As the merchant lay dying, his friends came to him one by one and all together. "It is not too late," they said, imploringly. "It is not too late to lift your eyes to God."

"I will die as I have lived," he whispered, defiantly. "I have seen what I have seen and I have done what I have done. And that has been my honesty." His eyes burned with dark fire as he closed them for the last time.

And now the soul of the merchant descends—down, down, down—down to the deepest hell from which there can be no escape for all eternity. The gates of this hell are immense. Slowly they open and slowly they close. And once they close there is nothing in all the worlds that can open them.

The soul of the merchant passes through the great open gate. Slowly, slowly, in perfect silence, the gates are closing after him.

And just at the very moment, the very instant the immense doors touch each other, the merchant lifts his eyes upward.

In that very instant a hand appears under the soul of the merchant and carries him to heaven.

This is a tale about the real meaning of *now*. It is a story about remorse, which is the bridge, the closing of the arch that enables a human being to cross the Socratic threshold, to become a human being who is capable of morality.

.　.　.

We are approaching the end of our inquiry. But no end is really an end unless it is also a beginning. How to understand this new beginning of a human life in the full sense of the word, "human"?

What must end within ourselves and, within that ending, what must begin, what must be born, if we are to become actually capable of morality, now?

The answer lies in another of Hillel's sayings, which will lead us to an entirely new understanding of the meaning of the universal moral law brought to our world by the great Abrahamic traditions and the saints and sages who have continually sought to revolutionize it inwardly. We have all lived our lives within the shadow of the idea of the universal moral law, we have all been shaped by it, our identities have been formed by it—whether we have tried to obey it or resist it. It is the law of our world, our culture, our daily life in all its aspects. And nothing is more urgent than the need to allow it to awaken us to a new life, in which the ideals of what is good are green again, in which the seed that is this idea takes root in our world and grows and breathes in us without pretense or deadly oppression. The idea of the moral law needs to grow and yield good fruit. For, as St. Paul also said, the earth groans in travail because of man.

Once again, Hillel, who is for us no more and no less than a representative of the interiorization of morality. Who is no more and no less than a representation of the countless saints and sages of all traditions who have offered a path leading to the transformation of man.

Only a representative! But what an immensity it is to meet an authentic representative of truth! It is like meeting a being who is only one angel among the countless millions that are said to crowd the endless firmaments of heaven.

Only one angel!

Fifteen

THE METAPHYSICS
OF MORALITY

My humiliation is my exaltation;
my exaltation is my humiliation.[44]

HILLEL

When I consider thy heavens, the work of thy fingers,
the moon and the stars, which thou hast ordained:
What is man, that thou art mindful of him? And the son
of man that thou visitest him?
For thou hast made him a little lower than the angels,
and hast crowned him with glory and honor.
Thou madest him to have dominion over the works of thy hands:
thou hast put all things under his feet.

PSALM 8:3–6

When the blessed Holy One desired—when it arose in His will—to create
the world, He gazed into Torah and created it. For every act of creation . . .
the blessed Holy One gazed into Torah and created . . . As He was about to
create Adam [Man], Torah exclaimed: 'If a human being is created and then
proceeds to sin, and You punish him—why should the Work of Your hands
be in vain, since he will be unable to endure Your judgment? He (YHVH)
replied, 'I have already prepared *teshuvah*, returning [remorse of conscience],
before creating the world.'[45]

gain we ask: where do we find ourselves?—not so much in our present groping inquiry, but in our life as man, in our being. Can we now situate the question of ethics in its truest setting? Can we try to glimpse the immense scale and difficulty of what we are trying to understand and what we are yearning for under the somewhat prosaic word, ethics; or under the seemingly intractable question, "Why can't we be good?"

The point is that we are speaking about nothing less than the whole sweep and drift of human life on earth—our life in relation to the greatness of surrounding nature—our planetary home under the "moon and the stars." We are speaking also of humanity as the inheritor of human civilization into which there flow—from the heights and expanses of countless peoples and nations, most long since dissolved in the passage of time—the creations of science, art, religion, economy, language and law, as well as the destructions of war, cruelty, perversity, barbarism, and the distortion of the work of the noblest of men and women through the ages. We are speaking as well of humanity's metaphysical essence and our predestined place in a living universe of inconceivable interlocking purposes and designs. We are speaking of philosophical man, who seeks to understand reality as such, and also of technological man who seeks to make nature serve every kind of human need and desire; of religious man, who seeks to obey God, and also of psychological man, the victim and the agent of subjective conditions of social class, race, childhood and the dramas of the bloodline. We are speaking of political man, legal man—with his man-made rights and duties, his man-made powers and honors, his man-made concepts of good and evil, reward and punishment, man-made glory—who seeks to organize and administer the infinitely complex outer life of human society, delicately poised, as of necessity it always is, on the narrow ridge dividing justice and injustice, hope and resentment, obedience and rebellion. And we are speaking of biological man, carrying within ourselves a human body awesome both in its microcosmic complexity and hierarchical order and in its fragility and brevity of life: the human biological body subject to merciless time and yet host to an indestructible eternal essential consciousness living and breathing within us and calling to us in chords too fine for us to hear, too beautiful for us to bear, closer to us than our "jugular vein," yet tragically remote from our coarse ego and our delusional fears and impulses.

All of this is man; yet it does not answer the psalmist's cry: "What is man that Thou art mindful of him?" On this side of the Socratic threshold, do we really behold *Man*? We may see wonders and marvels—art, science, religion, philosophy, soaring monuments, exquisite structures, cities, glories of form and color; we may hear angelic sounds and thrilling voices—but are these the sights and sounds of *Man*? Alongside these sights and sounds, what of a hundred million screams of slaughtered men, women and children, the insane noise of war; what of human hatred, fear and greed blinding and burning and enveloping the earth like the atmosphere of the lowest hell? Is this not also man? Doesn't the whole of the individual and collective history of the human race tell us that *what we have interpreted as man is not really man at all*? It is only parts of man that we see—glorious, inspiring parts that create wonders; and coarse, ugly parts of man that spawn monstrosities.

Should we not say instead that man as a species has not yet appeared on the earth? Obviously, there have appeared true, whole men and women—masters, sages and saints, some of whose names are still visible on the stones of the past, along with countless others unheralded and unknown even in their own era. Obviously, such men and women have lived and taught, some by example, some in their actions as a guide, some through the establishment of intentional communities and esoteric schools and teachings that have brought hope to mankind. Yes, obviously there have existed authentic, authentically *good,* fully human beings throughout the ages, men and women who now and now and now, again and again and again, stepped across the Socratic threshold and were able to love. But should we not say that such human beings, countless though they may have been and may be, are no more and no less than signs to us of what man is meant to be, not of what he as yet is? Can we not say that they are the future of man, the "future"—meaning that which is possible and even necessary, but which does not yet exist, and may not exist, ever, in our world, on our earth, as a species: as what—to use a Hebraic shorthand—God "intended" when he created his most beloved creation, whom he "visits" again and again under "the moon and stars"?

Now, at this point in our thought, having invoked, however faintly, the cosmic immensity of the being of the "future man," the fully human that is ourselves as man—at just this point we must immediately look to the "mustard seed," symbolically the smallest and yet deepest source of life. We are now speaking of the one nearly invisible "gap," the one invisible, but metaphysically unique movement in ourselves, in man—the movement that can arc like a current of electricity, bridging the two worlds separated by the Socratic threshold.

It is "the smallest of the small" that enables the birth of "the greatest of the great" within oneself. We are speaking of a movement in ourselves, in our uniquely human attention, that again and again can take us across the Socratic threshold and carry us into the world of genuine human action, which means action perfused by love and justice. In making this movement, which we have yet to define, man, as it has also been said, becomes "higher than the angels."

THE DOCTRINE OF ANGELS AND THE
OBLIGATION OFFERED TO MAN

Among the great men of former times there was a difference of opinion as to whether an Israelite was greater than an angel, or whether an angel stood higher than an Israelite, and each supported his view by Scriptural quotations.[46]

So begins a discussion by a certain Rabbi Hayim of Volozhin (1749–1821), the chief disciple of the renowned teacher known as the Gaon of Vilna, under whose influence there arose in nineteenth-century Europe a powerful school of Judaism bringing together mystical vision, magisterial scholarship, and rigorous application to daily life of the Mosaic commandments.

Rabbi Hayim of Volozhin defines the meaning of angels both in cosmic terms and as representing conscious forces within man. In reading these words, it will help to remember that at the heart of all ancient knowledge there lies a vision of the universe as a vast organic whole—vast not only quantitatively, or "horizontally," in terms of space, time, and physical force, but, most importantly, qualitatively vast, "vertically" vast in terms of levels and degrees of intelligence, purpose and consciousness; and—as it is expressed in the Jewish mystical tradition—vast in the fundamental determining influence of the complementary forces of love (*hesed*) and judgment (justice, *gevurah*). In this vision of the universe as an inconceivably immense living organism lies the principal difference between ancient cosmology and modern cosmology. Modern science, relying as it does mainly on external empirical verification and mental logic, is cut off from the more interior instruments of human perception that are the necessary means for discovering objective value and purpose in the world of nature and the cosmos.

Referring to the difference of opinion regarding the question of the status of the Israelite (that is, man as a follower of Truth or Torah) and the angels, the Rabbi of Volozhin goes on to say that both of these views are true, "but that each is true under a different aspect." It is the manner in which these two apparently contradictory views are both true that can help us grasp the significance of the one inner movement that can carry us across the Socratic threshold into the realm of moral power, the capacity to be good.

"For indeed," writes the rabbi, "an angel is greater than man, both in his actual essence and in his extreme holiness and wonderful conception of Deity. There can really be no comparison between them at all." That is, there exist in the universe energies of being and levels of spiritual intelligence ("conceptions of Deity") incomparably higher than those possessed by man.

But that is not the last word in this matter. And here the rabbi cites the mystical text known as *Zohar Hadash:*

> The conception [comprehension] of Deity of the Angels is exceedingly great, and there is nothing to which it can be compared, in the conception of those below them. A second degree in conception is that of the Heavens who conceive as nothing below them can conceive. A third degree in conception is that of the lowest kind, grounded in dust—the human conception of Deity, which is nevertheless more than any other sublunar creature can conceive.[47]

We need to be very clear about what is being said here, without being distracted, misled or repelled due to a literalism that often blinds our modern mind to the metaphysical language of symbolism. To repeat: beyond and above the level of the being of man there exist inconceivably higher levels of being, consciousness and intelligence. These higher levels are here called "angels" and "the heavens." At the level called "earth," however, man's degree of consciousness is supreme. Man is "lower than the angels," but at the same time incomparably higher than any other "sublunar creature." Man is uniquely *in between* the earth and the heavens.

> The nearest angels receive the Powers of the Influx of the Divine Reflection first; from them it descends to the heavens and all their hosts; and from them to man.[48]

But now the text carries us to the critical element in what might be called *the metaphysical definition of man*—man as human being, *the ethical animal.* And what this means will take us far beyond familiar definitions of man. Beyond what the science of evolutionary biology tells us; beyond what psychology tells us; beyond academic philosophy's conception of human rationality; beyond what anthropology tells us; and beyond what has conventionally been explained to us by many of our religious teachers.

Suddenly, the concept of what Man is explodes into the cosmos with one apparently familiar word: *action*. Man is the being uniquely capable of action.

But what can this mean?

Man, we are told, "has an advantage over the angels, and that is in his possibility to effect the Elevations by the intertwining of all the Worlds, Powers and Lights as a single Unity in his structure, something impossible in an angel . . ." That is to say, Man possesses the cosmically unique capacity to bring together into a harmonious whole nearly all the levels of intelligence and energy in the universe. In Man, and in Man alone, the worlds above and the worlds below can meet and blend into a Oneness or Unity that mirrors in its way the essential nature of the Creator and the essential "intention" of the Creator. And this unique power of Man is called *action*:

> An angel is in essence only *one* individual power, in whom there is no generalization of all the several worlds. Hence it is in no way within the power of angels to elevate, join together, or unify any world with the one [that is] spread above their heads, for they have no part in common with them. . . . Hence the angels are termed 'standing Seraphim' (Isaiah VI 2). 'I will give thee access among those that *stand by*' (Zech. III 7). Man alone is the one who elevates, joins and unifies the Worlds and their Lights by virtue of his deeds, inasmuch as he is comprised of all of them.[49]

By virtue of his deeds: that is, by virtue of his power to act, to *do*. It is in this capacity, with this capacity, that Man assumes cosmic significance and fulfills what he is made for.

> Thus, even an angel can feel an elevation and addition to his sanctity coming from him [man] as a result of human deeds, *since the angel is virtually a component part of man*. And even the soul[s] of man—[at all its levels of divine force] are devoid of this exalting and unifying power *until*

they descend into the World of Action in the human body. So is it written: "He blew the breath of life into his nostrils"—a soul to all the worlds . . ."[50]

And finally:

This matter is also involved in the vision of the ladder which appeared to Jacob our Father, peace be upon him. "The ladder is indeed the soul of man, the Throne of the Name Jehovah . . . and the angels of Elohim ascend and descend it." That is, the angels ascend and descend by medium of the ladder standing *on the ground,* the lower end of which is embodied in the physical frame of man.[51]

THE ETHICAL ANIMAL AND
THE MEANING OF OUR FREEDOM

But enough of the ancient symbology. It is of use to us only if we can feel in it the immense scale of what man is and is meant to be—the scale of what we are and are meant to be now and here in our present era. The ancient symbology is a language meant to communicate facts about the real world and the real structure of man, facts that cannot be verified or understood only with the senses and mental logic alone. The idea in the ancient teachings is that man is free to be either greater than the angels or else descend as a spoiled animal living in violence and fantastic dreams. The idea is that we are free to be—and are obliged to strive to become—beings through whom and in whom the highest energies of consciousness and eternity blend into a unity in relationship to all the forces of earth and passing time.

Then let us leave behind us the ancient language that so few of us in the modern world can understand, the ancient call that so few us can hear. We have come to a point in our inquiry where we can affirm something of ultimate importance. Even though the ancient language of religion and spiritual philosophy can hardly reach us, nevertheless we can confront the fact that we are called to be good, we are called to something we experience as moral duty, the duty to be moral, to be ethical, to love what is good and do justice to man. We cannot and we will not abandon the ethical imperative in our lives—no matter what we call it, no matter that we can no longer explain it because we have lost the fundamental support of metaphysical ideas that point us to the exalted nature of what we as man are meant to be. No matter that we believe we understand much more than we do simply because we can manipulate nature up to a point, manipulated as we ourselves are by our automatisms of desire and fear in the world around us; no matter that we see clearly that our knowledge without the development of our morality is bringing us to the edge of destruction; no matter, no matter—we know we are meant to be ethical, to care, to love, to do justice.

Twist and turn as we may, explain it or deconstruct it as we may, we know that though we may be animals, we are ethical animals. In everyone, in every place, in every occasion of our lives and culture we see that we are failing to be what we are meant to be—and we suffer from that, we run from one answer to another—religion, relativism, psychology, medical drugs, psychotropic drugs, mass movements, charismatic leaders, fundamentalisms of all kinds from the religious to the atheistic to the scientistic; we run here and there looking for our moral power, trying to exercise it even though all evidence screams out to us that we do not have this power, that we cannot be the moral beings we know, down deep, that we are meant to be.

Even when we turn away from the moral dimension and look simply for pleasure and happiness and the satisfactions of simple life—we cannot escape the fact that we are man, the ethical animal. We cannot escape the fact—unless we shut our eyes tightly and never open them again—that we cannot find meaning or happiness just for ourselves alone. We are obliged to love, to care, and there can be no meaning, no real happiness in our lives unless we discover how to serve what is greater than ourselves, and with that how to serve our fellow man, our neighbor. We are not constructed to be happy in selfishness. Many have tried and many have gone to their graves bitterly assured that there was no moral imperative out there, that duty was only to one's little self, or that there was no such thing as duty. But the bitterness itself is ample evidence that they lost their lives to an illusion about life, an illusion often even rooted in the ideals of honesty in front of so obviously immoral and unjust a world. And how many others have gone to their graves, and have taken millions with them, believing in themselves alone, assured in themselves alone that they and they alone knew what is good and what is just, knew the mind of God?

"God" or no God, pleasure or no pleasure, relativism or absolutism, philosophical subtlety or ham-fisted self-assurance—how much is it all the theater of the ego imagining it can be what we are meant to be without confronting the real metaphysical, biological, cosmic fact of our nature—that we are born into a cosmic obligation? That there is such a thing as duty, as the moral law, the moral imperative? Not necessarily as it was taught to us in our churches or in our social groups or political cells or self-protective societies or imagined historical or tribal priorities—no, not that . . . and yet, and yet, where did all those moral ideals originally come from, the ones we heard as children, however oversimplified or overcomplicated they had become, however mixed with those aspects of ourselves from which, in their purity, these ideals were meant to liberate us—namely, egoism, fear, self-pity, self-will, suggestibility?

There is no escaping it: all our attempts in the modern world to free ourselves from what we see as the oppression of outworn customs of social behavior have brought us no real happiness, no real hope, no real sense of meaning; all our attempts to free ourselves from the way mankind has twisted the great moral law and fashioned it into either a heartless tyrant built up out of our own neurotic guilt or a whoremaster drugging us with fantasies (in the ancient language, idols) of egoistic pleasure, egoistic money, egoistic power, egoistic freedom.

But wait—what is this freedom that we have won in our modern world? Surely it is better than the religious or political tyranny that threatens us at every side? Yes, of course, but why has it not brought us meaning? And without meaning, how can there be happiness?

We have been trying to think and think again about this question. But now, at this point in our inquiry, we can present the question more nakedly: There is no human happiness without human goodness. And our freedom, our political freedoms, our freedom of intellect, our freedom of speech—which means our freedom of human relationship—our freedom to associate, our freedom to express ourselves artistically, politically, philosophically—these are all freedoms *from* something, but what are they *for*?

In most cases, *the freedoms we have won in the modern world are purely and simply freedoms from the distortions of the moral law; they are freedoms from toxic misunderstandings of duty and obligation.* But having escaped from prison, what are we to do? Where are we to go?

Let us say it nakedly: Duty in its genuine sense, the moral law in its pure sense is not the grim, gray habit of life that these words are sometimes used to denote. On the contrary, pure duty, pure morality is intrinsically joyous; it is meant as a call to that in us which brings ultimate happiness and meaning to human life. In that sense we may say quite clearly what the freedom we cherish is *for* and not only what it is freedom *from*. The freedom we wish for is strictly speaking the freedom to obey the pure, undistorted moral law handed down to man from "above," and since "time beyond time."

All genuine freedom is the freedom to love and act justly toward man. Any other meaning of freedom is only for children, not adults.

Suddenly, the word "ethics" comes alive, like a puppet cutting its own strings and speaking directly to us. No longer is the word and what it refers to under the spell of bloodless philosophical concepts and arguments; nor held in place by stiff religious dogmas, nor controlled by political agendas, social resentments and noisy moralistic judgments. No longer need the word and what it refers to be manipulated as an instrument in the craving for power or profit. And, of paramount importance, no longer is our individual search for meaning and happiness defined by a childish reduction of the idea of what man is, of what we ourselves are and are meant to become.

Sixteen

A MEDITATION ON CROSSING
THE SOCRATIC THRESHOLD

What is truly human is beyond human strength.

EMMANUEL LEVINAS[52]

I wished to create around myself conditions in which a man would be continually reminded of the sense and aim of his existence by an unavoidable friction
between his conscience and the automatic manifestations of his nature.

G. I. GURDJIEFF[53]

I n both our personal lives and in the life of our world every great
problem urges us to take action; every crisis urges us to do something. Yet our own lives and the life of mankind show us how little
difference our actions really make in the long passage of time and events.
Again and again we repeat the same mistakes; we take resolute action, resolute decisions, only to find, sooner or later, that our actions have either
led us back to where we started or have taken us far away from where we
had hoped to go. Our resolution has weakened, shifted, deflected, perhaps inch by inch. And if, in the end, it seems otherwise, it is only because we have launched our little boat by chance into a broad rushing
current that takes us where it will—and, more often than not, we are
simply carried by this invisible current, leaving us merely to imagine that
we have chosen our direction and by our own will carried out our aim.

It is the same in the life of nations and the world. History goes round in circles—destruction provoking ideals and their consequent betrayal; beauty overcoming ugliness and then being cheapened and forgotten; great teachings enter the stream of history, also only to be distorted and exploited in the service of ignorance and brutality; knowledge is miraculously wrought from the apparently blind forces of nature and this knowledge inevitably becomes the plaything of the same blind forces operating within human nature. Progress made in one sphere is inevitably offset by barbarism in another. Human life, under the illusions of action, spins us round and round in a circle of repetition—what the ancient traditions call "the wheel of birth and death."

THE GREAT UNKNOWN

But in our personal life there are moments when the way out of this grim cycle appears. These are the moments when we stop inside and we simply look, we attend to what we are and what we know we are meant to be. These are moments when we live the one question of our being. And these moments show us a way, they show us that, far in the distance as it may be, real action is possible, real intelligence is possible, real will is possible. These are not moments of doubt, nor are they moments of revelation; they are not mystical ecstasy, they are not inspirations of genius or spiritual wisdom. These are moments of deep moral intention and they lead us to live through something *entirely misunderstood* in our lives and our culture. Something about which, as such, there exist no shelves full of books, something which modern psychology and literature have never clearly seen or noted. It is a completely unexplored place on the spectrum of human consciousness and life. It is the place in between impulse and act, the point of transition where the love of the good passes into the movements of our body, of our emotions and our thinking; where what we know to be right and true meets the forces of habit, fear, self-protection and all the illusions of identity that the world around us has thrust upon us.

Between every serious intention and the act which accompanies or follows it there falls the transition between two levels, two kinds of reality in ourselves—the inner ideal and the outer action. Between my love for the other and my manifestation toward him or her; between my ideal of sacrifice and struggle and my manifestation of it which is often cruel and hurtful; between my desire for justice and compassion and my manifestation of it in compromise or harsh self-righteousness; between my love of knowledge and the wish to serve others with it and my manifestation which is often arrogant and self-serving—between every higher intention and its attempted manifestation there falls this immense, invisible transition between worlds. Something of the higher, or the reaching towards the higher, has appeared in the mind or the feelings; some echo, however faint or partial, of the greatness of Man has appeared in us. But it is followed immediately by a movement at an entirely different level of reality and in an entirely different direction. It is like falling from heaven to earth or from earth to hell; from being to non-being, from one species, man, to another species—animal? plant? stone?

This transition takes only a second or a fraction of a second in time measured in its conventional way. But from another measurement of time, this transition is like the birth and death of a world. An entire metaphysical or human/cosmological period is there, an immensity of time outside of time, time in another dimension, in which what I do disconnects from what I intend. In this time out of time lies the whole secret of human moral, ethical, intelligent action. In the secret of this transition lies the whole, entire problem of the human species on earth. And the total centrality of this transition has not been seen or acknowledged in our psychology or in the religious teachings that we know. And it has not been seen or acknowledged, except in brief flashes which we do not know how to understand, in the processes of our everyday life.

This moment of transition, this place where the two worlds are meant to, but do not, meet is the great unknown of human life, and is the reason we fall and fail in almost everything serious or good that we try to do, as individuals, as a society, and as a species created, as is said, "in the image of God." It is the great unknown, far more important and unknown than what is conventionally called the "unconscious." Or, rather, it is an entirely new and essential way of understanding and working with what we call the unconscious, because we are speaking not simply about two parts of the mind, as we know it, but about two levels of being within the human mind—along with the potential appearance and development of a third, unknown, unifying function of the human mind, a third realm, the realm of metaphysical transition, metaphysical relation between worlds, the realm of the One Question.

This realm so strangely hidden from us—metaphysically hidden— requires of us an entirely new level of attention that must be worked for in our life of action. No psychoanalysis, no neurology, no computer models, no laboratory science of brain states knows about this realm of the human psyche. Its existence, its reality, its centrality has slipped entirely out of our civilization's definition of the human. And without remembering this meaning, this defining element in the structure of the psyche, our science, for example, can never make contact with our moral yearnings; our religion can never make real contact with our lawful physical and biosocial desires and needs, our art and literature can never really guide us toward action.

THE BIRTH OF THE HUMAN

To repeat: we rarely notice this transition, we rarely perceive this space in between what we are in our deepest heart and what we actually do and say. But this is the place where the two worlds exist together. This, we say again, is the unknown sphere of the birth of man. The two worlds at first, and for a long time, oppose each other, but man is meant to inhabit them both, and do so in a way that one world, one reality, the world of manifestation, submits to the higher, the inner world of pure attention. But the opposition of these two worlds must first, and for a long time, be seen and accepted, understood and *suffered* for what it is.

That suffering is called remorse of conscience.

The place where the two worlds can meet is the realm of the One Question. The real essential human question is always and in all its modes the contact between two worlds, two movements, two levels of reality, two systems of value, two identities. We need to see this question in every great, aching question of human life, every aching problem that we know is not answerable by external information, scientific theory, or religious dogma and moralism. These two realities are meant to be fused into a new union. To enable and sustain this meeting and blending of worlds within ourselves is the work of man. *It is the deepest root of man's birthright: the will and the capacity to love.*

And it begins with suffering the One Question in ourselves—not in words alone, but in experience and in the realm of forces confronting each other.

A TRANSFORMING FIRE

The obligation that is offered to us is to strive with all our being to serve what is good—while at the same time, also with all our being, to suffer in full consciousness the naked fact that it is beyond our strength. Then, and only then, can moral power be given to us. Such is the law of morality, seen from within. And, we may say, seen from above. Such is the metaphysics of morality.

It is very difficult.

But it is just this movement of *conscious suffering* that can take us again and again across the Socratic threshold by means of a force that touches the whole of man from another level within and above oneself.

Conscious suffering must not be confused with what we ordinarily speak of as "guilt." What we are speaking about here is a full experience of *seeing*—a full confrontation with our being; a vibrant acceptance of our incapacity to do what is good without masking the truth with self-pity or futile vows—an acceptance of the fact that our actions and all our manifestations are a result of our level of being. This act of seeing is the movement that brings the two worlds toward each other—the inner world and the outer world, the world of the inner aspiration toward love and justice, and the world of outer action and behavior.

Through experiencing the naked disconnection and contradiction between these two worlds, a metaphysical sorrow and yearning arises in man, a sense of infinite need, and thereby an openness to the forces above and within man that can, however briefly, make us whole and enable us to be what we are and to do what is right.

At the same time, in what is seemingly the great existential paradox of our destiny, we are obliged to try in every instance to obey the moral law, knowing of our fundamental weakness, yet also knowing of the fundamental power to act justly and love mercy that belongs to the fully human man. In a word, we are obliged to obey the moral law even though it is beyond our strength.

We are obliged to obey the moral law while working to become able to obey it. And this work is rooted in the striving at one and the same time to do what is good and to suffer consciously the sorrow of our incapacity.

The moral law, as we know it, the basic principles of Judeo-Christian ethics, may be understood as a rehearsal for the uncovering within oneself of the force of conscience, carried into human life through deep attention to the body, heart and mind. The moral law may be understood as a record left by men and women of greater being who set down what they discovered under the influence of genuine conscience. In this sense, *it is rooted in human experience;* it is not something "received" in a pseudo-religious trance or fabricated by social convention. It is not given as something man *can* do, but something he must *strive* to do with all his heart, all his mind, and all his soul. The moral law tells me to do what a man in the conscious state would do through the agency of a higher energy acting through the body.

But here we must be very precise in what we say. When we say that to obey the moral law is beyond human strength, this does not mean we cannot take actions to help our neighbor, to refrain from violence, to weigh the scales as justly as we can, to "care for the widow and the orphan," to fulfill our external obligations, to give time and attention to our neighbor and to those we love, to succor the poor and the helpless among us. To say anything else would be monstrous nonsense. What it does mean, however, is that we cannot hold inwardly to our aim, even if outwardly we hold to our behavior; it means we cannot activate the deeper sensitivity to the needs of the person before us, even though we are strictly obeying every ethical principle and rule. It means that in the end we often become moral automatons, doing the "right thing" externally, while inwardly we may plunge far, far away from the human attention needed for truly understanding what is good and what is merciful and what is just. It means we act morally by habit or by a power of choice that is far weaker than we imagine, and that we are far more susceptible to distraction and deflection than we know. In a word, we do not have the being of the person who is outwardly obeying the rules and principles. We love only when we are not "scratched." We do justly only when we are not in danger or frightened or in pain . . . of course, not always, not everyone. But on the whole, we are all poor, poor human beings living within a script written for fully human beings and having to beg inwardly for the help we need to fill the garments of fully human actors in the drama of human life.

And of course these moral rules are absolutely necessary for society to hold together in an outward sense. Where would we be without them? They hold the world together, more or less, patching over the gashing wounds of war and brutality and barbaric injustice, and hypocrisy and crime tearing ever and again at the body of human society, skin healing again and again under the scar tissue of new institutions, creations of great art, new knowledge (without the being to use it ethically). But our human civilization never heals completely and now and again, again and again, an upheaval of hatred and violence shows the world it has not understood the nature of man. Again and again every philosophy, every religion that we know is confounded by war and brutality—genocide, mass murder, unbearable injustice against nations, peoples and cultures. Yet the world holds together under the illusion of morality, the illusion that we can obey the moral law. No matter how much it is proved otherwise, we continue to feel "guilt" and make impotent promises to ourselves and our fellow men. Few are they who make no promises, but who work with great fervor and precision to suffer to see the lack of being that results in human evil. Few are they who can hear the voice of conscience and stay open to it long and deeply enough to cry for help from above and within, the help that appears mainly in the form of love for oneself even amid the shock of deep remorse. These few are the future of man.

THE SHOCK OF LOVE

And so, we must obey the law and within that "obedience" we must find help that will enable us not to cover over our moral incapacity. Which will enable our poor human functions to stay in view of our attention and not hide themselves only to act again in betrayal of the moral law. For should we see only the intrinsic weakness of our morality, there may appear a moral cynicism that makes up its own moral codes on the basis of superficial reasoning and preferences, or clever philosophical arguments. This cynicism about man is based on a cynicism about human nature, a profound distrust of our animal and socialized selves, a profound mistrust of our functioning. Our functions, our thoughts, our emotions, our instincts, cannot withstand the hatred or contempt directed at them by the moral relativists or, for that matter, by the moral absolutists. Man cannot bear to have his functions despised. They must be seen in such a way that they will trust our consciousness, will allow our consciousness to see them in all their manifestation and reality—so that eventually they will submit to the simultaneous shock of remorse and all-accepting love. The shock of a forgiveness rooted in truth, not in self-deception or self-arrogation or false assumptions of our moral power. This love, this shock of remorse, is the fire that can transform man into Man, self into Self, ego into Soul, me into *I*.

Seventeen

A KIND OF SUMMATION:
WHY CAN'T WE BE GOOD?

I am looking down at a hundred young teenagers and they are now looking back at me in silent anticipation. A moment ago the auditorium was a pandemonium of shouting boys and laughing girls and squeaking chairs—and a blur of arms and legs and all lengths and widths of young bodies. And now suddenly there is not a sound.

I am here to speak to these fourteen-year-old children about ethics. This is the freshman class of the Branson School, a distinguished private high school in the San Francisco Bay Area. I have been invited to help the school bring the study of ethics more deeply into the school's curriculum.

Already I have lectured to the three older classes—the seniors, juniors, and sophomores. And each time I was impressed by the deep unforced interest—the word "passionate" would not be amiss—in the subject. I had expected otherwise.

Looking out now at these freshmen, however, the youngest students in the school, I suspected the situation would surely be different. These were definitely *children:* some, standing next to me, came up not much higher than my waist. Even the girls, more mature of course than the boys, seemed not yet to have crossed the line that separates childhood from the beginnings of adulthood.

I began as I had with the other classes. Ethics, I said, has to do with the question: What kind of human being do you want to be?

Before starting, I had invited the class to ask anything they wished about what it means to be a good person. I was not two minutes into my talk when a small hand flew up in the second row. At first I tried to ignore it long enough to round off my opening remarks, but the small hand simply stayed straight up, rapidly opening and closing into a small fist.

And the moment I glancingly met the boy's eyes, he called out his question:

"Why do people get angry?"

It stopped me cold. I looked into his face and for a long moment I could find nothing to say.

Who was this child? I could not help but take his question very seriously, even seeing in it the whole problem of our common life: Why do our emotions take us into violence? Why do we so easily fear and hate one another—or simply shut down our sensitivities to each other?

Although everyone in the auditorium was waiting for me to turn my attention back to them, I could not take my eyes from this boy's face. I decided to speak directly to him as though it were only he and I in the room together.

I walked to the edge of the platform and looked down at him. He was a child, but he was not playing a child's game now. He was not being "smart." He was not trying to impress me or his friends and teachers. Or, if he was, it was only on the surface. Underneath the surface, behind the young eyes, I saw a man—a man only just coming into the chaos of human life in the world.

And I could not help but think of the one-legged man demanding of Hillel a clear, quick answer to a fundamental question of human life.

But I was no Hillel able in one wise and gentle reply to set a course of life for this young person.

"I don't know," I said. "It's strange, isn't it? I know that some things make me angry and some things make me feel kind, but I don't know *why* they do."

The boy became quiet. He was thinking. After a few seconds, he said: "Why don't you know?"

What a question!

I wanted to find a way to respond, but I felt the pressure building in the rest of the auditorium. Many other hands were going up.

Finally, I turned to the audience. "Here we are," I said, "we've immediately plunged into the heart of ethics. The question is not only what we ought or ought not to do, but what *are* we? What is a human being? And what are our emotions?"

I felt like someone in a foreign country who knows only the basic words of the language. My head was already swarming with thoughts about man's emotional nature and the need for self-knowledge as an ethical force, self-knowledge as a moral force—not information *about* oneself, but direct experience of oneself in the present moment of living.

Ideas started rearing in my mind like wild horses. No less than the one-legged man, these children needed to study real ideas about man and the universe, ideas that someday could guide their understanding of themselves and of other human beings. But I would have to speak about such ideas in the language of this foreign country of fourteen-year-olds.

The raised hands were sprouting all over the place. I called on a slight, olive-skinned girl sitting quietly with a group of friends in the middle of the auditorium. She spoke softly, her voice trembling:

"Why are we destroying the earth?"

Again, I was stopped. And again I felt it was just myself and this one nervous girl who existed in the room. I paid no attention to all the other hands, some waving urgently.

Finally, I answered:

"Your question makes me think of the achievements of the human mind, especially in science. It makes me think of how much we have come to know about nature and how much we are able to do with what we know. And at the same time how much we use our knowledge to destroy ourselves and our world. Maybe we all need to think more deeply about that contradiction in ourselves. It's as though the part of ourselves that makes scientific progress has no connection to the part of ourselves that wishes to care for others and for the world."

She looked puzzled. I went on:

"Don't we see the same kind of thing in our own personal lives? There is a part of ourselves that wishes to love and there is another part of ourselves that just wants what it wants for itself—whether it's knowledge or success or pleasure—and doesn't think at all about other people or about the earth."

I paused. Perhaps this was the moment to bring in the meaning of self-knowledge as the hidden root of ethics and morality: the need to *understand* the fundamental contradiction in ourselves between what we know to be good and what we actually do, the need to see ourselves deeply and resist the attempt to change ourselves by our own imaginary strength. But in order really to see this contradiction and to suffer it in a way that can bring new life to us, it was, paradoxically, all the more necessary to try to be what we wished to be toward our neighbor, to try with all our strength to obey the moral law—to be good. The words of Socrates were "Know thyself!" not "Change thyself!" And it was St. Paul, standing forever in front of this profound contradiction in himself and in man, who called on the help that can come to man only from another level of the inner being.

But what was I imagining? Wouldn't it be a great wrong even to try to speak about such things in this situation? After all, these were just children.

Weren't they?

My thoughts were interrupted by a crackling deep voice in the back of the hall:

"It's the multinational corporations!"

I answered quickly, "Yes and no!"

The boy simply went on. He was blond, athletically built, wearing a kind of white tennis sweater.

"It's all about money," he said. "They don't care what they do to poison the environment or destroy the rainforest or create poverty in Third World countries . . ."

I now interrupted him.

"You know," I said—and I was even surprised to hear myself saying it—"maybe they do care."

All the raised hands slowly went down. Smooth brows became furrowed.

I stood there feeling very exposed. Was I perhaps saying something that I myself didn't really understand—or even believe? When Socrates said to the world that no one does evil intentionally, that everyone acts according to what he considers good, what did he really mean? In fact, for many years, I never really appreciated that element of his teaching. Just as for many years I never really took seriously the words of Jesus, "Love thy neighbor as thyself." It was always obvious to me that, as my mother used to say to me, cautioning me when I was hurt by someone or shaken by the evidence of human evil: "Jerry, there are bad people in the world."

But now I saw something quite different in these famous words of Socrates. Perhaps he meant that even the greatest villain is still a human being who has two natures—one part that seeks the good and another that is drawn to obey impulses of personal fear or craving or violence—and that, like the tormented Mr. Prozi, an evil man is one who is utterly incapable of ever seeing the contradiction between his two natures, in whom there never has and never can exist a channel for the voice of conscience. Depending on the influences in which he develops, such a man can become anything from a widely respected artist or scientist or statesman to a petty, vengeful dreamer or thief or a dull, obedient soldier or bureaucrat or a monstrous tyrant engulfing the world in flames and anguish. Such a man or woman, who is forever barred from accepting, and perhaps after a point even from experiencing, the revelations of conscience—revelations which are given to man when, under the shock of grief, for example, the wall separating the two natures falls down. Such a man or woman may be socially good, that is, good within his culture or tribe or group, but under specific outer and inner influences he or she can at any moment turn to the manifestation of evil—violence, hypocrisy, injustice, cruelty, slavish obedience to "authority."

Of course, I resisted the impulse to speak these thoughts out loud to the children, the freshmen—except, except: just as these thoughts were racing through my mind I realized in my gut that what I was describing to myself was not simply one possible characterization of what might be called—in some sense of the word—human evil, I was not just describing "bad people," Could it be that I was describing *all* people?

In any case, I was describing myself!

And as though from a distance, I then heard myself saying to the boy in the tennis sweater and to everyone else:

"Maybe these bad heads of multinational corporations are also people like you and me. Maybe down deep we are all more alike than we imagine. Did that ever occur to you—or to any of us? You know, I never could understand these words of Jesus that I'm sure all of you have heard: to love your neighbor—or even your enemy—as yourself. I always used to think I am I and you are you—we are different beings. But now I begin to see what he may have meant—and, by the way, the same thing was said in the Jewish tradition long before. We need to understand that the person next to me or at the head of the corporation or even the person who is seeking to destroy me—that he is like I am. This is especially so, isn't it, when a person does something to hurt us or is angry at us. Is it possible to remember that we are also like that when we have lost our contact with our ideals and ethical principles?"

And again I remembered Hillel: "What is hateful to you, do not do to your neighbor."

I was immensely touched and surprised and relieved when the broad-shouldered boy in the tennis sweater quietly said, "I never thought of it that way."

Now I wanted to go on. I wanted to find the language or the excuse to let my thoughts develop. Because to say the other is like myself cannot and does not take us very far in the realities of "the streets of our lives" on the other side of the Socratic threshold. It cannot take us very far until we know ourselves fully and well. What point is there in saying the other is like myself unless I also know what I myself am? Yes, it can help us a little, a precious little, as a principle to moderate our reactions and judgments. But it does not go very far. Our reactions and judgments eventually, sooner or later, overwhelm that fine little principle.

So, once again, in order to be moral we are obliged to become *able* to be moral. We are obliged to seek out the ethics of self-knowledge.

By this time, I completely dropped the picture I had about what this talk and discussion would be like. As the questions came one after another—about war, sex and sexual identity, abortion; about the relativity of ethical principles in different cultures, about marriage and divorce, money and success; about standards of femininity and masculinity, about cheating and loyalty and helping the poor and righting the wrongs of racism, of what America is supposed to be—as the questions came one after the other I realized that the whole world was in this auditorium. It was not just a hundred fourteen-year-old children. It was a hundred incarnations of the One Great Question of who and what man is and of who and what we are supposed to be. They were incarnations, I say, in that all of these questions were brought with the passionate intensity of being questions about themselves—themselves as individuals. They were as personal as a question can get. They were asking about—*me, I.* They were asking about Carl, Jennifer, Kenneth, Tran, Lydia, Stephen, Fabio, Vicente, Alicia . . .

They were not asking the usual psychological questions of young adolescents—the personal questions and problems about the details of living that haunt almost all our lives to the very end—questions about popularity, personal appearance, status, recognition and appreciation. Of course they had such questions and problems, as do all of us. They were not asking questions about their personal worries and fears and desires and the complications that drive so many of them and us to seek much-needed relief in therapy and self-help programs or misdirected relief in alcohol or food or heartless sex. Their questions were questions about the world, about humanity as such, about other people's needs and suffering, about the future of the world, about the happiness of their parents and friends, about babies born and unborn—and at the same time their own personal anguish and need was pouring through these questions as the blood in our human bodies pours through every tissue, organ and cell within us. These young people yearn for one thing and one thing only—down under and behind every shout and cry of their lives: they yearn to love. And, without knowing it, they need, as do all of us, also without knowing it, to learn how to be able to love.

It cannot be denied: in these fourteen-year-olds care for others was fused with care for themselves—themselves not as this or that problem in this or that setting, but themselves as men and women, as human beings. And what did that word mean—"human being"? The answer was clear: a human being is the being who yearns to love, who is built to love and to act justly toward man—just as we have heard (but is it heard anymore?) since ancient times in our Western world and in the great teachings of the East, just as Moses, Hillel, Jesus, Mohammed, the masters of India, the Buddha, Socrates, and the whole angelic host of the spiritually wise have taught.

☞

The One Great Question: What is Man?

The One Great Answer: Man is the being who can love and who can do what love demands, be it sharp or tender, full of thunder or enwombed in silence.

☞

And at this moment I feel an ancient presence behind me whispering to me:

"Now, go and study!"

FOR FURTHER READING

It is futile to try to think seriously about the basis of ethics and morality without awareness of the assumptions we make about human nature, history, the earth, the universe, religion—everything. An uncritical or pseudo-critical acceptance of culturally prevalent views in these areas can be as misleading as the most eccentric speculations—and this is because many of what we take to be objective "facts" are subtly permeated with unexamined assumptions that have profound ethical implications. To take just one example: let us say a philosopher rejects religion as a fundamental source of ethical principles. In claiming this, he cites the seemingly obvious and commonly accepted fact that people from different religions hold very different views about right and wrong. But in so doing, he betrays ignorance of anything but the surface of religion and has not acquainted himself with the vision of mankind, reality, and ethical principles that constitutes the heart of all the great religious traditions of the world. One could cite many other examples from our culture's commonly accepted "facts" about the ancient world, the world of nature, and the human mind and body.

Several books listed here have therefore been chosen as a possible help toward appreciating how deeply the subject of ethics is embedded in and dependent upon our overall understanding of the world we live in.

Many of these titles have passed through numerous editions at various dates. The date given next to each title represents the year of the book's first publication in an English-language edition. Each separate grouping of books is followed by a brief commentary.

Robert Cushman, *Therapeia* (1958)
Pierre Hadot, *The Inner Citadel: The* Meditations *of Marcus Aurelius* (1998) and *What Is Ancient Philosophy?* (2002)
Marcus Aurelius, *Meditations,* translated by Maxwell Staniforth (1964)
Plato, *The Dialogues of Plato,* translated by Benjamin Jowett (1892)

One thing is clear: read Plato. But where to start, how to proceed? It is certainly possible and very worthwhile just to plunge into his inspired thought even if there is no lifeguard present. Many excellent translations of Plato exist, exhibiting fine scholarship. I still like one of the oldest, that of Benjamin Jowett. The language is a bit dated, but these translations help the reader, perhaps more than some others, to sense the transcendent dimension in Plato's thought. Nevertheless, for most of us it is nearly impossible to grasp the immense force of Plato's vision without a guide. There exist countless excellent studies of Plato's philosophy, but I have found Robert Cushman's *Therapeia* to be the most deeply sensitive presentation of what Plato is really all about—namely, the possible transformation of man and how this human possibility changes most of our commonly accepted views about morality.

As for the *Meditations* of Marcus Aurelius, there are very many translations available and new ones are constantly appearing, including a version that I am collaborating on with John P. Piazza. Because Marcus was writing this book as notes to himself, his language is sometimes highly compressed. Here, I am recommending one of the few translations that have been able to catch the essential meaning of Marcus's language while rendering it in graceful English.

In its ancient and most essential meaning philosophy is a preparation for and a partial accompaniment to the work of self-perfection. No one has illuminated this meaning of philosophy more cogently, clearly and authoritatively than the French scholar Pierre Hadot. His book on Marcus Aurelius is at the pinnacle of reflective scholarship, and the essays collected in Hadot's *What Is Ancient Philosophy?* demonstrate the role of lived philosophy through the life of our culture. Hadot also offers valuable reflections about the life that was actually lived in the centuries-long community known as the Academy of Plato.

René Guénon, *The Reign of Quantity* (1953) and *The Crisis of the Modern World* (1942)

Frithjof Schuon, *The Transcendent Unity of Religions* (1953)

The Life of Milarepa, translated by Lobsang Lhalungpa (1977)

Concerning the question of the nature and origin of religion, the writings of René Guénon and Frithjof Schuon are intellectually powerful demonstrations that religion—apart from anything else that we may make of it— originally comes to man from a source that is far deeper and higher than is imagined in the cultural consensus of our time. These writings constitute, as well, a formidable and startlingly comprehensive critique of modernity. One cannot put the Guénon book down without taking stock of all one's easy assumptions about our era's scientific and cultural progress and about the so-called "ignorance" of our distant ancestors. These books are not easy reading; they are deeply challenging and deeply rewarding.

Buddhism is one of the great ancient teachings that views human beings as intrinsically relational and compassionate, and which views the "lesser morality"—that is, the work of becoming capable of morality—as the spiritual and psychological practice that deeply allows the intrinsic power to love to break through as a force governing the movements of our lives. For Westerners, there may be no better introduction to this aspect of the heart of Buddhism than *The Life of Milarepa,* the autobiography of the most renowned saint in Tibetan Buddhist history. No reader will ever forget the wondrous severity this compassion takes in the hands of Milarepa's teacher, the Lama Marpa, whose sole aim is at any cost to awaken his beloved pupil from the sleep of the ego, releasing in him the force, latent in all human beings, of a boundless compassion that helped to change the face of an entire culture.

Hayim Nahman Bialik and Yehoshua Hana Ravnitzky, editors, *The Book of Legends: Legends from the Talmud and Midrash* (1992)

Martin Buber, *I and Thou* (1958)

Yitzhak Buxbaum, *The Life and Teachings of Hillel* (1994)

Theodor H. Gaster, *The Dead Sea Scriptures* (1976)

Nahum N. Glatzer, *Hillel the Elder* (1956)

Judah Goldin, *The Living Talmud: The Wisdom of the Fathers* (1955)

Emmanuel Levinas, *Nine Talmudic Readings* (1990)

Glatzer's lucid study *Hillel the Elder* is boldly suggestive of Judaism's profound fusion of inner spirituality and ethics. Buxbaum's *The Life and Teachings of Hillel* generously provides all the sayings attributed to Hillel and all that is written about him in the ancient commentaries. Buxbaum also offers his own heartfelt interpretations of Hillel's teachings. Goldin's *The Living Talmud* reveals the *Pirke Avot* ("The Wisdom of the Fathers") in a way that will give many readers a completely new perception of the ancient chain of rabbinic teachers all held together by the ideals of love, justice, and the dynamics of spiritual transmission from teacher to pupil.

Levinas' *Nine Talmudic Readings* stuns the reader by the endless profundity and contemporary relevance of the great Rumanian philosopher's reading of only a tiny sample of Talmudic passages: a profundity that makes of ethics a primal, ultimate word for what it means to be human. Levinas is gradually becoming known as one of the twentieth century's most powerful philosophers, but here he demonstrates that the depth of his revolutionary philosophical views are echoes of what he has seen in Judaism's understanding of the ethical as the very essence of man and God. Buber's *I and Thou* brought to the modern world its most influential statement of the ethical dimension of life as a mode of knowing the world that is as authentic and cogent—and perhaps more so—as anything offered by science. This book has been and can continue to be a powerful support for the work of understanding the world and each other from the intelligence of the heart and mind together, rather than from the isolated intellect alone.

The Book of Legends is a joyous, magnificent compendium of tales, parables, and lore from the classical rabbinic tradition. Here the reader will discover that the biblical vision of the fundamental moral essence of reality includes everything in life, and that the ethical vision of reality is both intensely realistic—more so than many of us can bear—and intensely visionary and wondrous: more so than we might have ever hoped to find.

What evidence do the Dead Sea Scrolls offer concerning the teachings of the spiritual communities in and around Jerusalem that may have influenced Hillel and his mission? Theodor Gaster's translations in *The Dead Sea Scriptures* have seemed to me a fine balance of scholarship and sensitivity to the profound and sometimes hidden spiritual intention behind many of these texts.

Anonymous, *The Cloud of Unknowing and the Book of Privy Counseling,* edited by William Johnston (1973)

Meister Eckhart, *A Modern Translation,* translated by Raymond B. Blakney (1941)

Søren Kierkegaard, *The Sickness unto Death* (1941)

Jean-Yves Leloup, *The Gospel of Mary Magdalene* (2002), *The Gospel of Philip* (2003) and *The Gospel of Thomas* (2005)

Thomas Merton, *The New Man* (1963)

The Nag Hammadi Library, James M. Robinson, general editor (1977)

Maurice Nicoll, *The New Man* (1950)

Elaine Pagels, *Beyond Belief* (2003)

The Philokalia, translated by G. E. H. Palmer, Philip Sherrard, and Kallistos Ware (1979)

The teachings given by Meister Eckhart and by the anonymous author of *The Cloud of Unknowing* show with unmistakable clarity the meaning of what we have called the inner morality at the heart of the Christian doctrine of love. This material is required reading for anyone who wishes to confront the question of the relationship between inner spirituality and ethical action. *The Philokalia* is a collection of texts written between the fourth and fifteenth centuries by spiritual masters of the Orthodox Christian tradition. These texts speak in practical terms of the inner work of opening the mind, heart and body to the action of the divine force of attention as the key to actually living as a Christian. These are some of mankind's most powerful and moving writings on this subject in all its vast applications.

The writings of Søren Kierkegaard have by now shaken the minds of tens of thousands of men and women throughout the Western world with the question of what it means actually to live Christianity. Of all his powerful books, *The Sickness unto Death* focuses most explicitly on man's two opposing natures and the obligation offered to the individual to incarnate the essential Self through an existential act embracing both eternity and time within oneself.

Two books with coincidentally the same title, *The New Man,* represent two luminous contemporary explorations of the practice of becoming Christian inwardly and outwardly. Thomas Merton's writings are known everywhere for the light they throw on the meaning of Christian love. Far less known is this beautiful and profound book by Maurice Nicoll, a Jungian psychiatrist who became a pupil of G. I. Gurdjieff. Nicoll's insights into the inner, psychological meaning of the parables of Jesus have helped many men and women feel in their whole being the meaning of spiritual symbolism not only in the New Testament, but in all the sacred writings of the world.

The whole question of what has been labeled "Gnosticism" is now surrounded by a jungle of commentary, speculation, blockbuster fiction, painstaking archaeological research, theological controversy, literary appropriation and even Hollywood merchandising. Elaine Pagels' writing, especially *Beyond Belief,* has created a bridge between the important discoveries of scholars working in this field and those who suspect that there is much in what is labeled "Gnosticism" that cries out for deep and unforced personal understanding by all serious seekers of truth. Here there is no better guide than the French spiritual commentator Jean-Yves Leloup. Readers of these books should be prepared to experience alternating waves of astonishment, joy, hope, and a quiet sense that the true essence of all genuine religion remains as unknown as one's own essential self.

Along with *The Dead Sea Scriptures* mentioned above, James Robinson's *Nag Hammadi Library,* a collection of texts from the astounding discoveries made in Upper Egypt in 1945, offers bountiful material for consulting one's own instincts and forming one's own personal opinion about the possible existence of genuine and beneficent esoteric communities in the time and place of Jesus and Hillel.

Walter B. Cannon, *The Wisdom of the Body* (1932)

Jean-Henri Fabre, *The Mason-Bees* (1925)

Peter Kingsley, *Reality* (2003)

Shimon Malin, *Nature Loves to Hide: Quantum Physics and the Nature of Reality* (2001)

Guy Murchie, *The Seven Mysteries of Life: An Exploration in Science and Philosophy* (1978)

Maurice Nicoll, *Living Time and the Integration of the Life* (1952)

Vladimir I. Vernadsky, *The Biosphere* (1986)

David Rains Wallace, *Bulow Hammock: Mind in a Forest* (1988)

It is impossible to take ethical thought past a certain point while carrying in one's mind the simplistically reductive worldview that speaks of reality itself as a blind automatism—a view that can properly be called not science, but scientism. Fortunately, there are many books that irresistibly communicate a vision of nature as everywhere giving evidence of a central universal intelligence and purpose. Jean-Henri Fabre's *The Mason-Bees,* Walter B. Cannon's *The Wisdom of the Body* and Vladimir I. Vernadsky's *The Biosphere* are three classics that retain all their power and authority despite decades of new scientific discoveries. *The Mason-Bees* is not only a wondrous account of purpose in nature, but an extraordinary testimony to the spirit of deep scientific inquiry. Such books show us that the mind of nature is revealed only to the observer who brings his heart along with his head. *The Wisdom of the Body* introduced the concept of homeostasis into the science of physiology and in so doing communicated, with empirical evidence, the vision of an awesome intelligence ordering and coordinating the countless processes and exchanges constantly taking place every instant in the human body. In *The Biosphere,* originally published in Leningrad in 1926, Vladimir Vernadsky presented a revolutionary theory of the earth itself as an integral dynamic system controlled by life as its organizing force. Vernadsky's work remains one of the foundations of today's deep ecology movement and the understanding of the earth—and beyond—as living self-relating entities.

Some more recent books carry on this tradition of scientific observation as a discipline of the whole mind and heart: David Rains Wallace's *Bulow Hammock* is an account of the profound and mysterious relationship between the mind and nature; here a pristine woodland in eastern Florida reveals itself as being as complex and self-organizing as the mind observing it. Guy Murchie's *The Seven Mysteries of Life* sweeps through the whole realm of science—from the electron to the cell to man to the universe—and, with the utmost sober respect for scientific honesty, unveils a cosmos of transcendent order and beauty. A remarkable contemporary expression of this perspective is Shimon Malin's *Nature Loves to Hide,* written by a recognized authority on quantum mechanics, General Relativity and cosmology. The title of this book says a great deal and may perhaps be taken to imply that even quantum events exhibit properties of "mind," just as the mind in ourselves is all too often hidden from us.

There is of course a great and vast tradition of philosophy that offers a vision of the universe as alive and purposeful. Maurice Nicoll's *Living Time* and Peter Kingsley's *Reality* are two recent accounts of the immense wisdom in the ancient vision of the universal world. The former is a truly life-changing book of great profundity and clarity about the mystery of time and the human Self, unlocking many doors to the inner teachings of Christianity and the spiritual philosophies of the West—especially Plato. The latter is the work of a consummate scholar who has spiritually and intellectually unearthed the powerful metaphysical vision and practical inner work that flowed through some of the masters who are now somewhat glibly referred to simply as "pre-Socratic." Far from being defined only as coming before Socrates, these powerful teachers are, so the author persuasively argues, at the high source and fountain of all that came later, and which was in some essential respects forgotten, by the time of Socrates.

G. I. Gurdjieff, *Beelzebub's Tales to His Grandson* (1950 and 2006)

In 1913, the spiritual teacher G. I. Gurdjieff appeared in Moscow with a teaching unlike anything known or heard of in the modern world, yet unfailingly faithful in its depths to the essence of spiritual tradition. Offering a vision of man's possible individual evolution and of mankind's fundamental responsibility to the evolving life of the earth, Gurdjieff challenges the categories and foundations of every facet of our civilization—its forms of religion, its science, its art, its forms of education, and, in the modern era, its belief in progress.

Beelzebub's Tales to His Grandson is the major written expression of Gurdjieff's teaching. It is a work of colossal originality and depth about the cosmic world and the life of man—the tragedy of his inner emptiness and the hope of the rediscovery of his own meaning. The book's spiritual force stems from the aim of Gurdjieff's writings: to serve first as an awakening shock and, ultimately, as a central source of guidance for the work on oneself that is the core of his teaching and the community that survives him. The book demands and supports the effort to free oneself from familiar categories of thought and to search for a quality of pure self-attention which gradually makes possible a direct experience of the book's profound message. Nowhere can there be found a more all-encompassing, reliable, troubling and compassionate introduction to the meaning of conscience.

NOTES

Quotations from the Bible are from the King James Version unless otherwise noted.

1. This story appears in the Babylonian Talmud, Shabbat 31a, and is widely quoted with only slight variations of "Now, go and study."
2. This saying of Jesus is cited numerous times in the New Testament, notably in Matthew 22:39. It appears also in the Old Testament in Leviticus 19:18 and elsewhere.
3. Nahum N. Glatzer, *Hillel the Elder: The Emergence of Classical Judaism* (New York: Schocken Books, 1966), 74–75. My emphasis.
4. Deuteronomy 6:4–7. Adapted: "upon" substituted for "in."
5. Exodus 3:14–15. This powerful and mysterious name of God has sometimes been translated in the Christian traditions as I AM THAT I AM. The name informs the Teacher Moses, who received this name atop the holy mountain, that God's essence is Being, but Being understood as the force of love and justice, which in turn reflect the action of the Higher (God) upon

all of reality and especially upon man. But man must sense the need for this action in order for it to act upon him and his life in a manner attuned to the essential nature of man.

6. Benjamin, Jowett, trans., *The Dialogues of Plato,* 2 vols. (New York: Random House, 1920), vol. 1, 770.

7. Ibid., pp. 361–384.

8. Edith Hamilton and Huntington Cairns, eds., *The Collected Dialogues of Plato* (New York: Bollingen Foundation, 1963), 307.

9. For a fuller depiction of Alcibiades' testimony, see my *The Heart of Philosophy,* in the chapter entitled "Socrates and the Myth of Responsibility" (New York: Knopf, 1982).

10. G. I. Gurdjieff, *Beelzebub's Tales to His Grandson* (New York: Penguin Putnam, 1999), 920.

11. Marcus Aurelius, *The Meditations of Marcus Aurelius,* 2:17, trans. Jacob Needleman and John P. Piazza (unpublished, 2005).

12. Pierre Hadot, *The Inner Citadel,* 2:2 (Cambridge, Mass.: Harvard University Press, 1998), 186.

13. Marcus Aurelius, *Meditations,* trans. Maxwell Staniforth; 8:34 with minor changes (Harmondsworth, England: Penguin, 1964).

14. Ibid., 5:11. Freely adapted.

15. Ibid., 3:12. Freely adapted.

16. Needleman and Piazza, 7:59.

17. Ibid., 2:5. Some changes.

18. P. E. Matheson, trans., *The Discourses of Epictetus,* I:26. In *The Stoic and Epicurean Philosophers,* Whitney J. Oates, ed. (New York: The Modern Library, 1940).

19. Ibid., 2:16.

20. Ibid.

21. *Discourses of Epictetus,* II:22, adapted from Matheson and from W. A. Oldfather, trans., *Epictetus Discourses* (Cambridge, Mass.: Harvard University Press, 1998).

22. Matheson, 20.

23. For a full description of this point, consult Hadot, *The Inner Citadel,* chap. 3, pp. 35–53.

24. See Hadot, p. 44.

25. Staniforth, *Meditations,* 5:23.

26. Ibid., 10:25.

27. Hadot, 6:7, p. 134.

28. Staniforth, 6:39.

29. Ibid., 8:52.

30. Ibid., 4:40.

31. The account given in the text is drawn mainly from the film *Obedience* by Stanley Milgram (1962). See also Stanley Milgram, *Obedience to Authority* (New York: Harper and Row, 1975), 13–14.

32. Taittiriya Upanishad, Part 2, 9.1. "Realizing that from which all words turn back. And thoughts can never reach."

33. Glatzer, *Hillel the Elder,* pp. 25–36. My emphasis.

34. Ibid., p. 26.

35. Ibid., p. 46. My emphasis.

36. Glatzer's phrase.

37. We need to remember that Hillel was only one—although certainly one of the greatest—in a vast chain of rabbinic spiritual teachers who came before and after him. He is being singled out because the historical facts clearly invite us to speculate about his association with an esoteric school, thereby giving us grounds for considering what specific new and subtle understanding is needed in our time for a renewal of the idea and the power of morality in our lives.

38. *Pirke Avot,* 1:14, as cited in Yitzhak Buxbaum, *The Life and Teachings of Hillel* (Lanham, Md.: Bowman and Littlefield, 1994), 268.

39. Raymond B. Blakney, trans., *Meister Eckhart* (New York: Harper and Row, 1941), 122.

40. Ibid., p. 123.

41. Ibid., p. 124. My italics.

42. Matthew 22:36–40.

43. William Johnston, ed., *The Cloud of Unknowing and the Book of Privy Counseling* (New York: Doubleday, 1973), 64.

44. *Leviticus Rabbah* 1:5, cited in Glatzer, p. 45.

45. Daniel C. Matt, trans., *The Zohar,* vol. 2. (Stanford, Calif.: Stanford University Press, 2004), 257.

46. Hayim of Volozhin, "Nefesh Hahayim," in *An Anthology of Jewish Mysticism,* trans. Raphael Ben Zion (New York: Yesod Publishers), 160.

47. Ibid., p. 161.

48. Ibid.

49. Ibid., p. 162.

50. Ibid. My emphasis.

51. Ibid.

52. Emmanuel Levinas, *Nine Talmudic Readings* (Bloomington, Ind.: Indiana University Press, 1994), 100.

53. G. I. Gurdjieff, *Meetings with Remarkable Men* (New York: Penguin Putnam, 1985), 270.

INDEX

Index

Index

ABOUT THE AUTHOR

The author of *The American Soul, Money and the Meaning of Life, The Heart of Philosophy, The New Religions, Time and the Soul,* and *Lost Christianity,* among other books, Jacob Needleman is professor of philosophy at San Francisco State University and former director of the Center for the Study of New Religions at the Graduate Theological Union, Berkeley, California. He was educated at Harvard, Yale, and the University of Freiburg, Germany. He has also served as research associate at the Rockefeller Institute for Medical Research and was a research fellow at Union Theological Seminary. In addition to teaching and writing, he serves as a consultant in the fields of psychology, education, medical ethics, philanthropy and business. He has also been featured on Bill Moyers's acclaimed PBS television series *A World of Ideas.* He lives with his wife, Gail, in Oakland, California.